100+ RECIPES MY HOME TO YOURS

breakfasts • slow cooker meals • casseroles • desserts sheet pan dinners • and so much more!

Julia Pacheco

SCAN HERE FOR MORE CONTENT

TABLE OF CONTENTS

Intro.. 6

    Breakfast.. 9

    Sides & Appetizers... 29

    Casseroles... 57

    Sheet Pan Dinners... 83

    One Pot Meals.. 105

    Slow Cooker... 139

    Super Quick Dinners..175

    Desserts... 201

Substitutions... 230

Conversions.. 232

Index.. 234

Intro

I dedicate this cookbook to my loyal YouTube subscribers and my followers, who encouraged me to publish my very own cookbook, and to my family who has motivated me along the way to never give up!

To begin, I have dyslexia and have always struggled reading lengthy cookbook instructions coupled with a long list of ingredients. Quite honestly, I wanted to create a cookbook that anyone could use. This cookbook is filled with creative, tasty meals that have been in my family for years and others that are new classics. When designing this cookbook, I sought to include realistic recipes with simple ingredients. No matter who you are, I hope you find this cookbook helpful!

I started this journey when I was only 20 years old! My husband and I were struggling to make ends meet, just like many other young couples do. I had to get imaginative in the kitchen to make a little go a long way. I always loved watching my mom cook when I was growing up and enjoyed helping out in the kitchen. It allowed me to experiment with food and led to my love of cooking for my own family.

Whether you are a family of one or many, these recipes are made for you! In the back of my cookbook, I have included some substitutions for common products that I use, along with a Standard US to Metric conversion chart.

And as for ALL of my amazing YouTube followers, you have no idea how much your love and support has meant to me and my family these past four years. You have encouraged and empowered me with your knowledge and positive feedback.

Last of all, I want to express my appreciation and love to everyone who has helped create my first ever cookbook. Thank you to my sweet husband, Will, for always being by my side. I am very thankful for my two daughters. I started my YouTube shortly after Brinley was born and she was the reason I never gave up or quit. Then I had Macie and she gave me motivation to create this book. I want to thank my wonderful parents for always loving me for me and pushing me to do hard things. Thank you to my sister Bailey, brother Brandon, and sister-in-law Alexis for always being so kind and helpful. Thank you to my close friend Cathy Yoder for guiding me to self-publish my very own book. Thank you to my great friend Heather Kennington who is the best photographer and book editor. Thank you to Lindsay Steele for helping me edit recipes and for taking on any task that I hand to you.

And thank YOU for being here today! I love you all! Don't Quit! Now let's get cooking!

– Julia

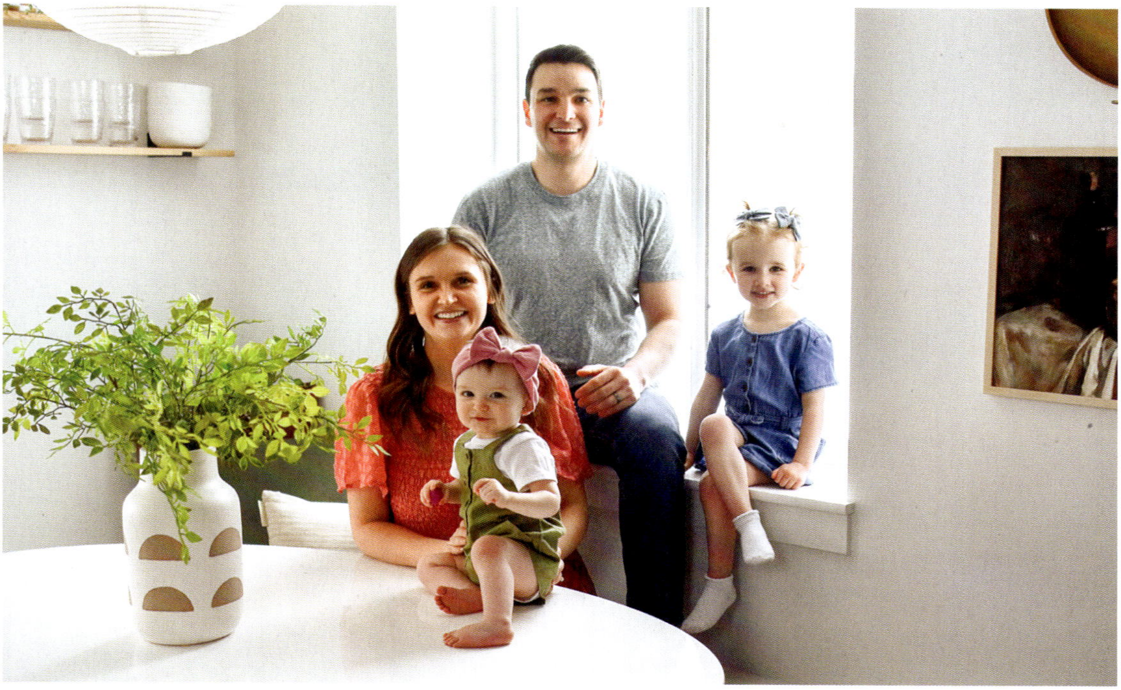

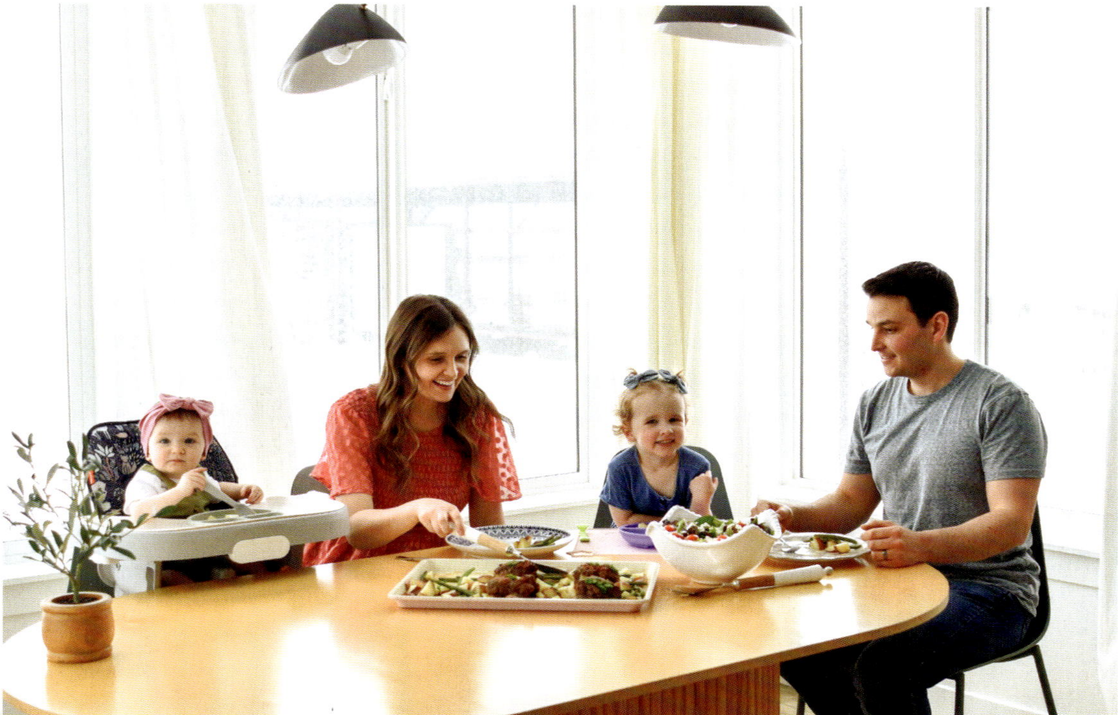

NOTES

BREAKFAST

On those crazy mornings when you want something sweet or savory, I have got you covered! These delicious breakfast combinations are a great way to start your day.

Crescent Roll Sausage Egg Casserole

A yummy pastry base, flavorful sausage, and fluffy seasoned eggs make this Crescent Roll Sausage Egg Casserole a delightful morning breakfast.

Prep time: 15 mins **Cook time:** 30 mins **Servings:** 4-5

INGREDIENTS

- 8 oz can refrigerated crescent rolls
- 1/2 lb breakfast sausage (sausage links or ground sausage will work)
- 6 eggs
- 1/2 tsp onion powder
- 1/2 tsp garlic powder
- 1/2 tsp paprika
- 1/2 tsp pepper
- 1/2 tsp salt

DIRECTIONS

1. Preheat oven to 350°F.
2. To a large pan over medium heat, add the sausage and cook through (if using sausage links, slice the sausage after cooking).
3. To a medium-sized bowl, add the eggs and all of the seasonings. Whisk to break the yolks.
4. Spray a 9×13 baking dish with non-stick spray. Unroll the crescent rolls and place them on the bottom of the baking dish, pinching the seams of the rolls together.
5. Sprinkle the sausage over the crescents, then pour the egg over the top of the sausage. Bake for 22-28 minutes, or until the egg has set in the middle. Top with your favorite toppings like chopped tomatoes, salsa, or cilantro. Enjoy!

Slow Cooker Breakfast Burritos

Breakfast Burritos in the slow cooker is one of my hacks for feeding a crowd. All you have to do is throw the ingredients in the slow cooker then wrap them up in a tortilla.

Prep time: 15 mins   **Cook time:** 30 mins   **Servings:** 4-5

INGREDIENTS

- 1 lb sausage
- 28 oz frozen bag potatoes O'Brien, thawed
- 1 1/2 cups cheddar cheese, shredded
- 12 eggs
- 1/2 cup milk
- 1/2 tsp salt
- 1/2 tsp pepper

DIRECTIONS

1. To a skillet over medium heat, cook the sausage and break it into crumbles. Remove any grease from the pan. I like to remove the excess grease by blotting a paper towel around in the pan with a spatula until it is absorbed.
2. Spray a slow cooker with nonstick spray and place the potatoes on the bottom. Place the cooked sausage on top of the potatoes, then sprinkle the sausage with the cheese.
3. To a medium-sized bowl, add the eggs, milk, salt, and pepper. Whisk to break the egg yolks and pour the egg mixture over the top of everything in the slow cooker. Do not stir.
4. Cover with a lid and cook on low for about 3 1/2 to 4 hours or until the egg has set and reached 165°F internally. Divide the mixture into cooked tortillas. Enjoy!

Sheet Pan Bacon, Eggs, and Potatoes

Sheet Pan Bacon, Eggs, and Potatoes is the way to go for making lots of yummy breakfast food with minimal cleanup.

Prep time: 10 mins   **Cook time:** 40 mins   **Servings:** 4

INGREDIENTS

- 20 oz refrigerated hash browns
- 1/2 tsp salt
- 1/2 tsp pepper
- 1/2 tsp Italian seasoning
- 1/2 tsp dried thyme
- 1/4 tsp dried basil
- 12 oz bacon
- 5-7 eggs
- 1/2 cup cheddar cheese, shredded

DIRECTIONS

1. Preheat oven to 400°F.
2. Spray a sheet pan with non-stick spray. Add the hash browns, and seasonings.
3. Stir to coat the hashbrowns in the seasonings. Spread hash browns out evenly and place the bacon strips over the top. Bake for 22 minutes.
4. Remove from the oven and crack the eggs over the top of the hash browns. Sprinkle the tops with salt, pepper, and the cheddar cheese. Bake for an additional 20 minutes, or until eggs are set. Enjoy!

Breakfast Power Cookies

Breakfast Power Cookies are full of nutritious ingredients, then scooped and baked like cookies for a fun-to-eat breakfast.

Prep time: 5 mins   **Cook time:** 12 mins   **Servings:** 6

INGREDIENTS

- 1/2 cup peanut butter
- 2 cups old-fashioned oats
- 1/3 cup semi-sweet chocolate chips
- 3 bananas

DIRECTIONS

1. Preheat oven to 350°F. Line a sheet pan with parchment paper or spray with non-stick pan spray.
2. To a large bowl add all of the ingredients and beat well. Scoop into 3 tablespoon-sized scoops and place on the sheet pan. Repeat until all of the cookie dough is gone. Bake for 12 minutes. Enjoy!

Egg & Ham Breakfast Enchiladas

Filled with ham, cheese, and green onions, then topped with even more cheese, Breakfast Enchiladas are a fun take on a classic Mexican dish.

Prep time: 15 mins **Cook time:** 1 hour **Servings:** 4-5

INGREDIENTS

- 1 lb honey ham, deli sliced
- 1 3/4 cups shredded sharp cheddar cheese
- 1 cup green onions, sliced
- 8-10 flour tortillas

Egg Mixture:

- 4 eggs
- 1 1/4 cup half and half
- 1 tbsp flour
- 1 tsp salt
- 1 tsp pepper

DIRECTIONS

1. Cut the ham into small pieces. Add the ham, one cup of cheese, and green onions to a medium-sized bowl and stir well.
2. Add the ingredients for the egg mixture into a medium-sized bowl and whisk well.
3. Grease a 9×13 baking dish with non-stick spray. Fill each tortilla with the ham mixture, then roll up and place, seam side down, into the bottom of the baking dish. Repeat with all of the tortillas and filling.
4. Pour the egg mixture over the top and cover the baking dish with plastic wrap. Place in the refrigerator for at least 6 hours, so the tortillas can absorb the egg mixture.
5. Preheat the oven to 350°F. Remove the plastic wrap, then cover the baking dish with aluminum foil and bake for 38 minutes. Remove the aluminum foil and sprinkle the remaining 3/4 cup of cheese on top. Bake for an additional 15-20 minutes, uncovered, until the cheese is melted and bubbly. Serve with your favorite toppings like sour cream, chopped tomatoes, cilantro, and green onions. Enjoy!

Breakfast Biscuit Casserole

Breakfast Biscuit Casserole has it all: yummy pastry base, savory sausage, and fluffy eggs.

Prep time: 10 mins   **Cook time:** 30 mins   **Servings:** 8

INGREDIENTS

- 1 lb breakfast sausage
- 1 can of biscuits (about 10 biscuits)
- 9 eggs
- 1/2 tsp pepper
- 1/2 tsp salt
- 1/4 cup water

DIRECTIONS

1. Preheat oven to 350°F. Grease a 9×13 baking dish.
2. To a large skillet over medium heat, add the sausage. Break it up and cook through. Remove any excess grease from the pan. Set to the side.
3. Cut each biscuit into four smaller pieces. Place each of the biscuit pieces on the bottom of the baking dish. Sprinkle the sausage evenly over the biscuits.
4. In a medium-sized bowl, crack the eggs and season with salt and pepper, and add the water. Whisk to break the yolks. Pour the egg mixture over the top of the sausage.
5. Bake for 25-30 minutes, or until the egg has set and the biscuits look golden brown on top. Enjoy!

German Pancakes

German Pancakes breakfast is a fluffy, baked pancake dish that is perfect to make for a crowd. It's a favorite in our household.

Prep time: 10 mins **Cook time:** 20 mins **Servings:** 4-5

INGREDIENTS

- 5 tbsp butter
- 6 eggs
- 1 cup flour
- 1 cup milk
- 1 tsp vanilla
- dash of salt

DIRECTIONS

1. Preheat oven to 425°F. While the oven is warming up, put the butter in a 9×13 baking dish and place in the oven until the butter is melted.
2. In a blender, combine the flour, eggs, milk, vanilla, and salt. Cover and blend until smooth. Pour all the batter into the baking dish with the melted butter.
3. Bake for 20-25 minutes, or until the edges are golden brown and puffy.
4. Serve with maple syrup, a sprinkle of powdered sugar, and fruit. Enjoy!

Slow Cooker Hash Brown Casserole

Slow Cooker Hash Brown Casserole is a perfect celebratory breakfast. Prep everything the night before, cook in slow cooker, and breakfast will be ready in the morning.

Prep time: 10 mins   **Cook time:** 7 hours   **Servings:** 4-5

INGREDIENTS

- 10 oz can cream of mushroom soup
- 1/2 cup sour cream
- 1/2 tsp pepper
- 30 oz bag frozen hash browns
- 14 oz kielbasa sausage, sliced into half moons
- 1 white onion, diced
- 1 red bell pepper, diced (optional)
- 2 cups cheddar cheese, shredded

DIRECTIONS

1. To a medium-sized bowl add the cream of mushroom soup, sour cream, and pepper then whisk to combine.
2. Spray a large slow cooker with non-stick spray. Add the hash browns, sausage, onion, bell pepper, 1 cup of the cheese, and the cream of mushroom soup mixture. Stir until incorporated. Sprinkle the remaning cheese on top Cook on LOW for 7 hours. Enjoy!

Slow Cooker Breakfast Potatoes

Frozen hash browns are pretty good, but making your own Slow Cooker Breakfast Potatoes is not much effort and they always end up so delicious!

Prep time: 10 mins   **Cook time:** 3-5 hours   **Servings:** 4-5

INGREDIENTS

- 3 lbs baby red or golden potatoes
- 1 white onion, diced
- 1 tbsp minced garlic
- 2 tsp seasoning salt
- 2 tsp paprika
- 2 tbsp butter, cut into pieces
- 2 tbsp olive oil
- optional: red bell pepper, diced

DIRECTIONS

1. Cut the potatoes into quarters or bite-sized pieces.
2. Spray your slow cooker with non-stick spray.
3. To the slow cooker, add the potatoes, onion, garlic, seasonings, butter, olive oil, and bell pepper, if using. Stir well.
4. Cover and cook on LOW for 4-5 hours or HIGH for 3 hours, or until the potatoes are fork tender. Enjoy!

SIDES & APPETIZERS

Have you been invited to a party or family get together? Need a great side dish or appetizer to wow your crowd? These recipes will not disappoint!

Parmesan Zucchini Skillet

Caramelized zucchini and sweet corn are topped with savory Parmesan cheese, zesty lime juice, and fresh cilantro for a unique side dish.

Prep time: 5 mins   **Cook time:** 10 mins   **Servings:** 4-5

INGREDIENTS

- 3 medium zucchinis, diced
- 2 tbsp olive oil
- 2 tbsp minced garlic
- 1 cup canned corn, drained
- 1/2 tsp dried oregano
- 1/2 tsp dried basil
- 1/4 tsp dried thyme
- 1/2 tsp salt
- 1/4 tsp pepper
- juice of 1 lime
- 1/2 cup Parmesan cheese
- 2 tbsp fresh cilantro

DIRECTIONS

1. Add the oil to a large skillet over medium heat. Once hot, add the diced zucchini, minced garlic, corn, and seasonings. Cook for about 7-9 minutes, stirring occasionally, or until the zucchini is golden brown.
2. Remove from heat and stir in the lime juice, Parmesan cheese, and cilantro. Enjoy!

Twice Baked Potato Casserole

Creamy, cheesy potatoes are topped with bacon and even more cheese or a delicious and hearty side dish.

Prep time: 20 mins   **Cook time:** 20 mins   **Servings:** 4-5

INGREDIENTS

- 10 medium Russet potatoes
- 1/2 lb bacon, diced
- 4 tbsp sliced butter
- 3/4 cup sour cream
- 4 tbsp cream cheese
- 5 green onions, chopped
- 2 cups shredded sharp cheddar cheese
- 3/4 cup milk
- 1/2 tsp salt
- 1/2 tsp pepper
- 1/2 tsp dried thyme

DIRECTIONS

1. Preheat oven to 350°F.
2. Peel and dice the potatoes. Add the potatoes to a pot of boiling water and boil until fork tender, about 8-10 minutes. Drain and set to the side.
3. Cook the diced bacon in a skillet over medium heat until cooked through. Move to a paper towel-lined plate to cool and absorb excess grease.
4. Add the potatoes, sliced butter, sour cream, cream cheese, green onions (reserve some for garnish), bacon (reserve some for garnish), 1 cup of cheese, milk, salt, pepper, and thyme to a large bowl and mix well with a potato masher or hand mixer. Taste and add more milk if too dry, and more salt and pepper as needed.
5. Grease a 9×13 baking dish. Pour the potato mixture in sprinkle the remaning cheese on top and bake for 20-25 minutes or until the cheese is melty. Broil for the last 1-2 minutes. Top with the reserved green onions and bacon. Enjoy!

Avocado Corn Salad

This fresh salad is bursting with flavor and richness. It's the perfect side for a cookout or weeknight dinner at home.

Prep time: 15 mins **Ready to Serve** **Servings:** 4-5

INGREDIENTS

- 1 large English cucumber, diced
- 1 red onion, diced
- 1 cup cherry tomatoes, sliced
- 3 avocados, diced
- 1-2 ears of corn, cut off cob
- 1 lemon, juiced
- 1 tsp salt
- 1/2 tsp pepper
- 1/2 tsp dried basil

DIRECTIONS

1. Combine all of the ingredients in a large bowl. Stir well and serve immediately or refrigerate and serve later.

Classic Side Salad

With fresh veggies and unique toppings, this Classic Side Salad is the perfect accompaniment to any main dish.

Prep time: 10 mins   **Ready to Serve**   **Servings:** 4-5

INGREDIENTS

- 5 cups spinach or spring mix salad greens
- 6 baby carrots, chopped
- 1 cup cherry tomatoes, sliced
- 1 avocado, diced
- 4 green onions, sliced
- 1/4 cup feta cheese
- 1/4 cup Dried Sweetened Cranberries and Honey-Roasted Almonds Salad Topper
- dressing of your choice (I like to use Light Italian or Parmesan Ranch variations)

DIRECTIONS

1. Clean the greens and chop the vegetables, avocado, and green onions. Add the greens to a large salad bowl, followed by the vegetables, avocado, and green onions. Sprinkle with feta cheese and Salad Topper. Drizzle with your favorite dressing and enjoy!

Ranch Bacon Pasta Salad

This Ranch Bacon Pasta Salad will have everyone asking for seconds. It's creamy, savory, and full of veggies too!

Prep time: 15 mins   **Chilling Time:** 1 hour   **Servings:** 4-5

INGREDIENTS

Pasta Salad

- 1 cup cooked crumbled bacon (about 6 slices)
- 12 oz rotini pasta (or other short cut pasta)
- 1/2 cup cubed sharp cheddar cheese
- 1/4 cup sliced green onions
- 1 cup sliced cherry tomatoes
- 1 cup sweet peas
- 2 cups fresh spinach

Ranch Dressing

- 1 1/2 tsp dried dill
- 1 1/2 tsp dried chives
- 1 1/2 tsp onion powder
- 1 1/2 tsp garlic powder
- 1/2 tsp salt
- 1/4 tsp pepper
- 1/3 cup mayonnaise
- 1/3 cup sour cream
- 3 tbsp milk
- 2 tbsp fresh lemon juice

DIRECTIONS

1. Cook the pasta according to the package directions. Drain and let cool completely.
2. In a large bowl, whisk together all the ranch dressing ingredients.
3. Add the cooled rotini and the remaining ingredients to the bowl with the dressing. Mix well, coating everything with the dressing. Refrigerate for at least one hour before serving. Enjoy!

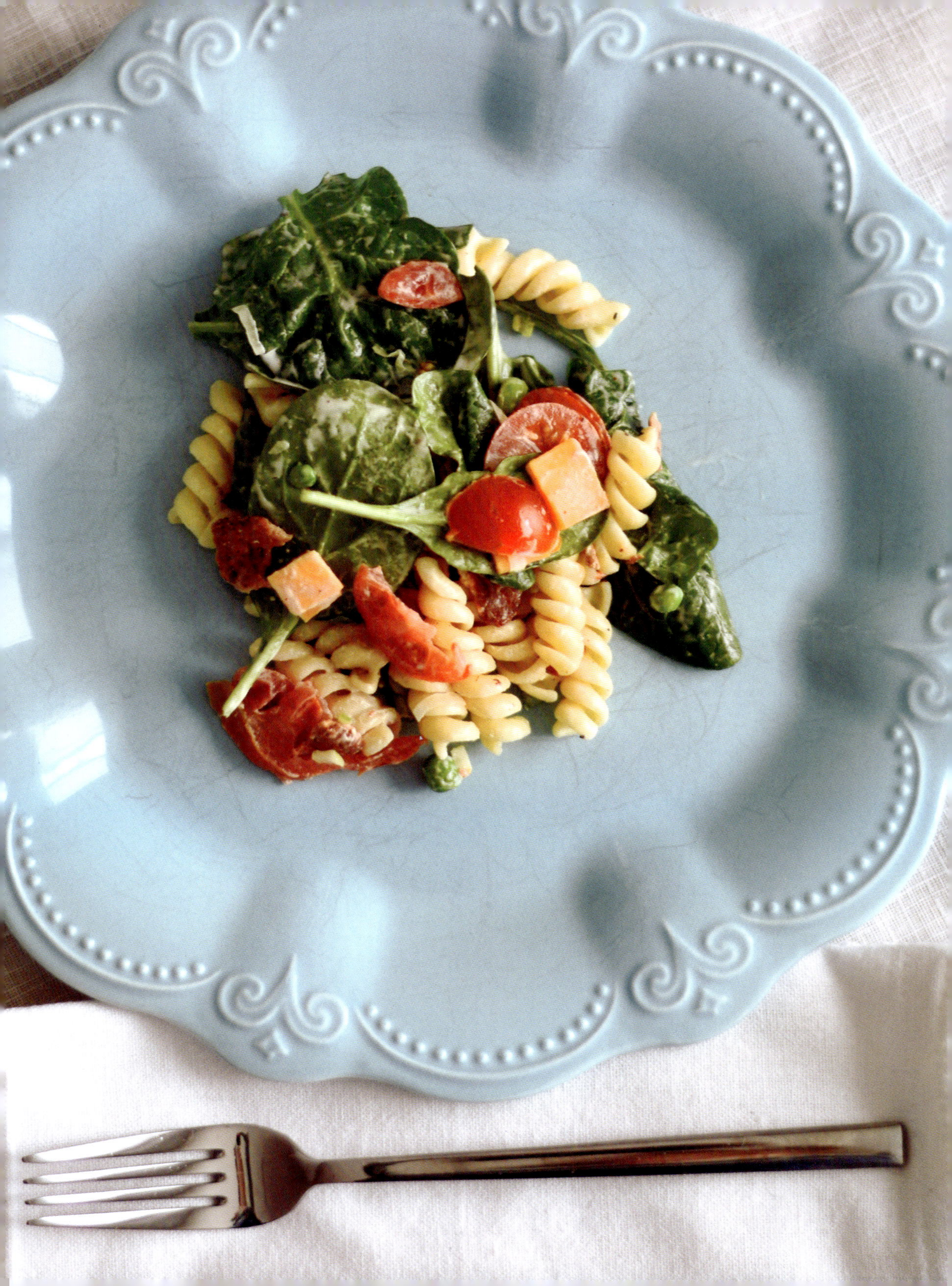

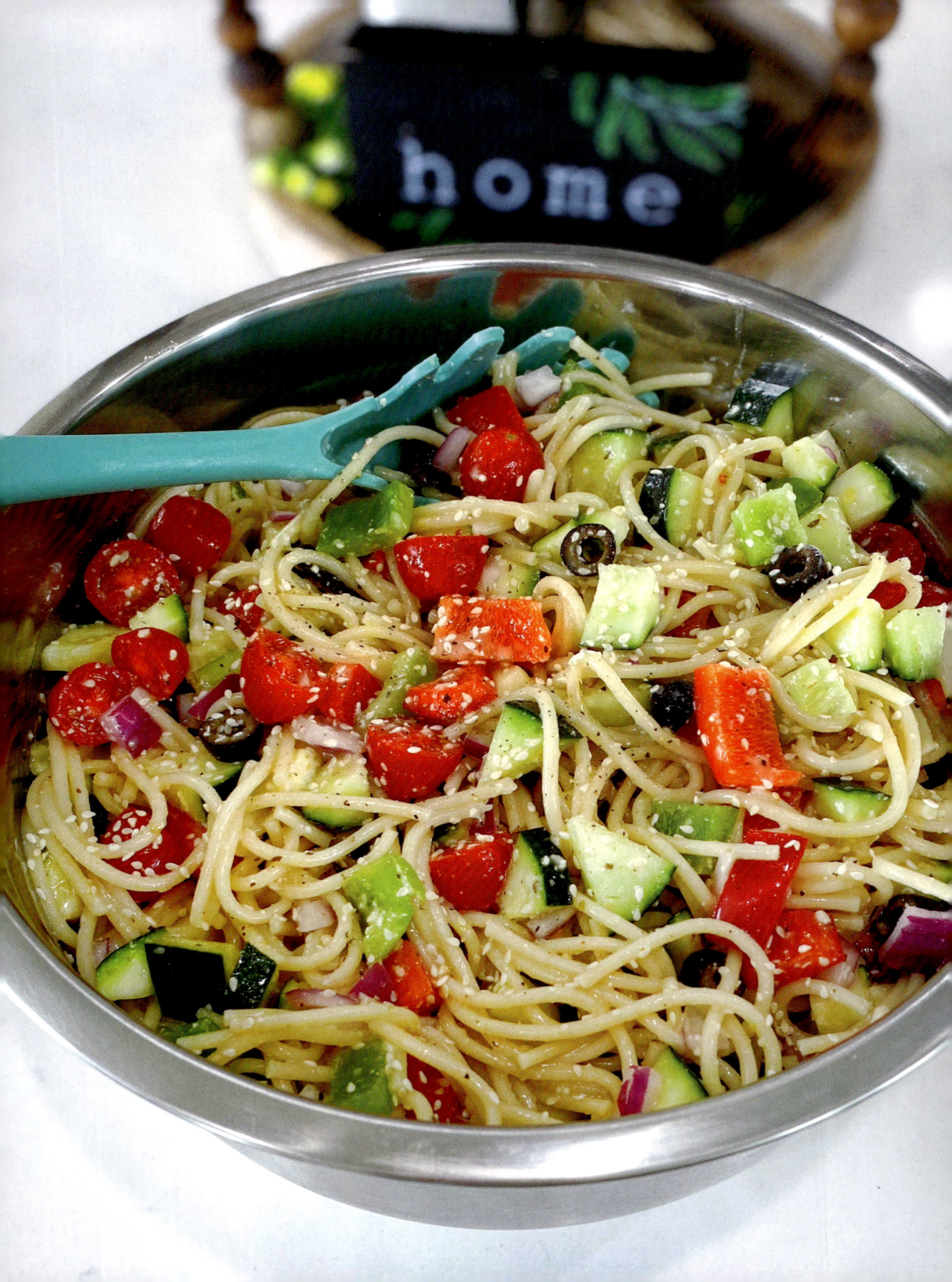
home

California Spaghetti Salad

With crunchy fresh veggies and zesty Italian dressing, California Spaghetti Salad is sunny and bright, just like its namesake.

Prep time: 10 mins **Chilling time:** 10 mins **Servings:** 6

INGREDIENTS

- 1 lb spaghetti noodles, broken into smaller pieces
- 2 cups cherry tomatoes, sliced
- 1 cucumber, sliced
- 1 green bell pepper, diced
- 1 red bell pepper, diced
- 1 medium zucchini, diced
- 1 red onion, diced
- 2.25 oz black olives, sliced

Dressing

- 16 oz Italian dressing
- 1/4 cup grated Parmesan cheese
- 1 tbsp sesame seeds

DIRECTIONS

1. Cook the spaghetti according to the package instructions. Drain and rinse with cold water and place drained pasta into a large bowl.
2. To a small bowl add the Italian dressing, Parmesan cheese, and sesame seeds. Whisk well. Pour the dressing over the pasta and stir to combine.
3. Add the chopped veggies to the bowl. Stir well and refrigerate for at least one hour. Enjoy!

Garlic Herb Mashed Potatoes

Garlic Herb Mashed Potatoes are creamy, salty, savory, buttery, and luscious. Everyone will be swooning over these amazing mashed potatoes!

Prep time: 20 mins   **Cook time:** 20 mins   **Servings:** 4-5

INGREDIENTS

- 4 lbs golden potatoes
- 6 tbsp butter
- 1 tbsp minced garlic
- 2 tsp dried rosemary
- 3 tsp salt
- 1-2 tsp pepper
- 1 tsp dried thyme
- 1 cup milk + more if needed

DIRECTIONS

1. Bring a large pot of water to a boil.
2. Peel the potatoes and cut them into large chunks. Place the potatoes in the water and boil until fork tender, about 15 minutes. Strain the potatoes and set them aside.
3. Place the pot in which the potatoes were cooked back onto the stove over medium heat. Melt the butter down, then stir in the garlic and seasonings. Let cook for 1-2 minutes until the garlic is fragrant.
4. Add the potatoes back into the pot with the milk and mash them with a potato masher. Stir them to combine with the garlic butter and seasonings. Serve immediately.

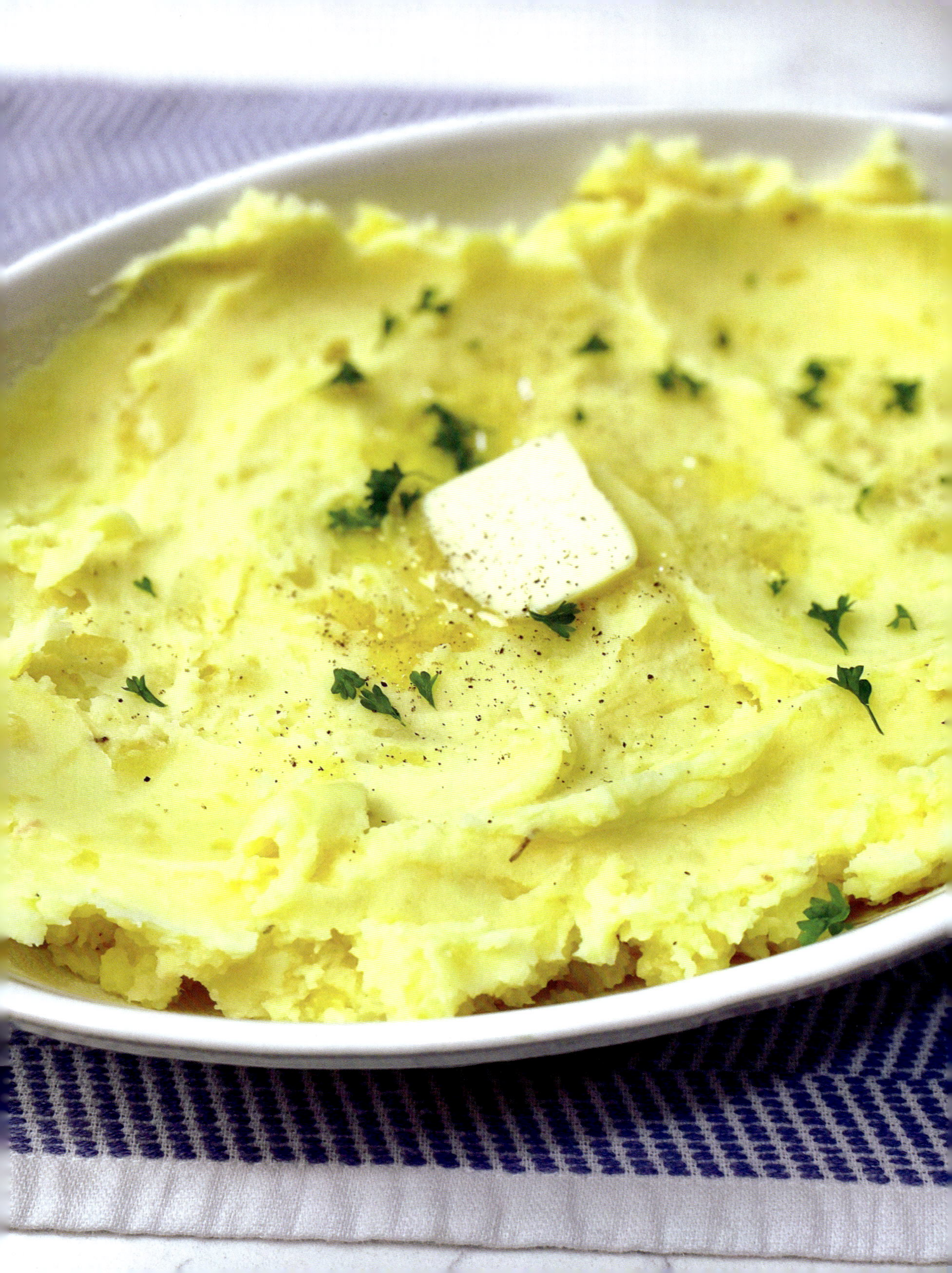

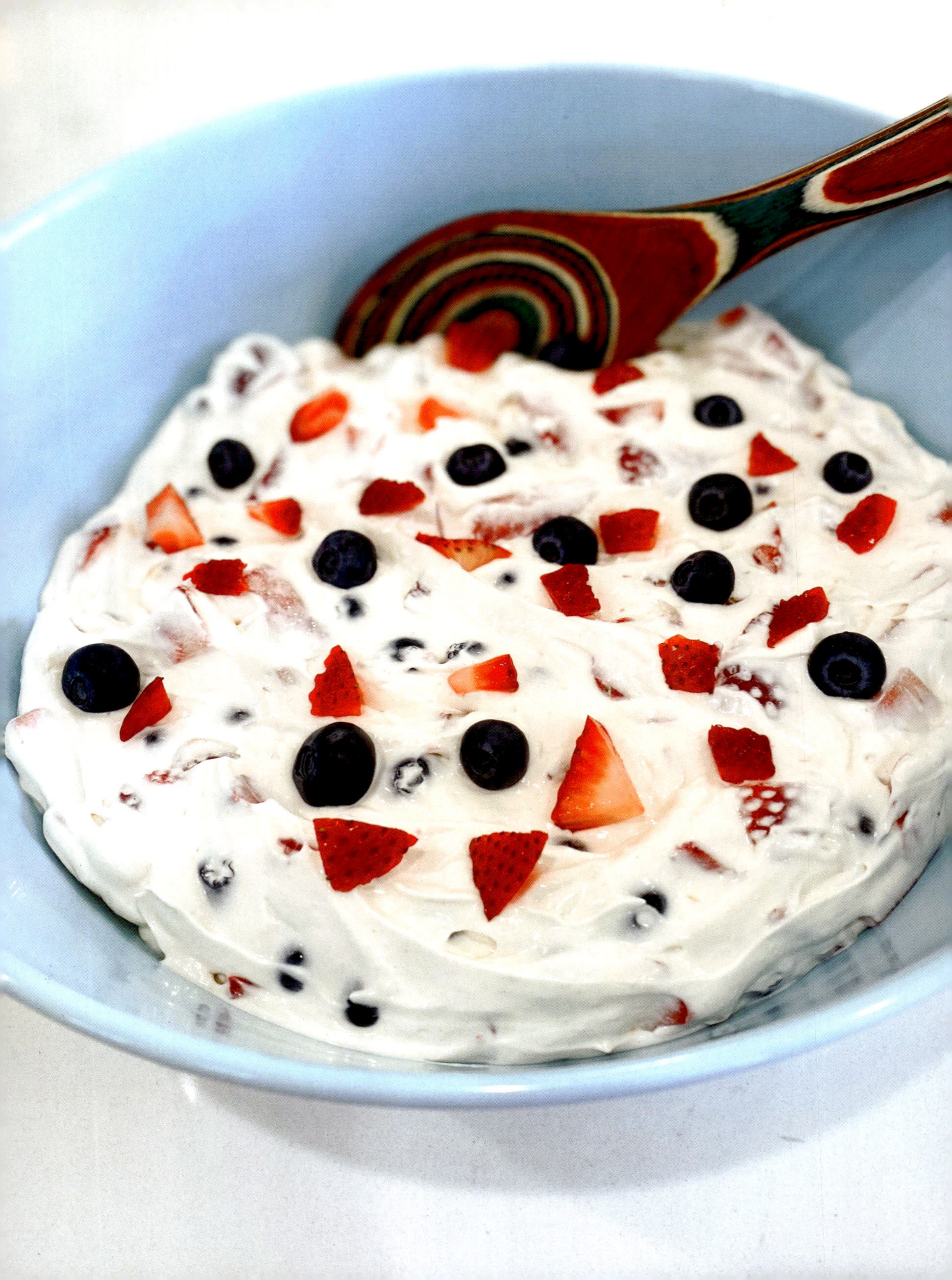

Red White & Blue Cheesecake Fruit Salad

This sweet and creamy fruit salad is the perfect patriotic side dish to serve at your summer cookout.

Prep time: 15 mins   **Chilling time:** 1 hour   **Servings:** 6

INGREDIENTS

- 12 oz whipped topping
- 3.4 oz box cheesecake pudding mix
- 12 oz strawberry yogurt
- 1 tsp vanilla extract
- 2 pints fresh blueberries
- 1 lb fresh strawberries, sliced
- 2 cups mini marshmallows (optional)

DIRECTIONS

1. To a large bowl add the whipped topping, pudding mix, yogurt, and vanilla extract then stir well. Refrigerate for one hour to set.
2. Add the blueberries and strawberries (and the mini marshmallows, if using) to the bowl with the whipped topping mixture. Stir well and serve immediately, or store in the fridge to serve later.

BBQ Chicken Roll Ups

BBQ Chicken Roll Ups are a fun, savory roll that are perfect as an appetizer for game day or a weeknight meal in.

Prep time: 15 mins   **Cook time:** 15 mins   **Servings:** 4-5

INGREDIENTS

- 3.8 oz can refrigerated pizza crust (or similar size)
- 1/2 cup BBQ sauce, any brand works
- 16 oz canned chicken, drained (or any type of cooked shredded chicken)
- 1/3 cup sliced green onions
- 1/2 cup shredded cheddar cheese

DIRECTIONS

1. Preheat oven to 425°F. Unroll the pizza crust on a large surface slightly flatten the dough with a rolling pin. Spread the BBQ sauce over the crust and sprinkle with the chicken, onions, and cheese.
2. Roll the dough up like a cinnamon roll, starting from the long side of the rectangle, then slice into 3-inch slices.
3. Place onto a greased sheet pan and bake for 15-18 minutes, or until golden brown. Enjoy!

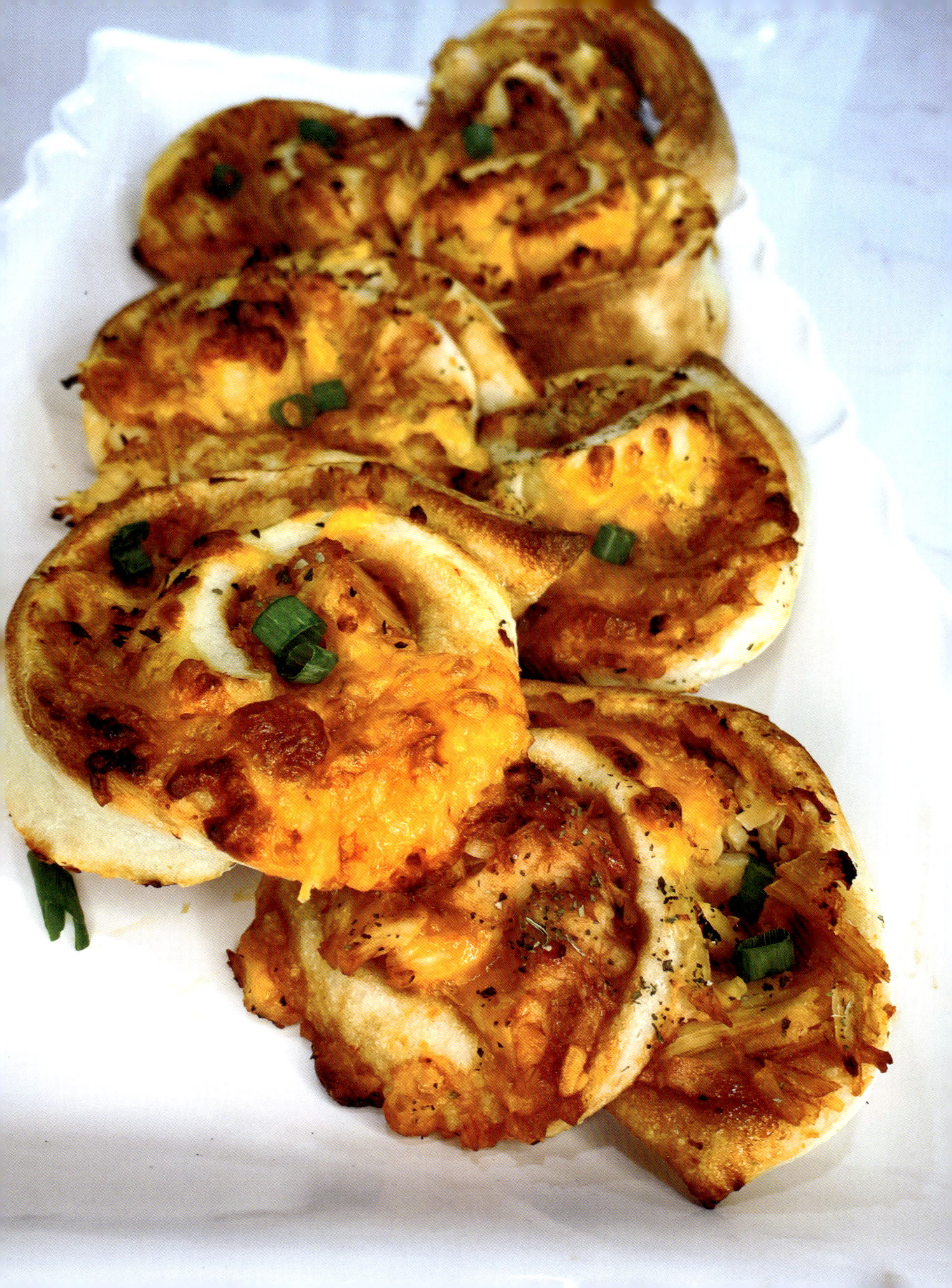

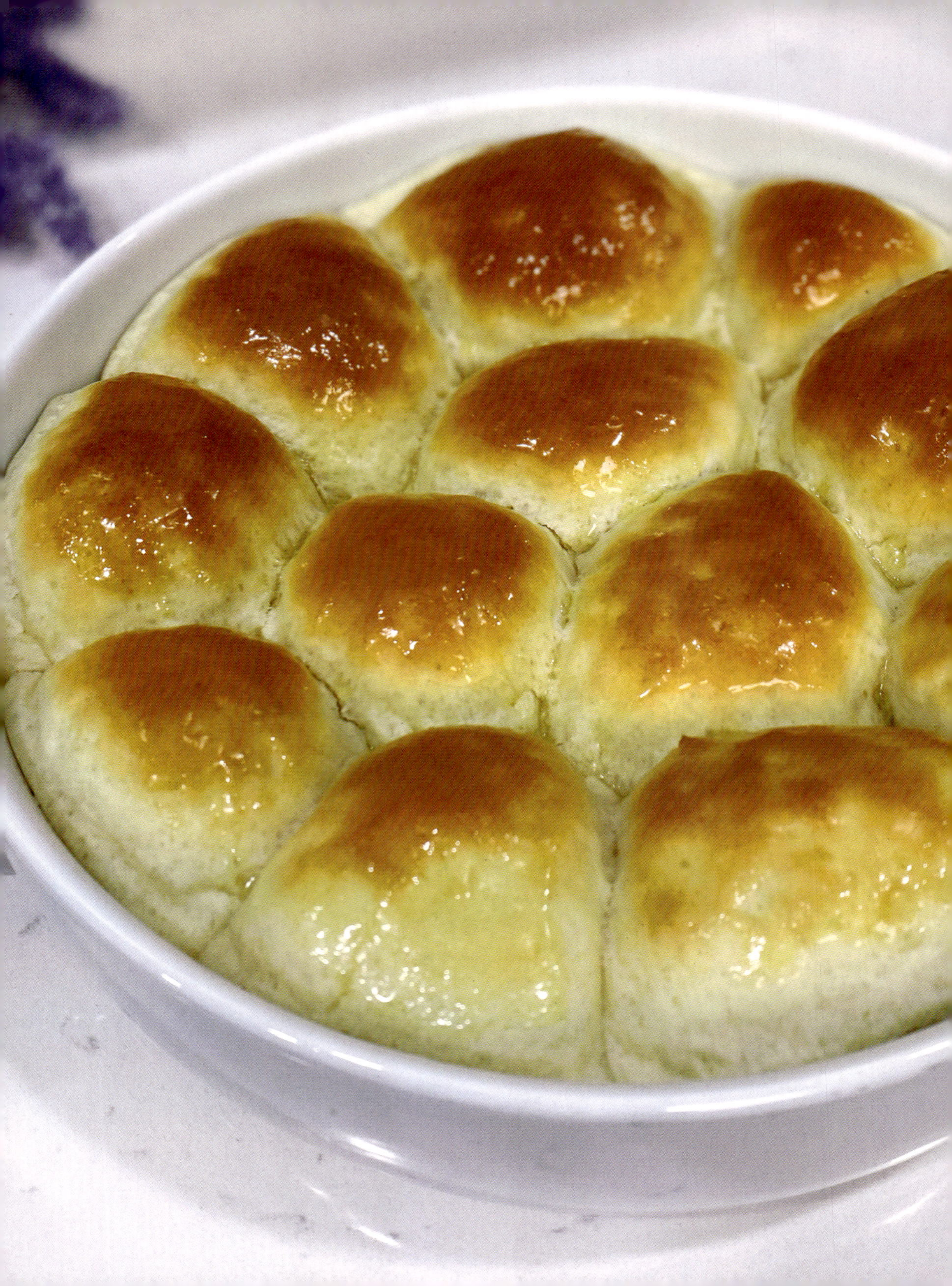

Easy One Hour Dinner Rolls

These One Hour Dinner Rolls are super soft and pillowy and can be made from start to finish in under 60 minutes.

Prep time: 25 mins   **Cook time:** 25 mins   **Servings:** 15

INGREDIENTS

- 3/4 cup milk
- 3/4 cup water
- 4 tbsp butter, softened
- 1/4 cup sugar
- 1 1/2 tsp salt
- 3 1/2 – 4 1/2 cups all-purpose flour
- 2 tbsp rapid-rise yeast

DIRECTIONS

1. Add milk, water, butter, sugar, and salt in a small bowl and heat in the microwave for about 1 minute. Stir well and pour into a stand mixer or large bowl. Whisk in yeast and let sit for 10 minutes. With a dough hook attachment, add about 3 1/2 cups flour and mix on medium speed. Add in additional flour incrementally until the dough is soft but not sticky. Mix for about 6-9 minutes.
2. Divide the dough into 15 even pieces and roll into balls. Place the dough balls in a greased 9×13 baking dish.
3. Cover with a clean dish towel and set it in a warm place to rise for about 20 minutes, or until doubled. While the rolls are still rising, set the oven to 350°F.
4. Bake for 15-18 minutes. After the rolls are finished baking, brush the tops with melted butter.
5. Let cool for a few minutes before serving. Enjoy!

Classic Coleslaw

Tangy, a little sweet, and a tad crunchy, this Classic Coleslaw recipe is the only one you'll ever need!

Prep time: 5 mins   **Chilling time:** 2 hours   **Servings:** 4-5

INGREDIENTS

- 16 oz bag of shredded cabbage or coleslaw mix
- 1/2 cup mayonnaise
- 1 tbsp sugar
- 1/2 tsp black pepper
- 1 tsp salt
- 1 tbsp lemon juice
- 1 tbsp apple cider vinegar or white vinegar

DIRECTIONS

1. To a medium-sized bowl, add all of the ingredients and stir well. Cover the bowl and refrigerate for at least 2 hours. Serve and enjoy!

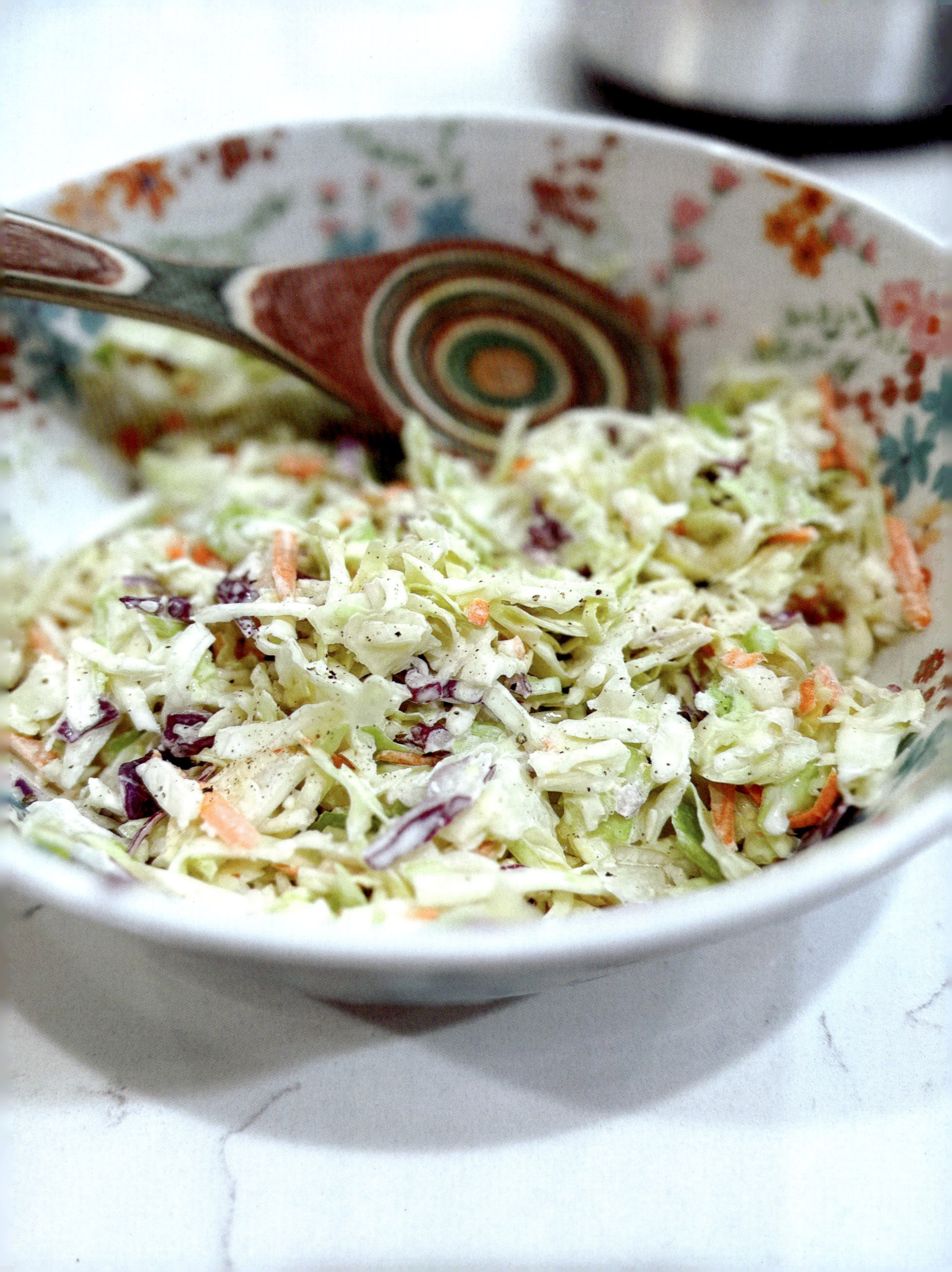

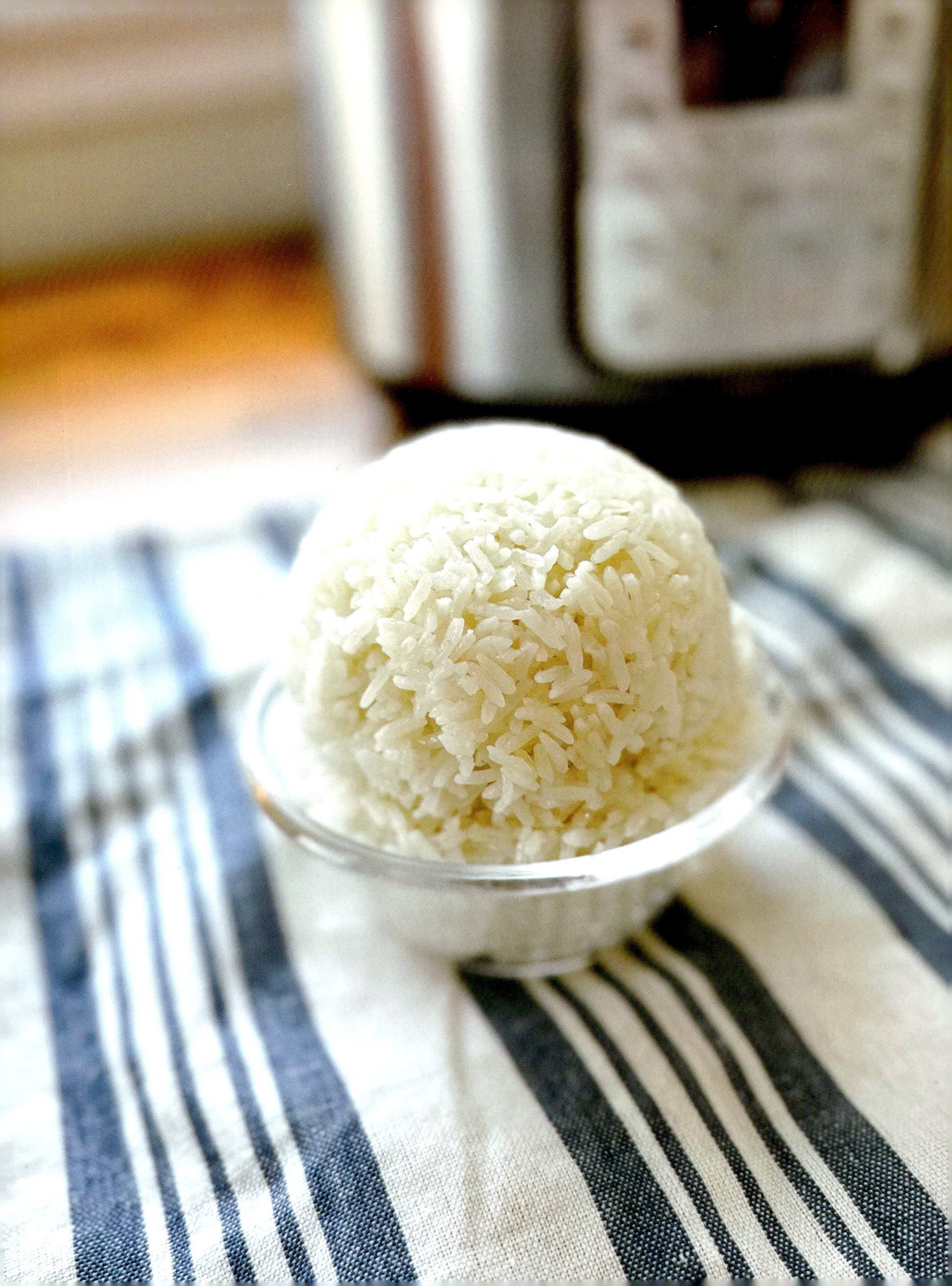

Electric Pressure Cooker White Rice

Electric Pressure Cooker White Rice takes the guesswork out of quantities and cooking times; you'll get perfect rice every time!

Prep time: 10 mins **Chilling time:** 15 mins **Servings:** 4-5

INGREDIENTS

- 1 tbsp olive oil
- 1 cup jasmine rice or long-grain white rice
- 1 1/2 cups cold water

Seasonings (optional)

- 1 tbsp taco seasoning for Mexican cuisine
- 1 tbsp Italian seasoning for Italian cuisine
- 1 tbsp any other seasonings you love

DIRECTIONS

1. Rinse the rice in a mesh strainer under cold water until the water runs clear. This will rinse away any excess starch so the grains remain separate.

2. To your pressure cooker, add the oil, rice, water, and seasonings. Stir, then place the lid on top, set the valve on the lid to the sealing position, press the 'Rice' button, then press Start (some pressure cookers don't have a start button but if yours does, press Start). Once the cooking time has elapsed, open the steam valve for a quick release. Stir and serve.

Potato Salad

Prep time: 10 mins   **Cook time:** 10 mins   **Servings:** 6

INGREDIENTS

- 10 medium Russet potatoes
- 1/2 cup Italian dressing
- 1 tbsp yellow mustard
- 3 hard boiled eggs, chopped
- 1 small yellow onion, chopped
- 1/2 cup mayo
- 1/4 cup sour cream
- 3 stalks celery, chopped
- 6 baby dill pickles, chopped
- 1 tbs dill pickle juice
- dash salt and pepper

DIRECTIONS

1. Peel and cut potatoes into bite-size pieces. Place in a pot of boiling water and cook until fork tender (about 8 minutes).
2. Strain and let cool them cool off.
3. In a large bowl, add cooled potatoes with Italian dressing and give it a good stir. Place in fridge for 2 hours to chill.
4. Add in mustard, eggs, yellow onion, mayo, sour cream, celery, pickles, pickle juice, salt, and pepper and stir to combine. Chill for another hour or longer!

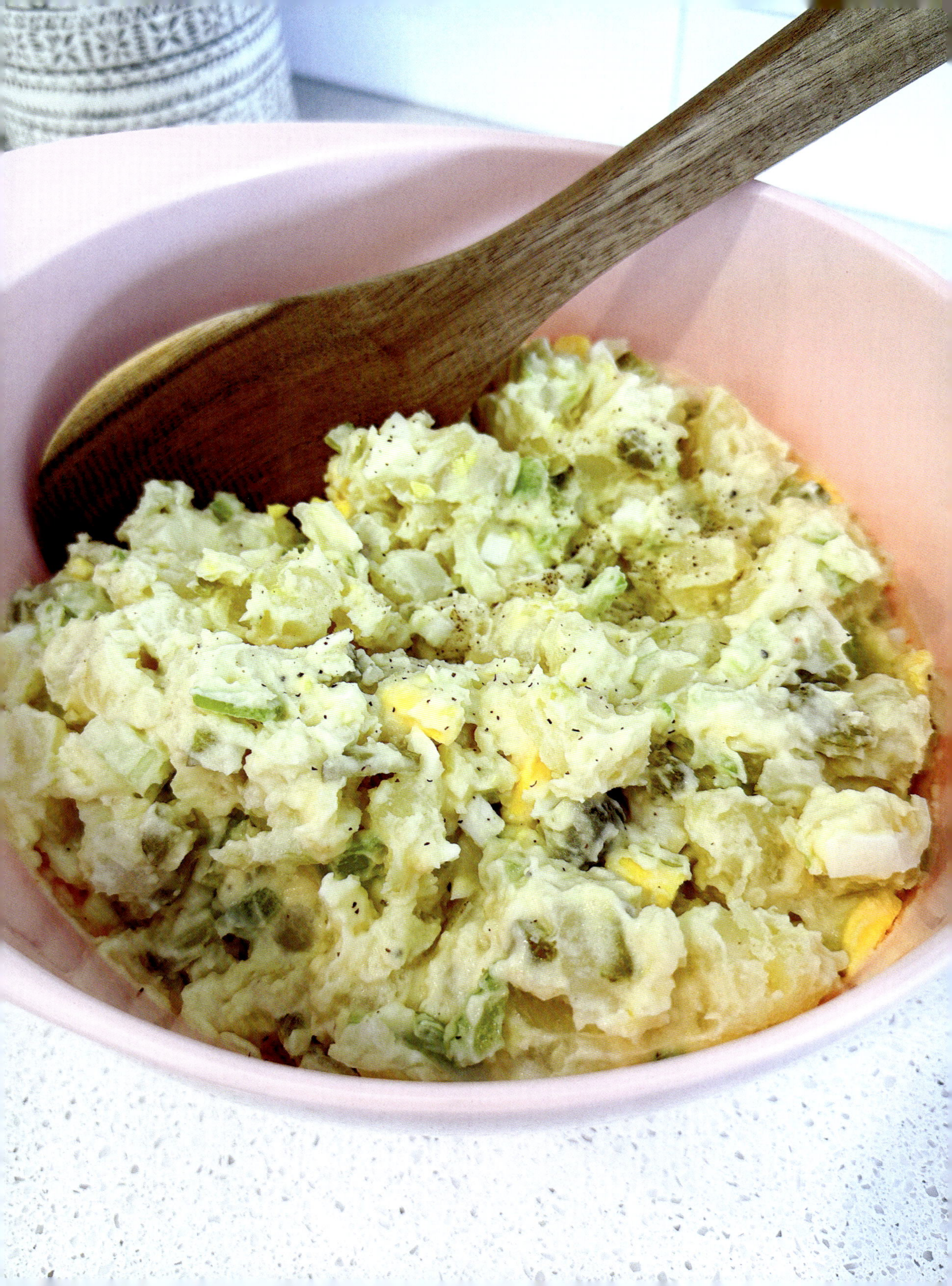

NOTES

CASSEROLES

The following casseroles are perfect for any season. You will want to make them over and over again. Your family will love them!

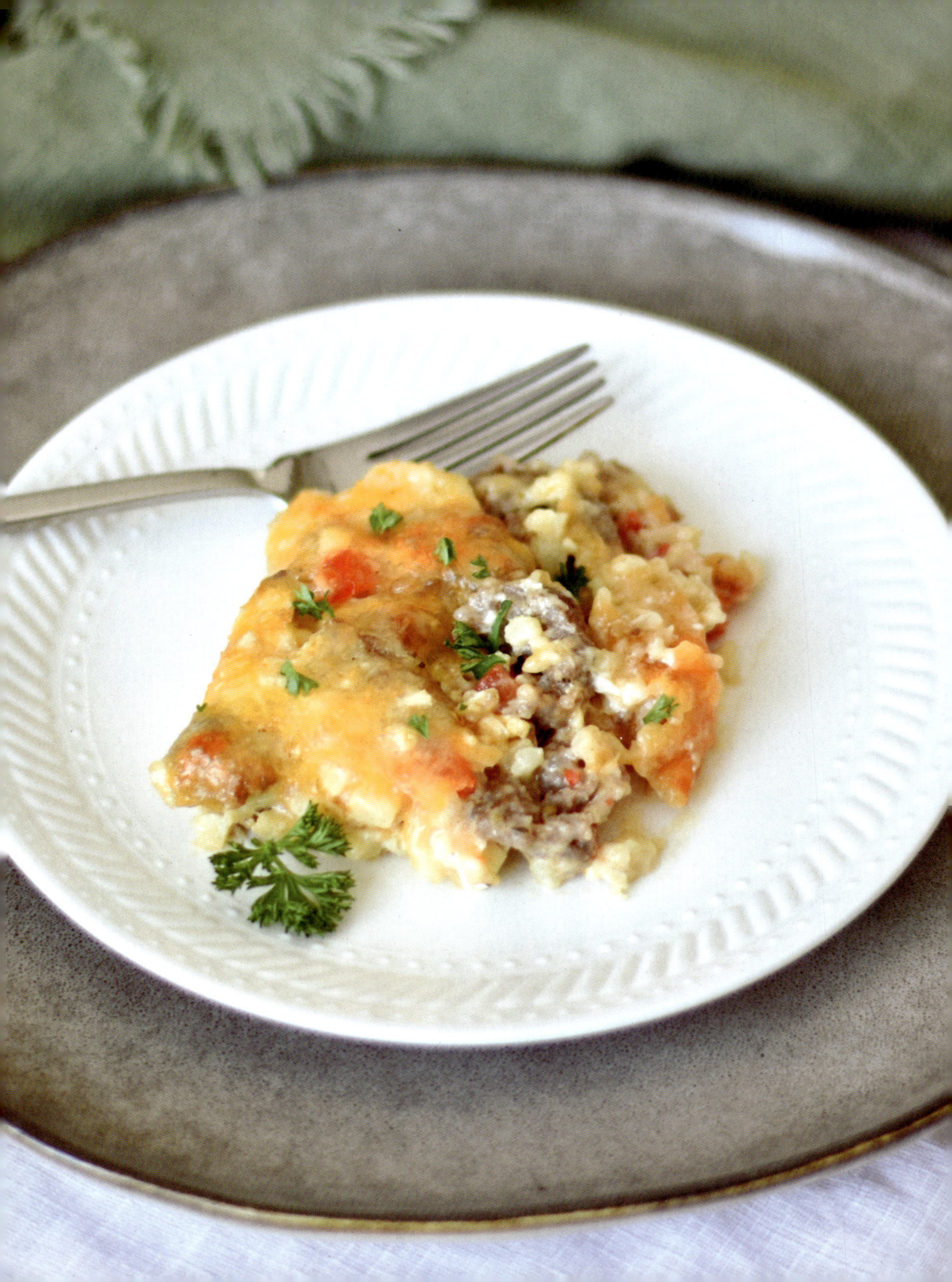

Sausage Casserole with Cauliflower Rice

Italian sausage and veggies bake together with lots of cheese for a creamy and comforting casserole dish.

Prep time: 20 mins **Cook time:** 20 mins **Servings:** 4-5

INGREDIENTS

- 1 tbsp olive oil
- 1 red bell pepper, diced
- 1 lb Italian sausage
- 5 oz softened cream cheese, cubed
- 6 cups frozen cauliflower rice
- 1/2 tbsp Italian seasoning
- 1 1/2 cups shredded sharp cheddar cheese

DIRECTIONS

1. Preheat oven to 375°F.
2. Add oil to a skillet over medium heat. Once hot, add bell pepper and sauté for 2 minutes. Add the sausage and cook through. Once cooked, remove any excess grease. Remove the skillet from heat and add the cubed cream cheese. Stir until the cream cheese is melted.
3. To a medium-sized bowl, add the sausage mixture, cauliflower rice, Italian seasoning, and 1/2 cup of cheese. Stir to combine.
4. Grease a 9×13 baking dish and pour the mixture in. Top with the remaining cheese and cover with aluminum foil. Bake for 25 minutes, then remove the foil and bake for an additional 12 minutes, uncovered. Enjoy!

French Onion Pork Chops

Pork chops are smothered with savory French onion sauce and topped with cheese and crispy onions for a decadent and easy meal.

Prep time: 10 mins   **Cook time:** 40 mins   **Servings:** 6

INGREDIENTS

- 8 boneless pork chops
- 1/2 cup French onion dip
- 1 cup shredded sharp cheddar cheese
- 1 cup crispy fried onions

DIRECTIONS

1. Preheat oven to 350°F.
2. Add the pork chops to a greased 9×13 baking dish, placing them side by side. Spread the French onion dip evenly over the tops of the pork chops. Sprinkle the cheese over the French onion dip, then sprinkle the crispy fried onions on top of the cheese.
3. Bake for 35-40 minutes or until the pork chops reach an internal temperature of 145°F. Enjoy!

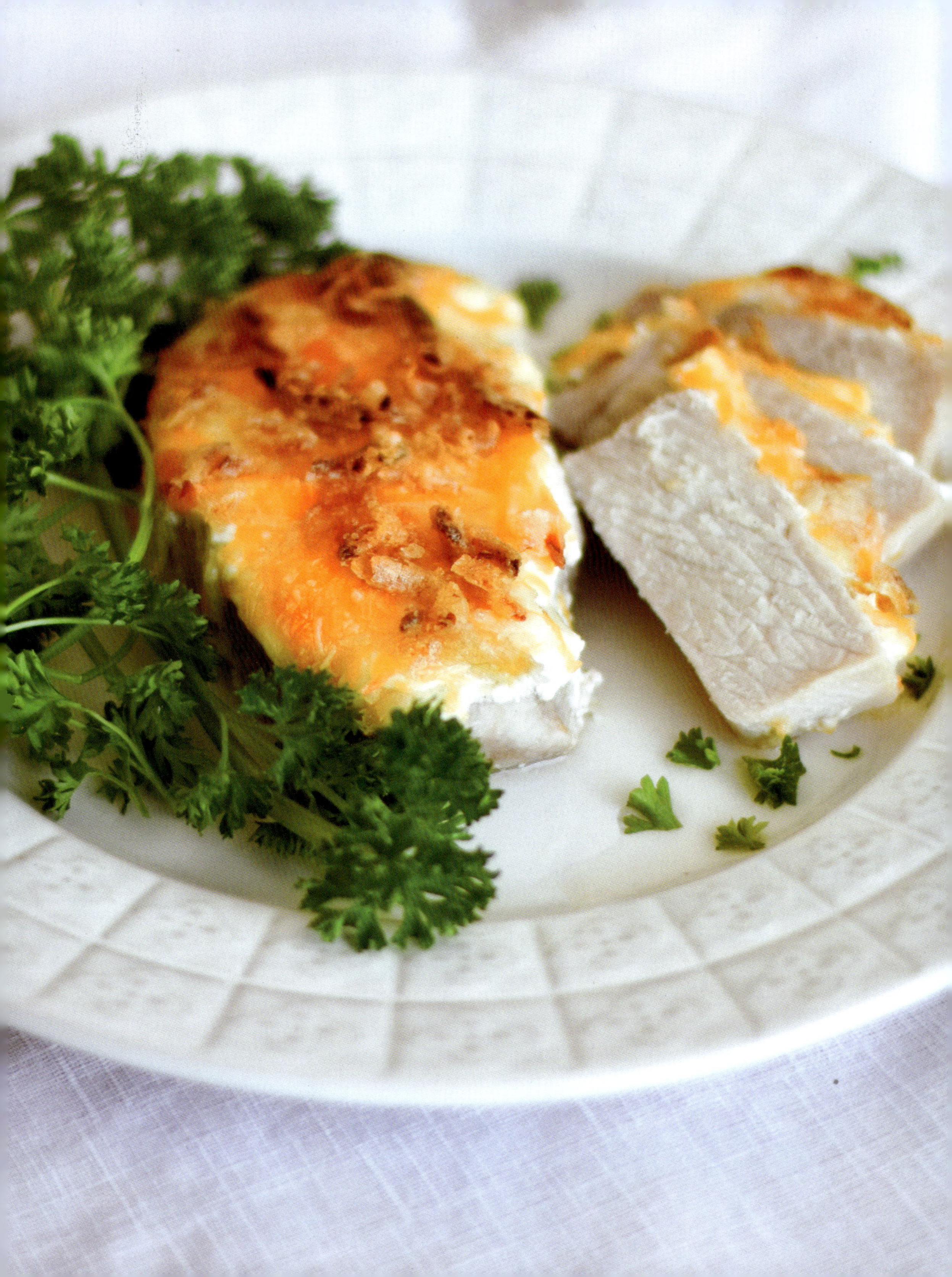

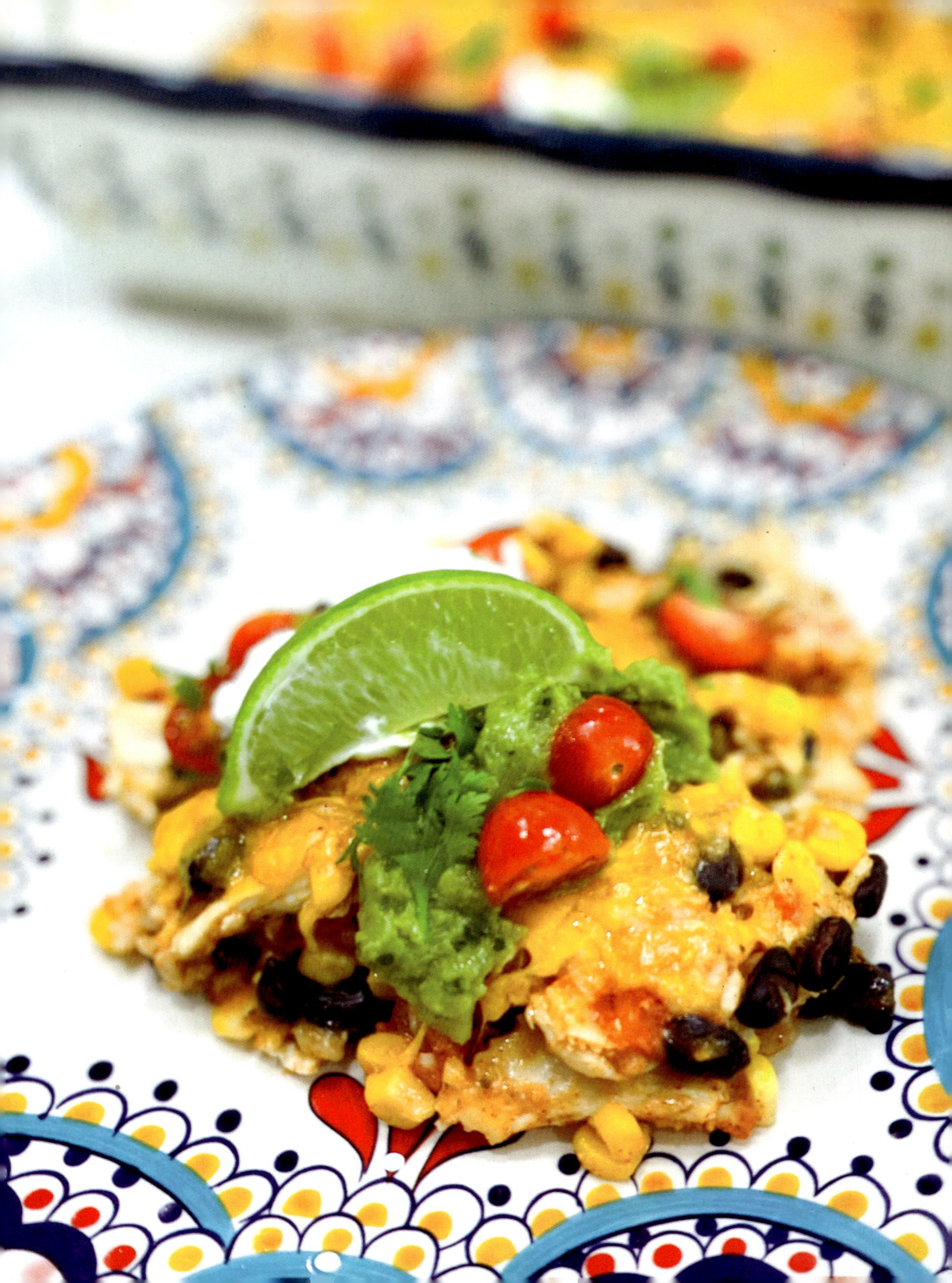

Fiesta Chicken Casserole

Chicken, rice, tomatoes, corn, and black beans are enveloped in a creamy and spicy sauce for a perfect blend of comfort and zing. This Fiesta Chicken Casserole is one of my most popular recipes!

Prep time: 10 mins   **Cook time:** 35 mins   **Servings:** 4-5

INGREDIENTS

- 4 cups cooked shredded chicken
- 1 cup uncooked instant rice
- 10 oz can Diced Tomatoes and Green Chiles
- 2 tbsp taco seasoning
- 3 tbsp milk
- 15 oz can corn, drained
- 10 oz can cream of chicken soup
- 15 oz can black beans, drained and rinsed
- 1 1/2 cups shredded cheddar cheese
- toppings like shredded lettuce, diced tomatoes, and sliced avocado (optional)

DIRECTIONS

1. Preheat oven to 350°F.
2. To a large bowl, add all of the ingredients except 1/2 cup of the cheese. Stir well.
3. Grease a 9×13 baking dish with non-stick spray. Pour the casserole into the baking dish. Sprinkle the remaining cheese on top and cover with aluminum foil. Bake for 30 minutes, then remove foil and bake for an additional 10 more minutes.
4. Top with your favorite toppings and enjoy!

Chicken Stuffing Casserole with Zucchini

Chicken Stuffing Casserole with Zucchini is creamy, savory, carb-y, and totally delicious! If you're a stuffing fan, you will love this.

Prep time: 15 mins **Cook time:** 45 mins **Servings:** 4-5

INGREDIENTS

Creamy Sauce

- 3 tbsp butter
- 3 tbsp all-purpose flour
- 3/4 cup chicken broth
- 1/2 cup milk
- 1/2 tsp salt
- 1/2 tsp pepper

Casserole Mixture

- 6 oz box Savory Herbs Stuffing mix
- 4 tbsp melted butter
- 2 zucchinis, diced
- 1 yellow onion, diced
- 4 cups shredded rotisserie chicken
- 1/2 cup sour cream
- 1/2 tsp salt
- 1/2 tsp pepper

DIRECTIONS

1. Preheat oven to 350°F.
2. To a large skillet over medium heat, add the butter. Once it melts down, whisk in the flour. Once the flour turns a golden color, slowly whisk in the broth and milk. Lastly, whisk in the salt and pepper. If your creamy sauce is too thick, whisk in more water until your desired consistency. Set to the side. If you want to skip this step, you can use a 10 oz can of cream of chicken soup instead.
3. To a large bowl, add the stuffing and 4 tbsp of melted butter and stir well to coat the stuffing. Remove 3/4 cup of the stuffing and set aside. This will be the topping for the end.
4. To the bowl with the majority of the stuffing, add in the creamy sauce, zucchini, onion, chicken, sour cream, salt, and pepper. Stir well to incorporate the ingredients.
5. Spray a 9×13 baking dish with non-stick spray. Spread the casserole evenly in the baking dish and top with the reserved stuffing. Bake for 40-45 minutes. Enjoy!

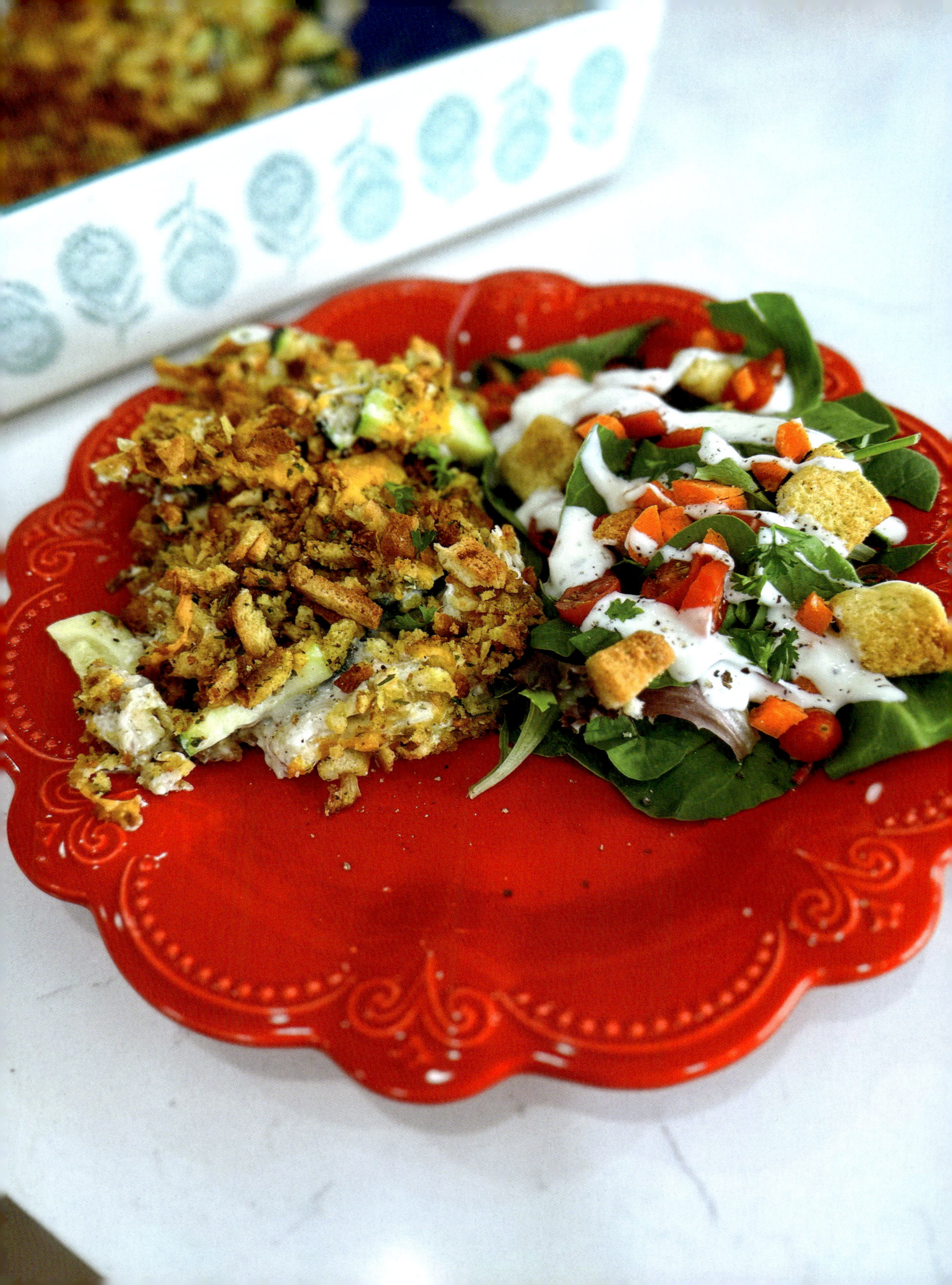

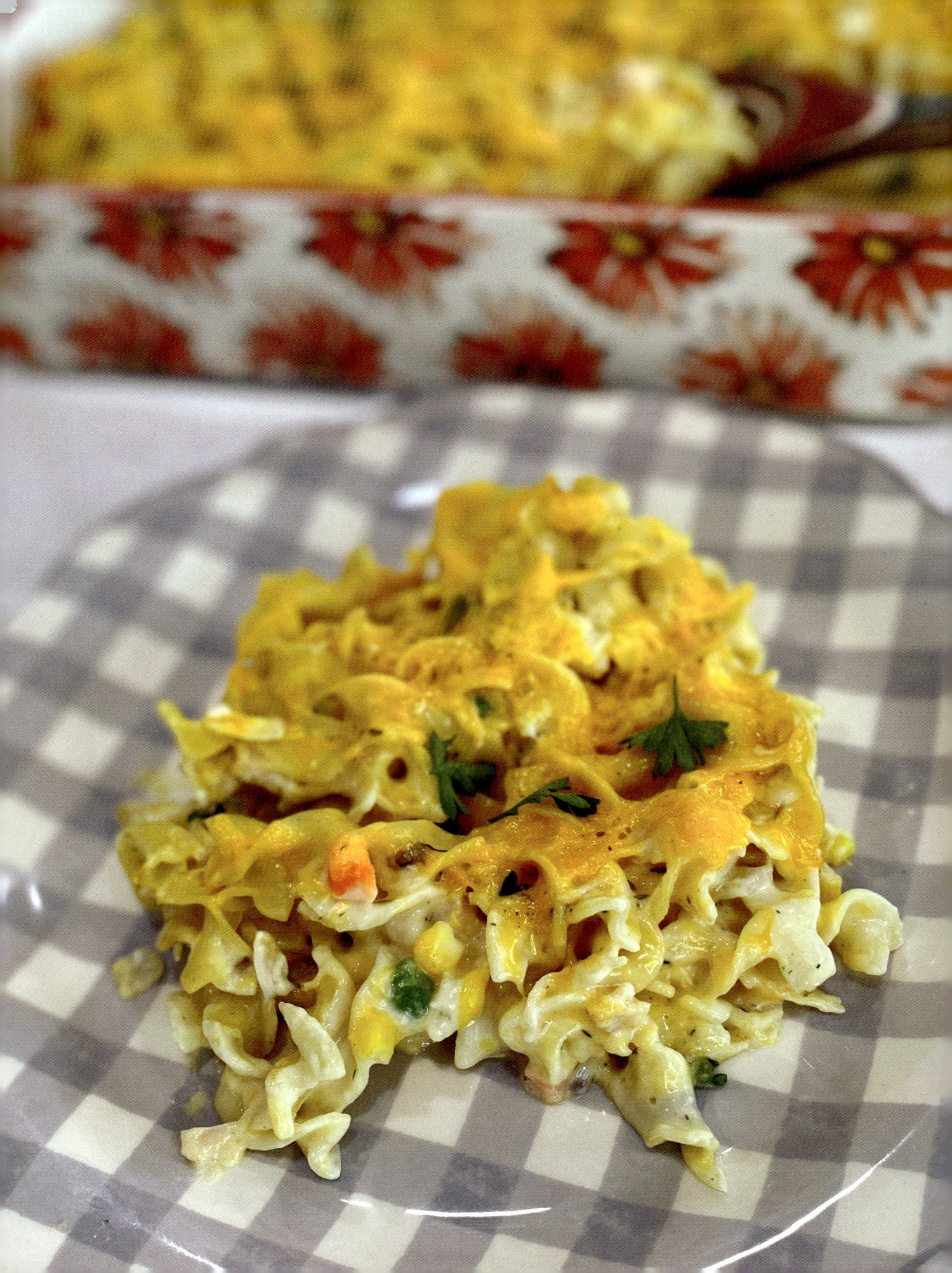

Chicken Noodle Casserole

Chicken Noodle Casserole is one of my favorite pantry meals. It uses mostly canned or frozen goods that I always have in my pantry at home.

Prep time: 15 mins   **Cook time:** 30 mins   **Servings:** 4-5

INGREDIENTS

- 12 ounces egg noodles
- 10 oz can cream of chicken soup
- 10 oz can cream of mushroom soup
- 1/2 cup sour cream (use light sour cream for less fat)
- 3/4 cup milk
- 12 oz can of chicken, drained (or use any cooked shredded chicken)
- 1 cup shredded cheddar cheese
- 1/2 yellow onion, diced
- 1 cup frozen mixed vegetables
- 1/2 tsp garlic powder
- 1 tsp salt
- 1/2 tsp pepper
- 1/2 tsp dried thyme
- 1/2 tsp onion powder

DIRECTIONS

1. Preheat oven to 350°F.
2. Grease a 9×13 baking dish with non-stick pan spray.
3. To a large pot of boiling water add the noodles and cook according to the package instructions. Strain and set aside.
4. To a large bowl, add both cans of soup, sour cream, milk, chicken, 1/3 cup of the cheese, onion, mixed vegetables, and seasonings, then stir well. Stir in the cooked egg noodles.
5. Pour into the baking dish and sprinkle with the remaining cheese. Bake for 28-30 minutes or until cheese is melted and bubbly. Enjoy!

Cheesy Pierogi Casserole

Cheesy Pierogi Casserole is one of those meals that uses just a handful of ingredients but tastes amazing. You will love this unique casserole.

Prep time: 5 mins **Cook time:** 56 mins **Servings:** 4-5

INGREDIENTS

- 24 oz jar marinara sauce
- 16 oz package frozen cheese pierogi
- 16 oz jar Alfredo sauce
- 1/2 cup grated Parmesan cheese

DIRECTIONS

1. Preheat oven to 350°F.
2. Grease a 9×13 baking dish with non-stick spray. Pour half of the marinara sauce into the bottom of the pan and spread evenly.
3. Place the pierogis next to each other in the dish and pour the remaining marinara sauce over the top. Pour the Alfredo sauce over everything and spread evenly. Sprinkle the top with Parmesan cheese. Cover with aluminum foil.
4. Bake for 40 minutes. Remove the foil and bake for an additional 15 minutes. Enjoy!

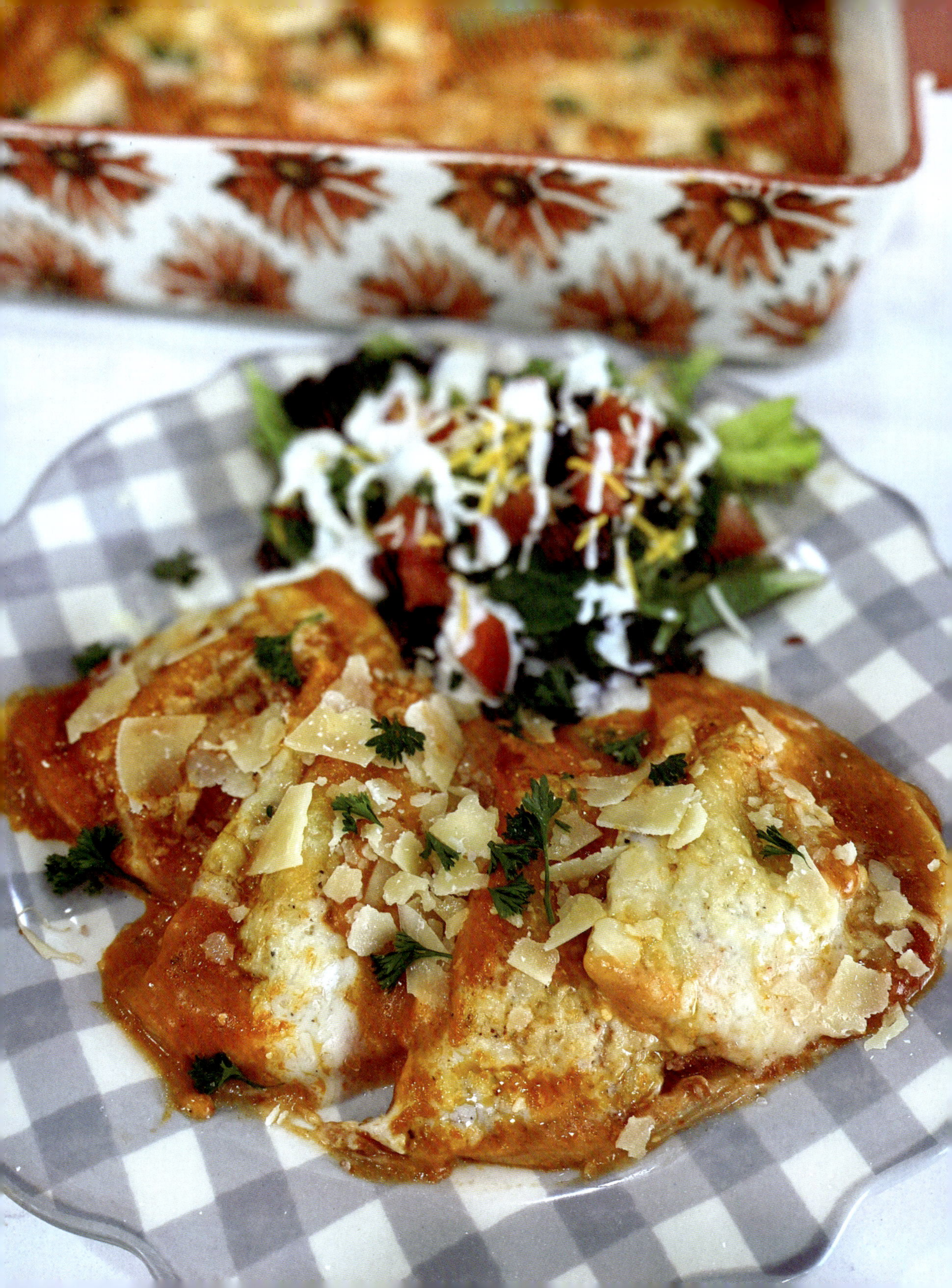

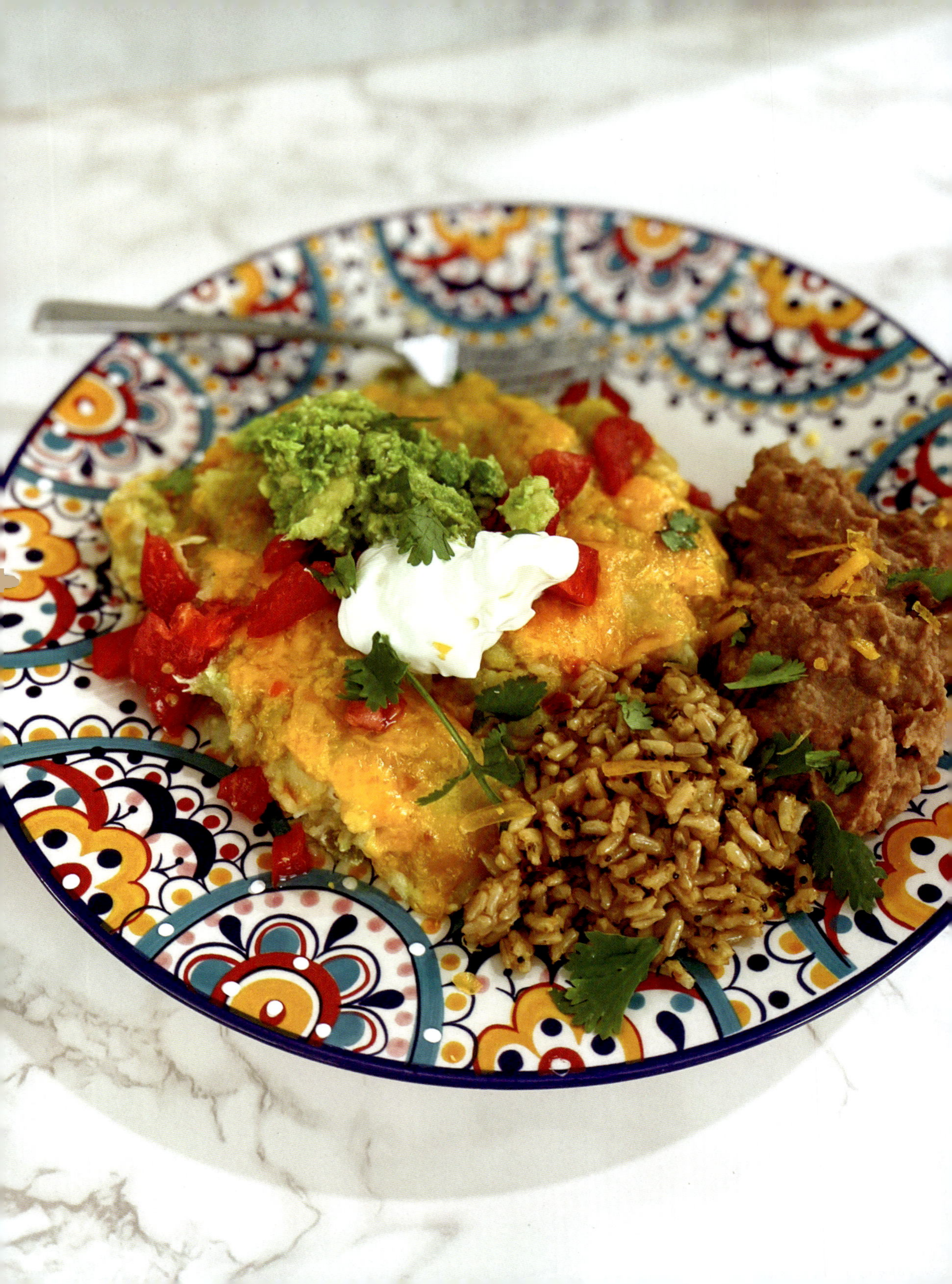

Green Chile Chicken Enchiladas

Cheesy, a little spicy, and super flavorful, these Green Chile Chicken Enchiladas are a great weeknight meal.

Prep time: 15 mins   **Cook time:** 30 mins   **Servings:** 4-5

INGREDIENTS

- 2 1/2 cups cooked shredded chicken
- 2 cups sharp cheddar cheese, shredded
- 4 oz can green chiles
- 3/4 cup sour cream
- 1/2 tsp salt and pepper
- 20 oz green chile enchilada sauce
- 12-14 small corn tortillas

DIRECTIONS

1. Preheat the oven to 350°F.
2. To a bowl, add chicken, 1 cup of cheese, green chiles, sour cream, and salt and pepper, and stir to combine.
3. Spray 9×13 baking dish with nonstick spray.
4. To a small pot over the stove, add enchilada sauce and bring to a boil.
5. One by one, dip each tortilla in the hot enchilada sauce. Then fill each with 2-3 tbsp of the chicken mixture, roll up, and place seam side down in the baking dish. Repeat until the baking dish is full. Pour the rest of the sauce on top and top with remaining cheese.
6. Bake for 25-30 minutes. Enjoy!

Baked Manicotti

Baked Manicotti is such a delicious and decadent meal that's not too hard to make at home. Make tasty, restaurant-worthy manicotti at home in under an hour.

Prep time: 20 mins	**Cook time:** 20 mins	**Servings:** 4-5

INGREDIENTS

- 15 oz ricotta cheese
- 1 3/4 cup mozzarella cheese
- 3/4 cup Parmesan cheese
- 2 eggs
- 1 tsp Italian seasoning
- 1 tsp salt
- 1/2 tsp pepper
- 24 oz marinara sauce
- 6 oz manicotti pasta

DIRECTIONS

1. Preheat oven to 350ºF.
2. Cook manicotti according to the package instructions.
3. To a medium-sized bowl add the ricotta, 1 cup of mozzarella cheese, Parmesan, eggs, and seasonings. Stir well. For easy filling, place this cheese mixture in a large Ziploc bag and cut a small hole in the corner of the bag.
4. Grease a 9×13 baking dish with nonstick spray and pour half of the marinara sauce into the bottom of the dish.
5. Fill each manicotti shell with 3-4 tablespoons of the cheese mixture. Place into the baking dish side-by-side. Pour the remaining sauce over the top and top with the remaining mozzarella cheese. Bake for 40 minutes. Enjoy!

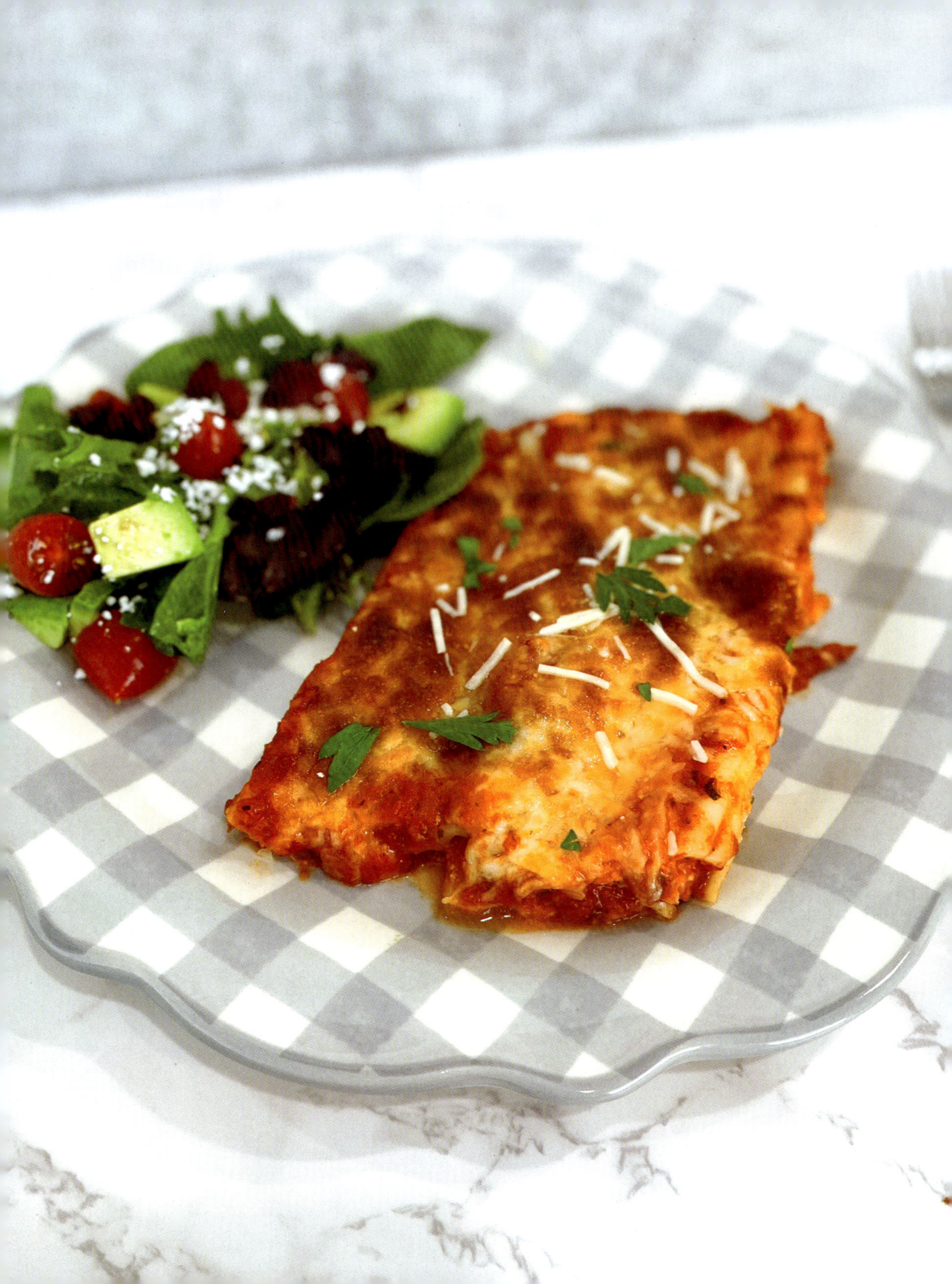

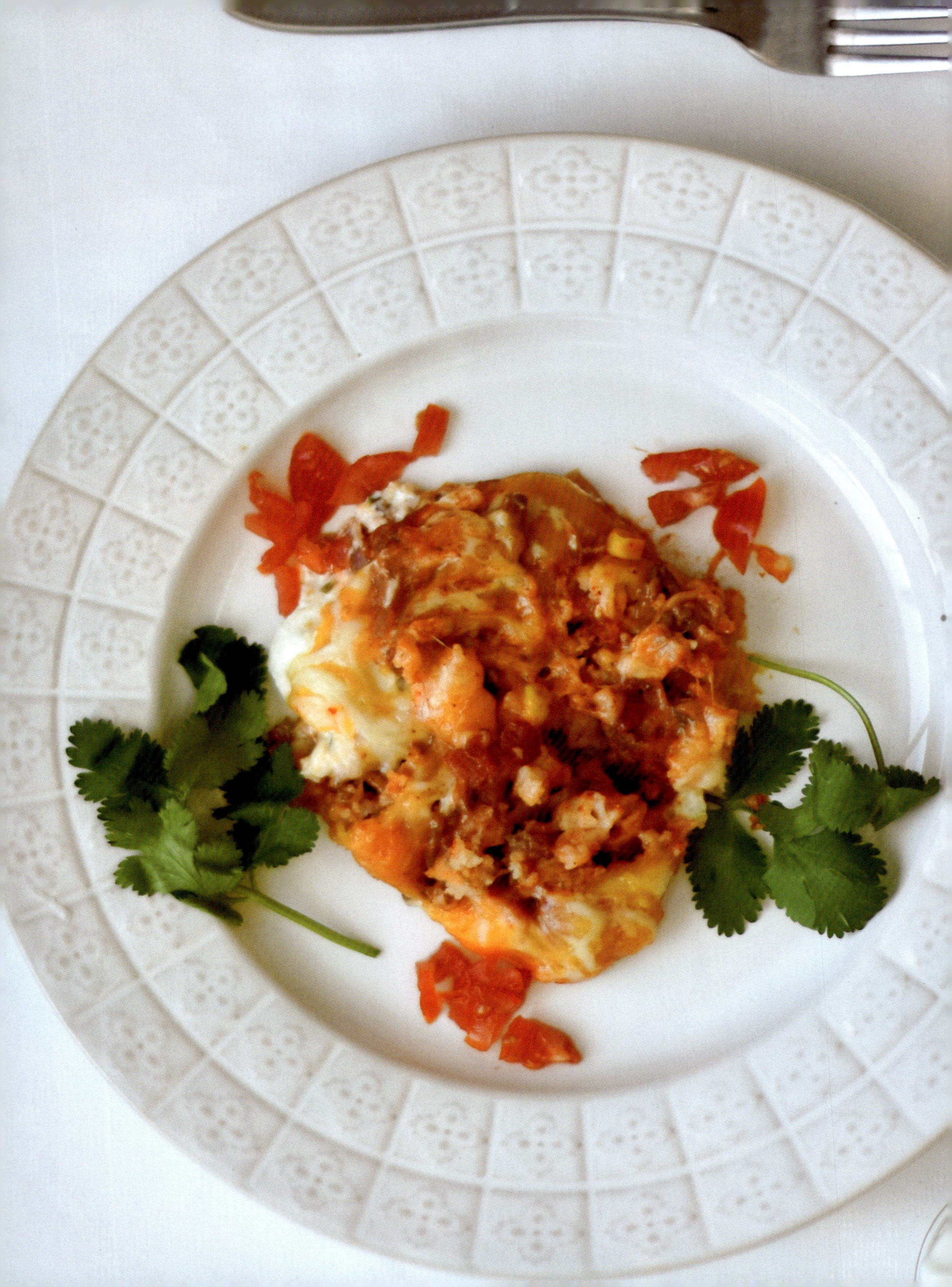

John Wayne Casserole

Yummy biscuit crust is topped with delicious layers of ground beef, veggies, and lots and lots of cheese. This John Wayne Casserole will become a family favorite!

Prep time: 15 mins   **Cook time:** 40 mins   **Servings:** 6

INGREDIENTS

- 1 lb ground beef
- 1/2 white onion, diced
- 1 1/2 tbsp taco seasoning
- 1/4 cup water
- 1 can Diced Tomatoes and Green Chiles
- 1 can corn, drained
- 1 cup shredded sharp cheddar cheese
- 1 cup mozzarella cheese

Biscuit Mixture
- 2 cups all-purpose baking mix
- 1 cup water

Creamy Mixture
- 1/4 cup mayonnaise
- 7.5 oz chive and onion cream cheese
- 1/8 tsp pepper
- 1/8 tsp garlic powder

Toppings (optional)
- chopped cherry tomatoes
- sour cream
- more cheese
- cilantro

DIRECTIONS

1. Preheat oven to 325°F.
2. Add the ground beef and onion to a skillet over medium-high heat, and cook until the beef is cooked through. Remove any excess grease, then add in the taco seasoning and water and simmer for 3 minutes. Add in the can of corn, and stir to combine.
3. Make the biscuit mixture by combining the all-purpose baking mix and water in a small bowl. Stir until well combined and set aside.
4. Whisk the ingredients for the creamy mixture together in a small bowl. Set aside.
5. Grease a 9×13 baking dish with non-stick spray. Spread the all-purpose baking mix mixture evenly in the bottom of the pan. Pour the ground beef mixture on top, then spread the creamy mixture over the ground beef, then sprinkle with the cheddar and mozzarella. Bake for 40 minutes. Let sit for 10 minutes. Top with your favorite toppings and enjoy!

White Chicken Mushroom Spinach Lasagna

Chicken and veggies are layered between creamy white sauce, lots of cheese, and noodles for a delicious take on lasagna.

Prep time: 15 mins   **Cook time:** 40 mins   **Servings:** 5

INGREDIENTS

- 1 white onion, diced
- 8 oz white mushrooms, sliced
- 2 tbsp olive oil
- 1 tbsp minced garlic
- 1 tsp dried basil
- 1 tsp dried oregano
- 1/2 tsp salt
- 2 cups fresh spinach
- 2 cups cooked shredded chicken
- 2 1/2 cups chicken broth
- 1 1/2 cups whole milk
- 1/4 tsp nutmeg
- 1/4 cup all-purpose flour
- 1/4 cup Parmesan cheese
- 9 oven-ready lasagna noodles
- 2 1/2 cups mozzarella cheese

DIRECTIONS

1. Preheat oven to 375°F.
2. Add olive oil to a large skillet over medium heat. Once hot, add in the sliced mushrooms, diced onion, minced garlic, dried basil, dried oregano, and salt. Stir well and let cook for 5-10 minutes, or until the veggies are soft and there is no more liquid in the pan.
   Stir in the spinach and chicken until everything is well combined and pour the mixture into a separate bowl and set aside.
3. To make the sauce, add the chicken broth, milk, nutmeg, and a dash of salt to the pan where you cooked the veggies. Whisk the mixture together and bring to a simmer. Slowly whisk in the flour a little at a time. Make sure you whisk it in slowly or your sauce will become clumpy. Whisk until it starts to thicken about 5-8 minutes. Whisk in Parmesan cheese for 1-2 minutes or until it melts.
4. To assemble the lasagna, grease a 2 qt baking dish and pour 1 cup of sauce in the bottom of the pan
5. Add a layer of lasagna noodles over the sauce (you might need to break the noodles up to fit in all of the space on the baking dish), then add a layer of the chicken vegetable mixture, then sprinkle 3/4 cup of mozzarella cheese on the top. Repeat two more times for a total of three layers.
6. Cover with aluminum foil and bake for 25 minutes. Remove the foil and bake, uncovered, for an additional 15 minutes. Enjoy!

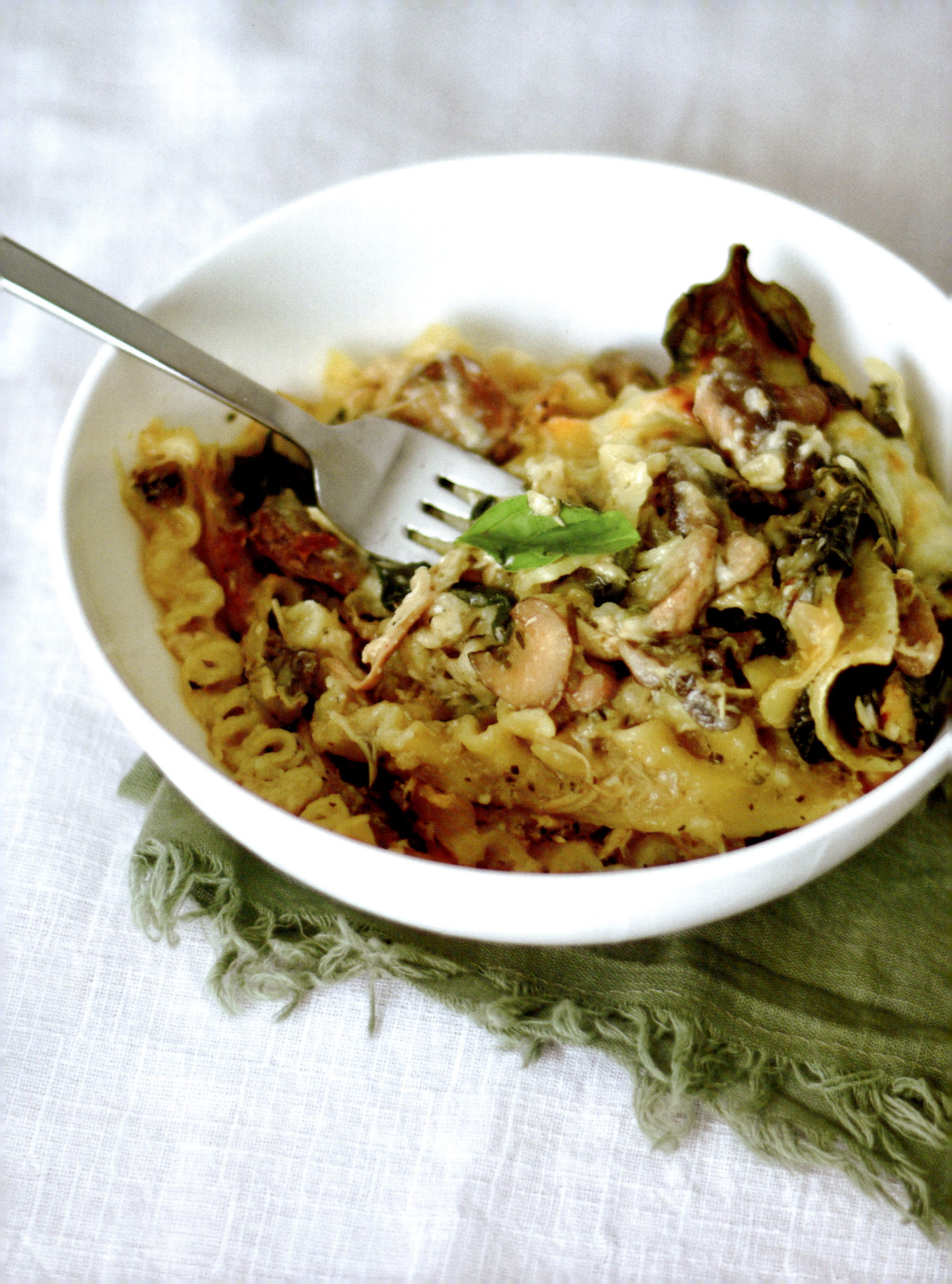

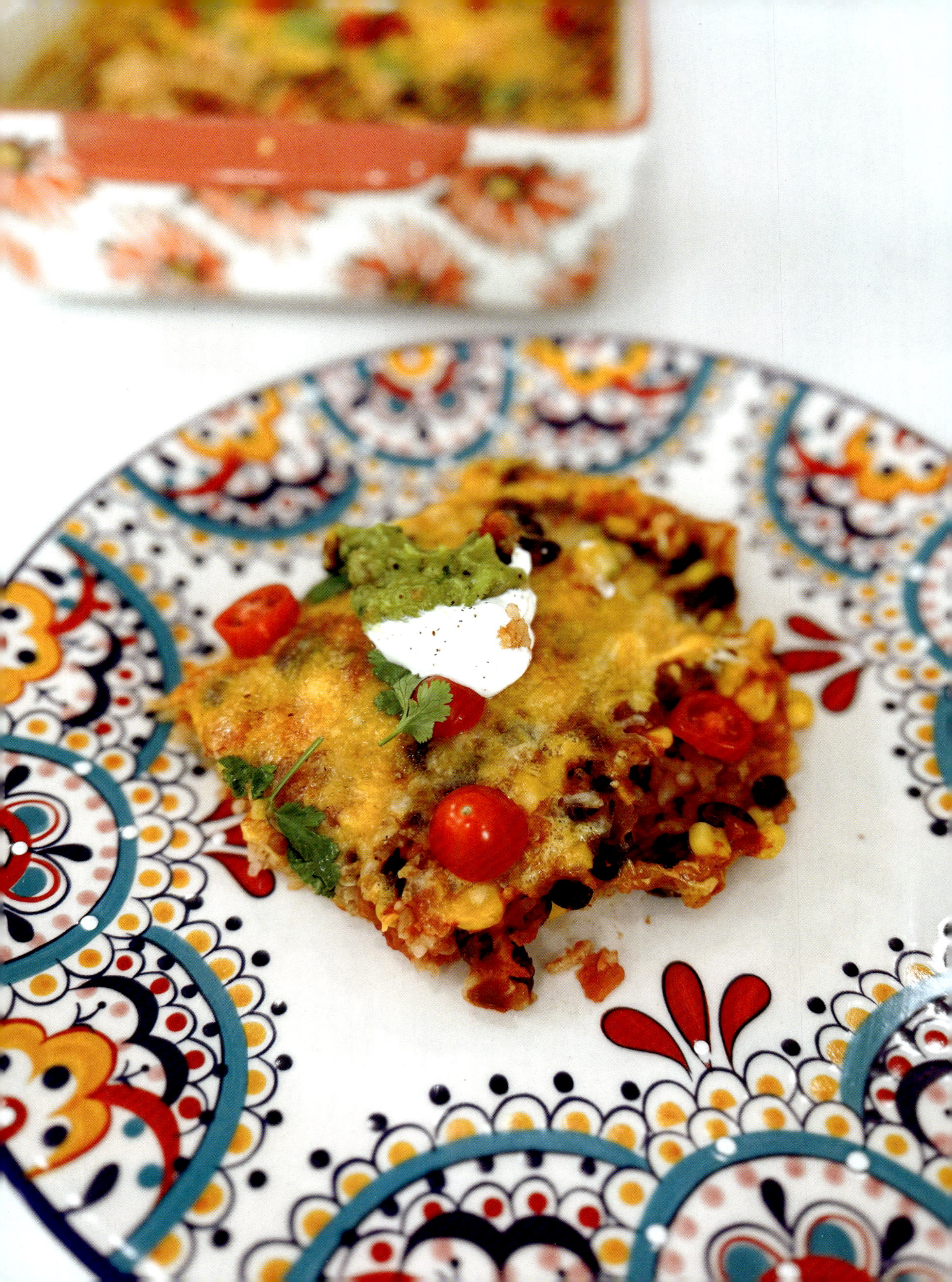

Vegetarian Mexican Casserole

Seven ingredients, five minutes of prep time, and one baking dish create the most delicious and easy Vegetarian Mexican Casserole.

Prep time: 5 mins   **Cook time:** 1 hour   **Servings:** 4-5

INGREDIENTS

- 1 cup uncooked jasmine rice or white rice
- 15 oz can corn, drained
- 15 oz can black beans, drained and rinsed
- 1 1/2 cup salsa (any salsa works)
- 2 cups vegetable broth
- 1 tbsp taco seasoning
- 1 1/2 cups Mexican style cheese

Toppings

- avocado, sour cream, diced tomatoes, shredded lettuce, etc (optional)

DIRECTIONS

1. Preheat oven to 375°F.
2. Grease a 9×13 baking dish with non-stick pan spray.
3. Directly into the baking dish, add the rice, black beans, salsa, vegetable broth, taco seasoning and 1/2 cup of cheese.
4. Stir to combine the ingredients and cover with foil. Bake for 50 minutes. Remove from the oven, discard the foil, and stir the ingredients around in the baking dish. Top with the remaining cheese. Bake for an additional 12 minutes, uncovered, or until the cheese is melted. Top with your favorite toppings and enjoy!

French Onion Chicken Casserole

French Onion Chicken Casserole has classic French flavors, tender chicken, and lots and lots of cheese. What more could you want?

Prep time: 20 mins   **Cook time:** 30 mins   **Servings:** 4-5

INGREDIENTS

- 2 tbsp butter
- 1 large yellow onion, sliced
- 2 large chicken breasts
- 2 tsp paprika
- 1/2 tsp salt
- 1/4 tsp pepper
- 10 oz can French onion soup
- 1/4 cup water
- 1 tbsp balsamic vinegar
- 3/4 cup mozzarella cheese, shredded
- mashed potatoes, rice, or cooked egg noodles, for serving

DIRECTIONS

1. Preheat oven to 350°F.
2. To a large skillet over medium heat, add the butter and onion. Once simmering, put the lid on the pan and turn the heat to low. Let the onions cook for 10-12 minutes, stirring often, until golden brown. Remove onions with a slotted spoon and set aside, keeping the excess drippings in the pan.
3. Season the chicken on each side with paprika, salt, and pepper. Turn the heat to medium-high and add in the chicken to the pan in which onion were cooked. Sear for 2-3 minutes on each side to brown the chicken on the outside. This will create a golden brown crust on the outside of the chicken (chicken does not need to be cooked through at this point).
4. Add the cooked onions, French onion soup, water, and balsamic vinegar and let simmer for 2-3 minutes to thicken the sauce.
5. Grease a medium-sized casserole dish with nonstick spray. Add the entire mixture to the baking dish and cover with mozzarella cheese. Bake for 25-30 minutes, or until the chicken is cooked through. Serve over mashed potatoes, rice, or egg noodles.

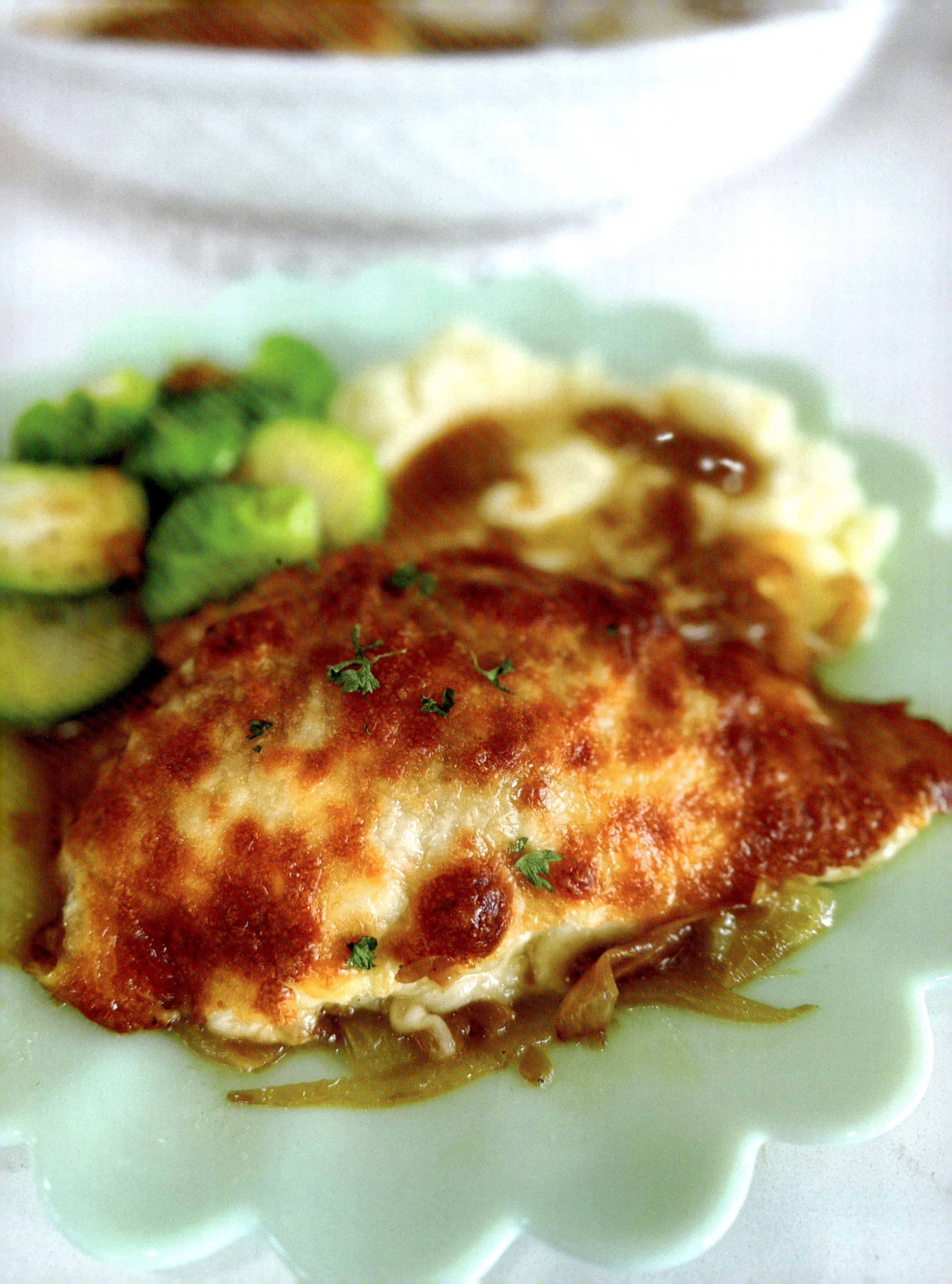

NOTES

SHEET PAN DINNERS

Are you looking for an easy, healthier version for dinner tonight? Look no more. These sheet pan meals have it all. Lots of flavor, easy preparation and cleanup, and savory roasted vegetables. Whether you are single or have more people to feed, these recipes have it all!

Sheet Pan Loaded Quesadillas

This is a GIANT LOADED SHEET PAN QUESADILLA! I'm talking a sheet pan-sized quesadilla to cut into pieces and share. You'll love it!

Prep time: 15 mins   **Cook time:** 20 mins   **Servings:** 4-5

INGREDIENTS

- 1 lb ground beef
- 1 diced white onion
- 2 tbsp taco seasoning
- 1/2 cup water
- 1 can black beans, drained and rinsed
- 1 can of corn, drained and rinsed
- 1/4 cup salsa
- 8 large burrito-sized tortillas
- 1 1/2 cups colby jack and cheddar cheese, or any type you prefer

Equipment

- 2 sheet pans

DIRECTIONS

1. Preheat oven to 425°F.
2. In a skillet over medium heat, cook ground beef and onion completely through and remove any excess grease.
3. Add in taco seasoning and 1/2 cup water. Stir together and bring to a simmer for about 1-2 minutes.
4. Add in black beans, corn, and salsa. Combine and remove the pan from heat.
5. On a greased sheet pan, place 6 tortillas with about 1/3 of each tortilla hanging off the pan. Now place a tortilla in the center.
6. Pour the cooked meat into the center of the tortillas and spread evenly. Top with cheese.
7. Place a tortilla on top in the center, and fold over the first layer of tortillas to completely cover the top of the quesadilla.
8. Spray the bottom side of the second sheet pan and place on top of the giant quesadilla with light pressure applied.
9. Bake for 20 minutes, with the second pan on top. After 20 minutes, remove the top pan and broil for an additional 1-3 minutes until desired crispness is achieved.

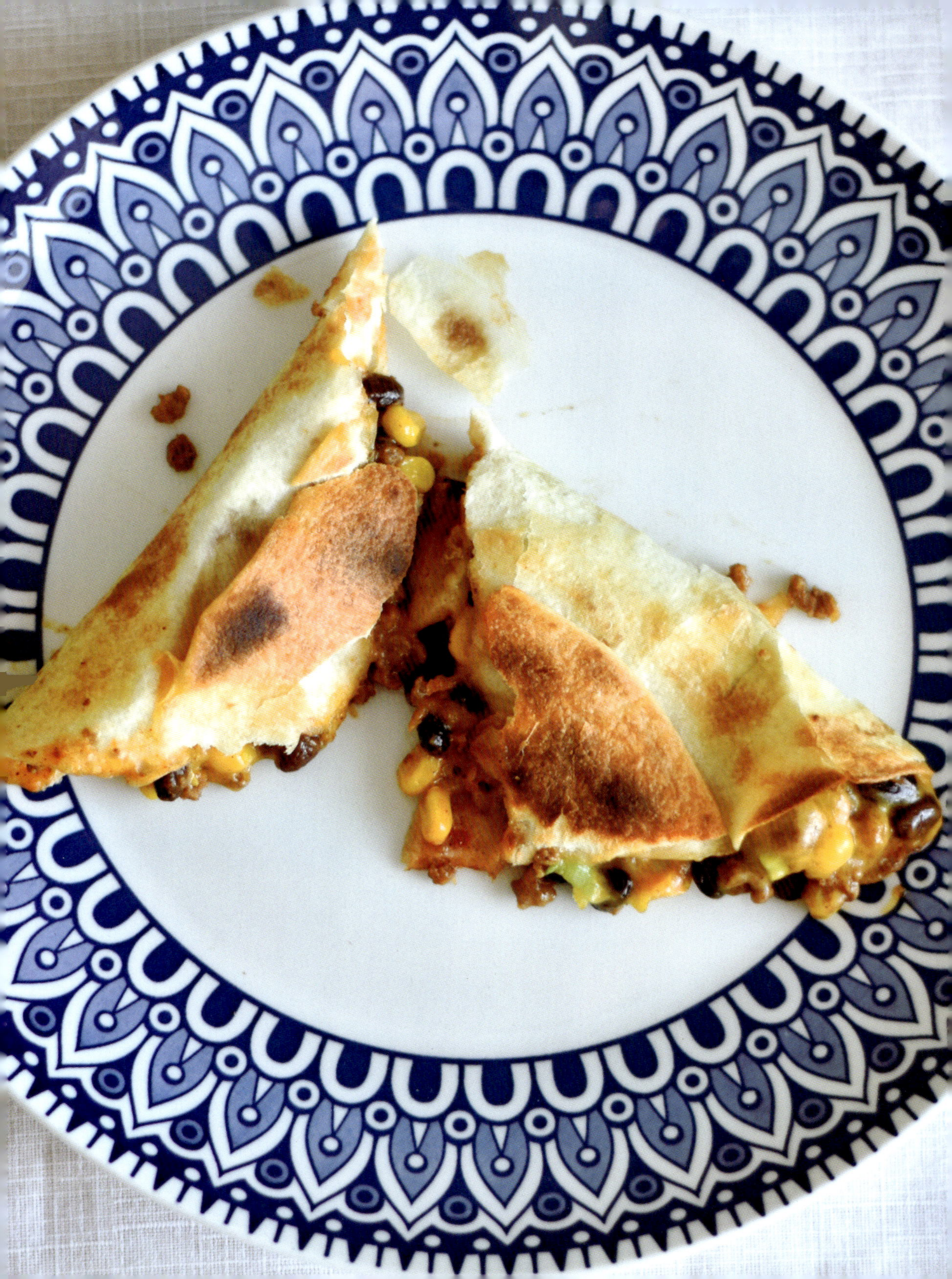

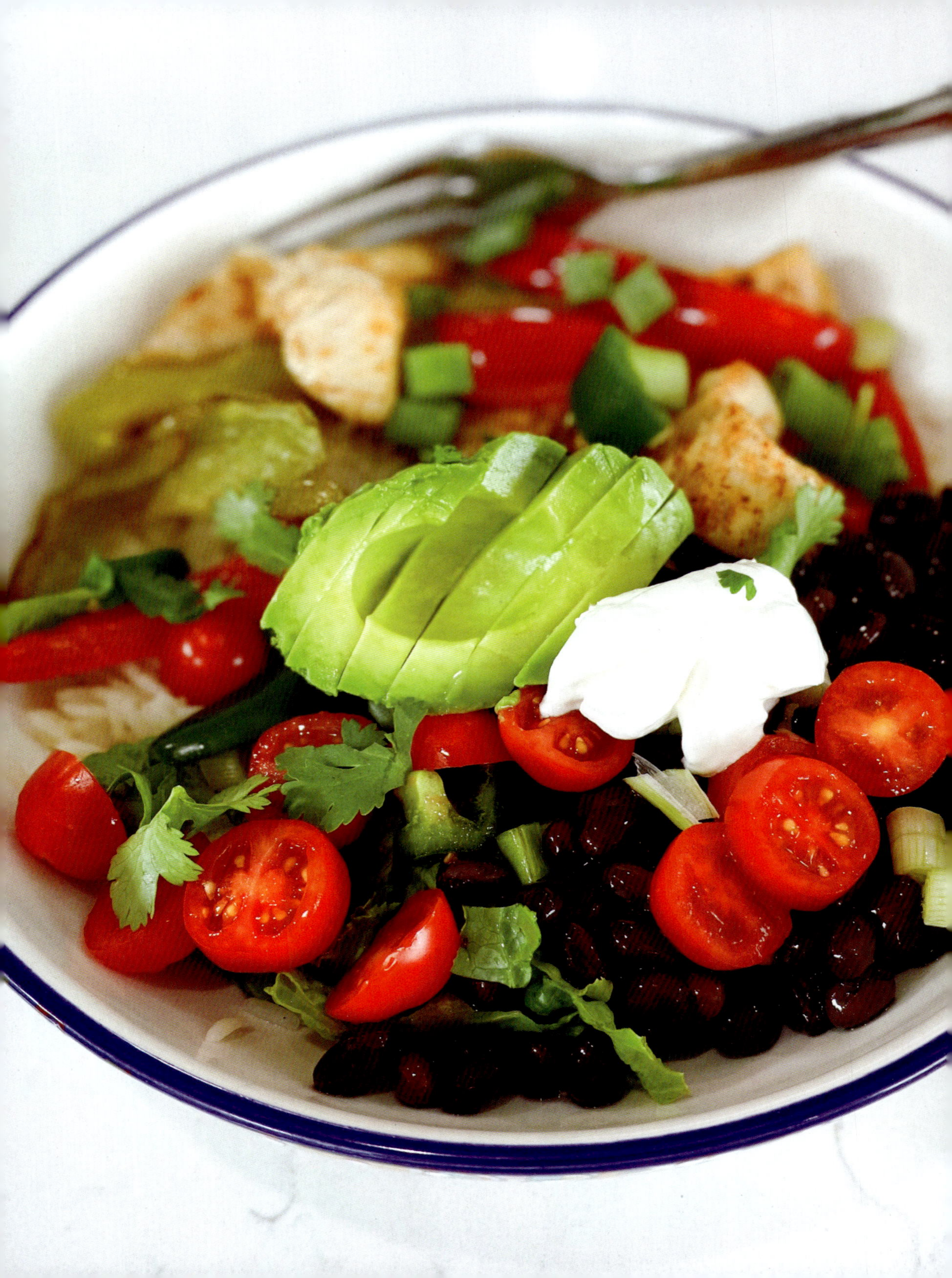

Sheet Pan Burrito Bowls

Build burrito bowls with zesty lime chicken, fajita veggies, rice, and all of your favorite toppings.

Prep time: 10 mins **Cook time:** 25 mins **Servings:** 5

INGREDIENTS

Chicken
- 1 yellow onion, diced
- 1 green bell pepper, sliced
- 1 red bell pepper, sliced
- 1 1/2 lbs chicken breast, cubed
- 3 tbsp olive oil
- 1 tsp cumin
- 1 tsp onion powder
- 1 tsp oregano
- 1 tsp chili powder
- 1 lime juiced

Burrito Bowls
- cooked white rice
- toppings like black beans, shredded lettuce, sliced tomatoes, avocados, cilantro, sour cream

DIRECTIONS

1. Preheat oven to 425°F.
2. Combine the chicken, oil, seasonings, and lime juice in a large bowl and stir to coat evenly.
3. Line a large sheet pan with parchment paper. Spread the peppers, onions, and chicken on the sheet pan. Bake for 25 minutes or until the chicken reaches an internal temperature 165°F.
4. Place the chicken and peppers in bowls over cooked rice, along with your favorite toppings. Enjoy!

Sheet Pan Burgers with Onions and Potatoes

These Sheet Pan Burgers are fantastic- bake the patties atop onions, so the burger comes out perfectly and the onions are caramelized!

Prep time: 15 mins   **Cook time:** 25 mins   **Servings:** 4

INGREDIENTS

Hamburgers

- 1 lb lean ground beef (higher fat ground beef will turn out greasy)
- 3 tbsp breadcrumbs
- 2 tbsp yellow mustard
- 1 tbsp Worcestershire sauce
- 1 large yellow onion, sliced thin
- 1 tbsp olive oil
- 1 tsp salt
- 1/2 tsp pepper
- sliced cheese
- hamburger buns
- lettuce
- tomato
- mayo
- mustard
- ketchup
- pickles

Potatoes

- 1 lb baby golden potatoes, diced
- 2 tbsp olive oil
- salt and pepper, to taste

DIRECTIONS

1. Preheat oven to 425°F.
2. To a medium-sized bowl, add the beef, breadcrumbs, mustard, and Worcestershire sauce. Mix with your hands until everything is incorporated. Set aside.
3. Line a sheet pan with aluminum foil. Place onions on the pan and drizzle with olive oil, sprinkle with salt & pepper, and toss to coat.
4. Form the ground beef mixture into 4 patties.
5. Gently nestle each hamburger on top of the onions.
6. Place the potatoes on one side of the baking sheet and drizzle with olive oil and salt and pepper.
7. Place pan in the oven and cook for approximately 25-28 minutes, or until patties are brown around edges and no longer pink in the center.
8. Remove from oven and top with cheese. Build burgers with buns, patties, and onions, then customize with your favorite hamburger toppings. Serve the potatoes on the side. Enjoy!

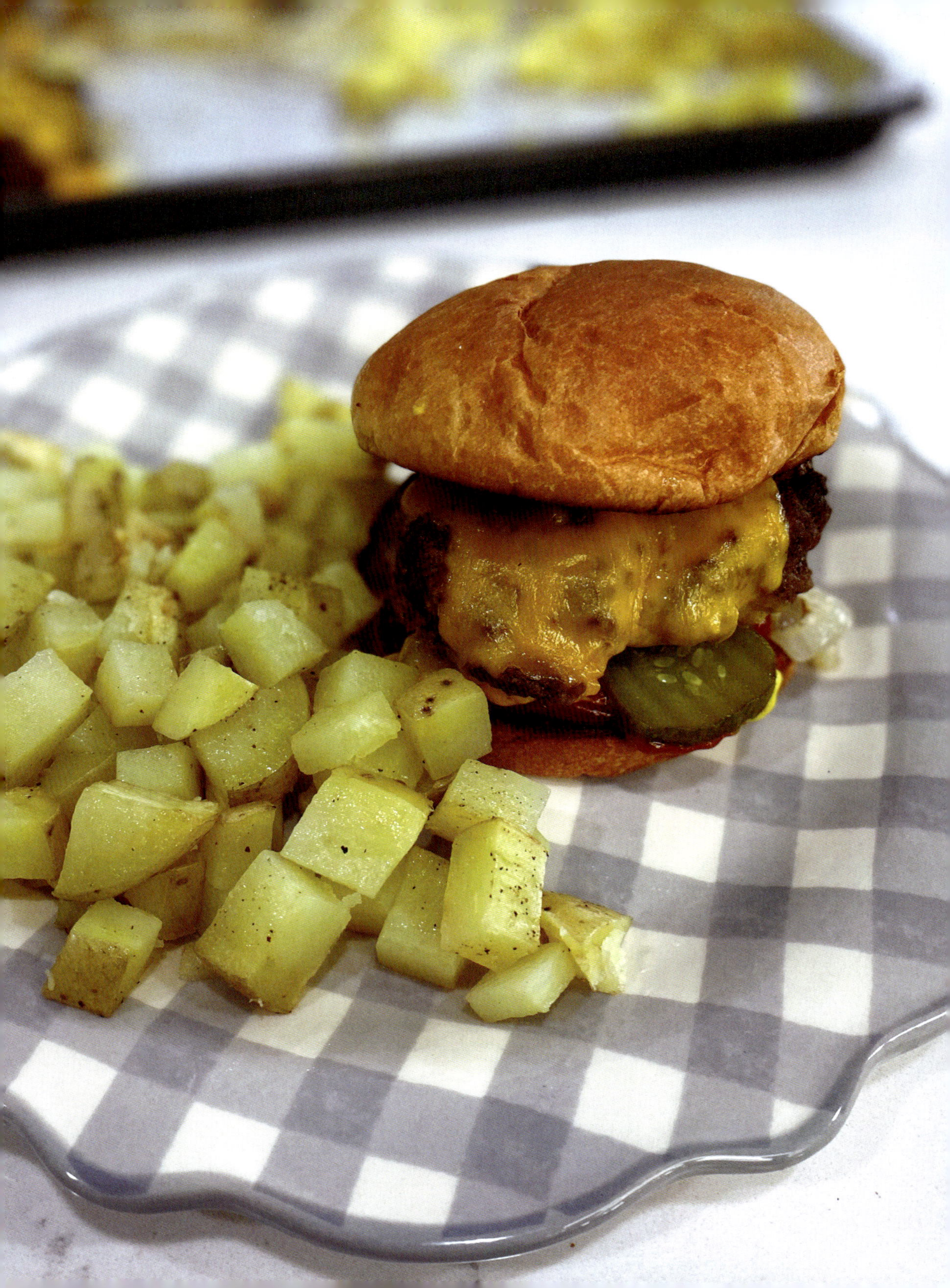

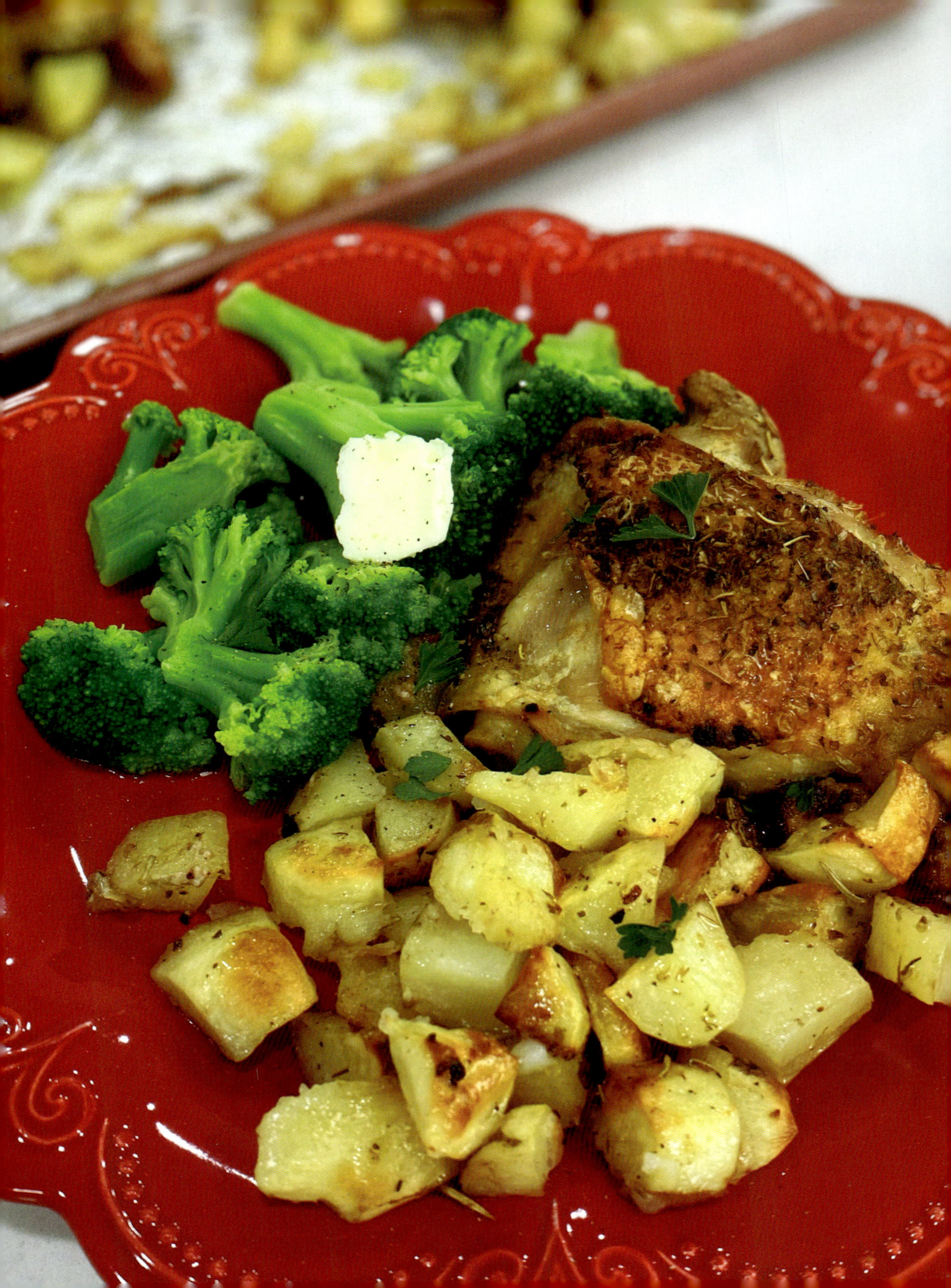

Sheet Pan Greek Chicken Thighs and Potatoes

These Sheet Pan Greek Chicken Thighs are flavored with lemon, garlic, and herbs and turn out juicy and flavorful. They're going to be one of your new go-to meals!

Prep time: 5 mins   **Cook time:** 1 hour   **Servings:** 4

INGREDIENTS

- 4 bone-in, skin-on chicken thighs
- 1 1/2 lbs Russet potatoes, peeled and diced into bite-sized pieces
- 1 tbsp dried oregano
- 2 tsp salt
- 2 tsp dried rosemary
- 1 tsp black pepper
- 2 lemons, juiced
- 3 tbsp olive oil
- 2 tbsp minced garlic
- 1/2 cup chicken broth

DIRECTIONS

1. Preheat oven to 425°F.
2. Line a sheet pan with aluminum foil.
3. To a large bowl add all of the ingredients except the chicken broth and stir to coat everything well. Dump all ingredients onto the sheet pan and scatter around the pan. Place the chicken skin side up. Drizzle the broth around the pan.
4. Bake for 30 minutes. Remove from the oven and flip the potatoes. Bake for 30 more minutes, or until chicken is completely cooked through. Enjoy!

Mozzarella Stuffed Meatloaf

This Mozzarella Stuffed Meatloaf is a fun take on a classic weeknight dinner and is so decadent and delicious!

Prep time: 10 mins   **Cook time:** 25 mins   **Servings:** 4-5

INGREDIENTS

Vegetable Ingredients

- 1 1/2 lbs red potatoes, cut into bite-sized pieces
- 12 oz bag frozen green beans
- 2 tbsp olive oil
- dash salt and pepper

Meatloaf Ingredients

- 1 lb lean ground beef
- 2/3 cup Italian style breadcrumbs
- 1 tbsp minced garlic
- 1/3 cup ketchup, divided
- 1 tbsp Worcestershire sauce
- 1 tbsp yellow mustard
- 1 egg
- 1 tsp onion powder
- dash salt and pepper
- 5 oz mozzarella cheese, cut into bite-sized cubes

DIRECTIONS

1. Preheat oven to 400°F.
2. Line a large sheet pan with aluminum foil, then spray with nonstick spray.
3. To a large bowl, add the potatoes, green beans, olive oil, and a dash of salt and pepper. Mix to coat the veggies in the oil and seasonings, then place the vegetables on the sheet pan and spread out evenly.
4. To a large bowl, add all of the meatloaf ingredients except for the cheese. Only add 2 tbsp of the ketchup, reserving the rest for later. Stir to combine.
5. Form into 4-6 small meatloaves then stuff them with some of the mozzarella cheese cubes. Make sure the mozzarella isn't sticking out of the meat or else the cheese will spill out of the meatloaf.
6. Place the mini meatloaves on the sheet pan around the vegetables and brush the remaining ketchup over the top of the loaves. Bake for about 25-30 minutes or until the mini meatloaves are cooked through (when the meatloaves reach an internal temperature of 160°F). Enjoy!

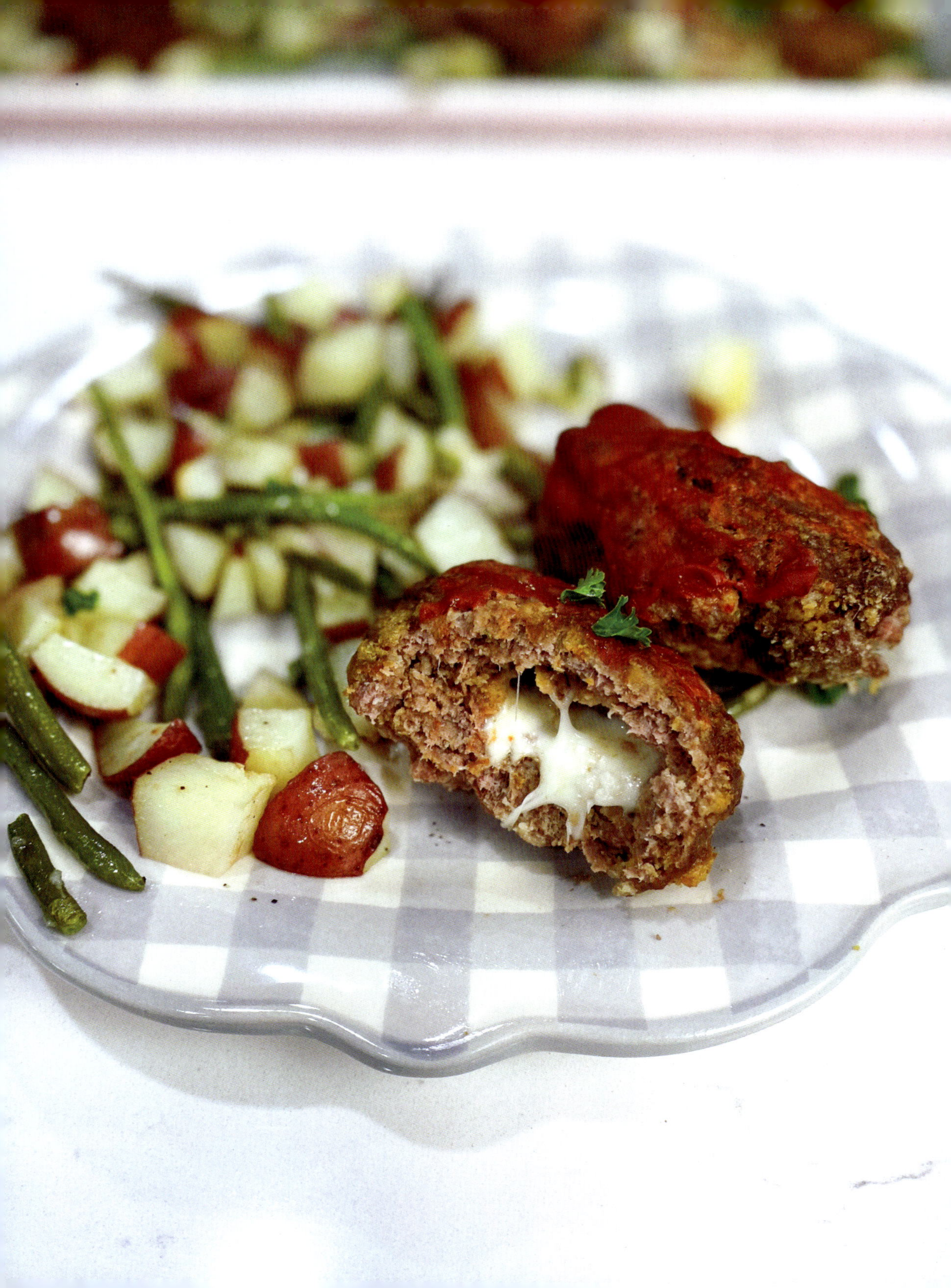

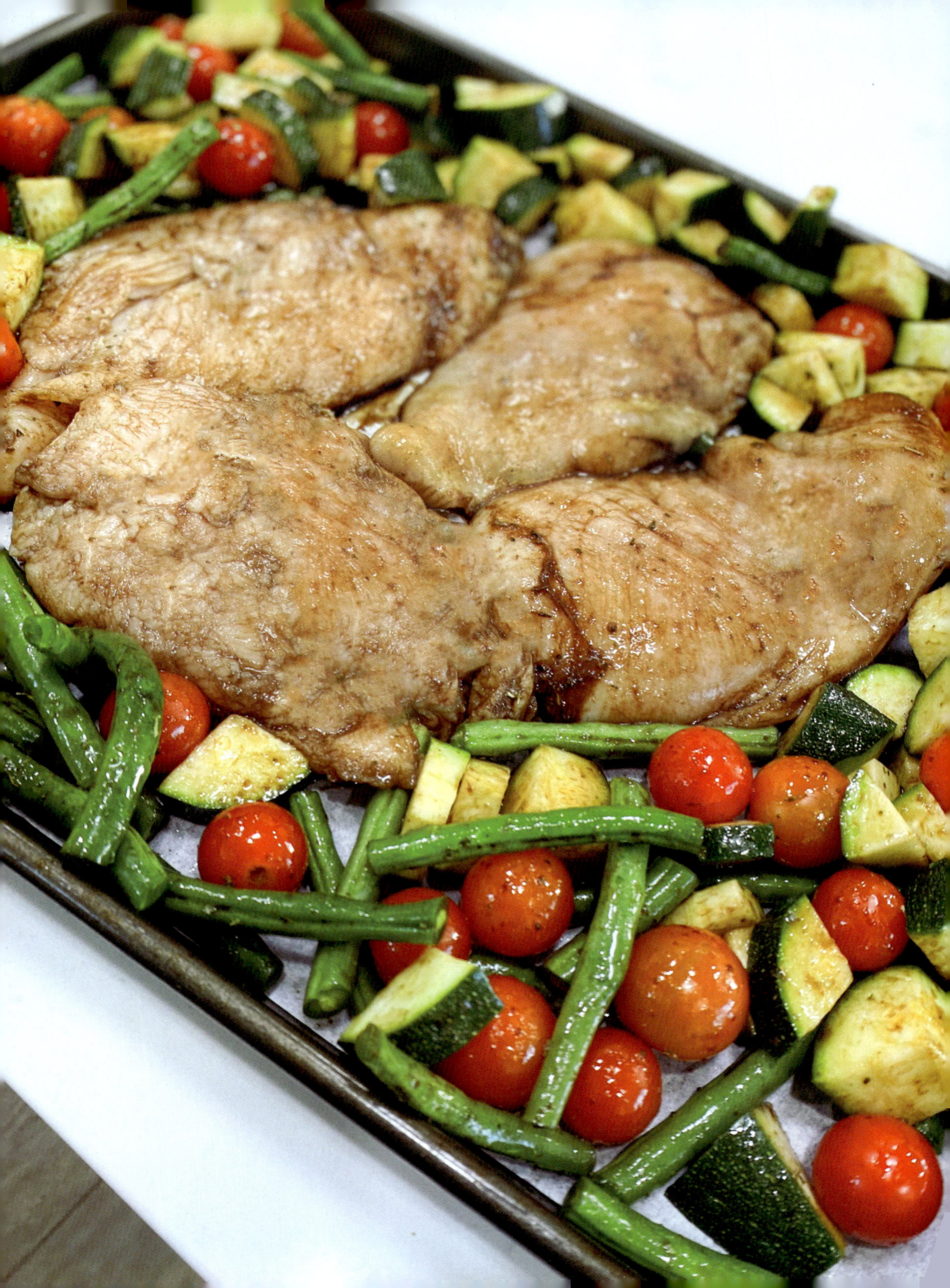

Italian Chicken and Vegetables

Zesty Italian marinade, chicken breast, and veggies topped with parm make this Italian Chicken and Vegetables a delicious and easy weeknight meal.

Prep time: 10 mins   **Cook time:** 30 mins   **Servings:** 4

INGREDIENTS

- 1 1/2 lbs chicken breast
- salt and pepper, to taste
- 3 tbsp olive oil
- 1/4 cup balsamic vinegar
- 1 tsp garlic powder
- 2 tsp Italian seasoning
- 1 1/2 cups cherry tomatoes
- 2 medium zucchini, cut into half moons
- 2 1/2 cups green beans, trimmed
- 1/4 cup Parmesan cheese, finely grated

DIRECTIONS

1. Slice each chicken breast in half horizontally to make the chicken thin. This will help make your chicken extra tender and help it cook more quickly.
2. Season the chicken with salt and pepper and place it into a large gallon-size plastic bag.
3. To a small bowl add olive oil, balsamic vinegar, garlic powder, and Italian seasoning and whisk well. Pour half of this mixture into the bag with the chicken and place in the refrigerator to marinate for at least one hour.
4. Preheat the oven to 425°F.
5. Place all of the vegetables into a large bowl with the remaining marinade and stir to coat the vegetables well.
6. Spray a rimmed baking sheet with nonstick spray and arrange the marinated chicken and vegetables evenly across the sheet pan. Bake for 25-30 minutes or until the chicken is completely cooked through. Sprinkle the Parmesan cheese over everything. Enjoy!

Sheet Pan Balsamic Chicken with Bacon, Potatoes, & Brussels Sprouts

Sheet Pan Balsamic Chicken with Bacon Potatoes and Brussels Sprouts is an easy, mouthwateringly delicious sheet pan meal.

Prep time: 15 mins   **Cook time:** 30 mins   **Servings:** 4-5

INGREDIENTS

Balsamic Marinade

- 1/3 cup balsamic vinegar
- 3 tbsp lemon juice
- 1 tbsp olive oil
- 1 tbsp minced garlic
- 1/2 tsp salt
- 1/2 tsp pepper

Sheet Pan Meal

- 1 lb Brussels sprouts, halved
- 2 lbs chicken breast, cut into large chunks
- 6 raw strips of bacon, cut into bite-sized pieces
- 1 1/2 lbs golden potatoes, cut into bite-size pieces

DIRECTIONS

1. Preheat oven to 375°F.
2. Combine all of the marinade ingredients in a large bowl and whisk well. Place the chicken breast chunks into the sauce mixture and set to the side.
3. Line a sheet pan with parchment paper. Place the potatoes, Brussels sprouts, and bacon pieces all around the sheet pan. Place the chicken pieces around the vegetables. Pour the leftover marinade all over the vegetables.
4. Bake for 30-35 minutes or until the chicken is cooked through and the bacon is crispy. Enjoy!

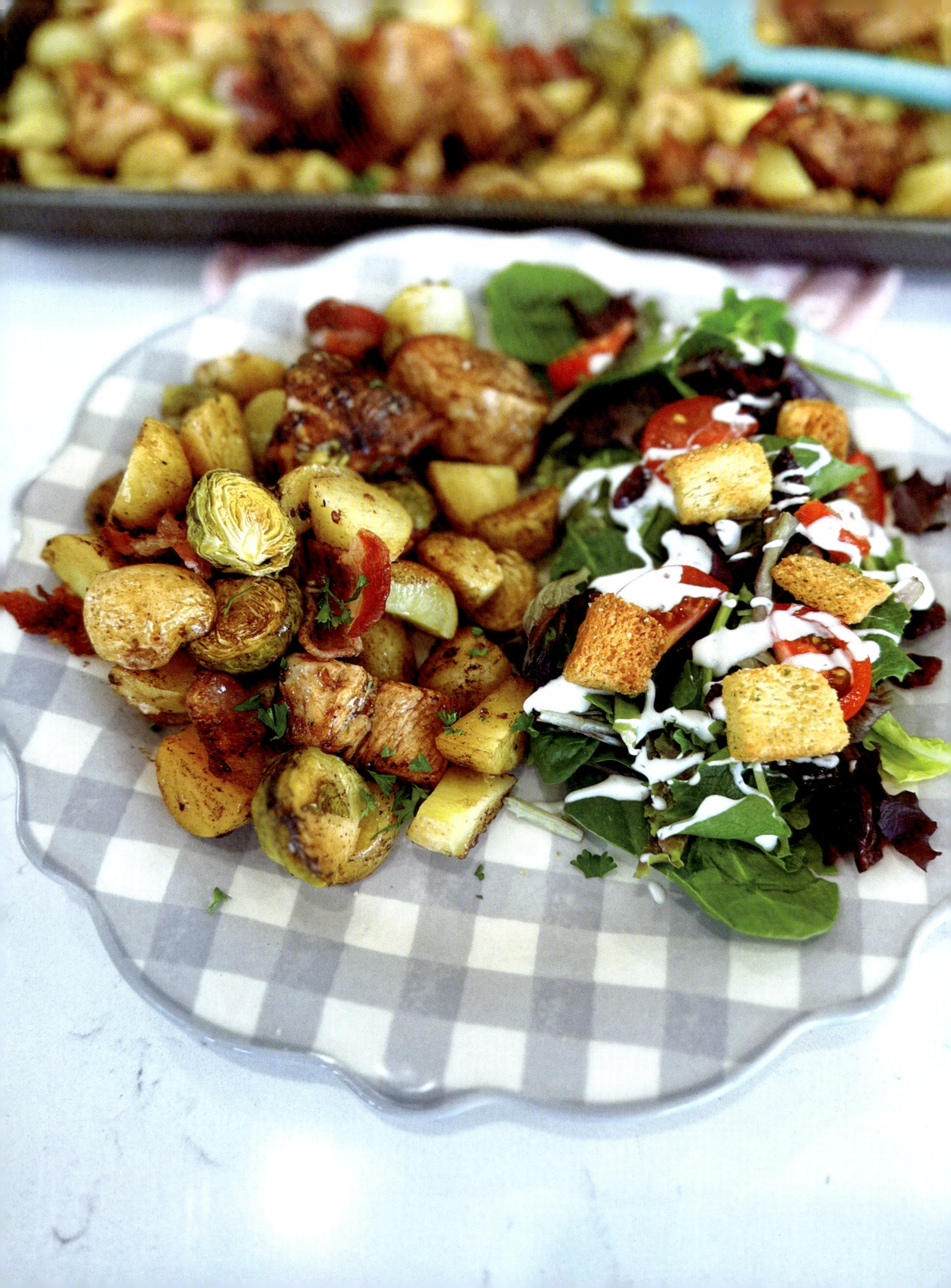

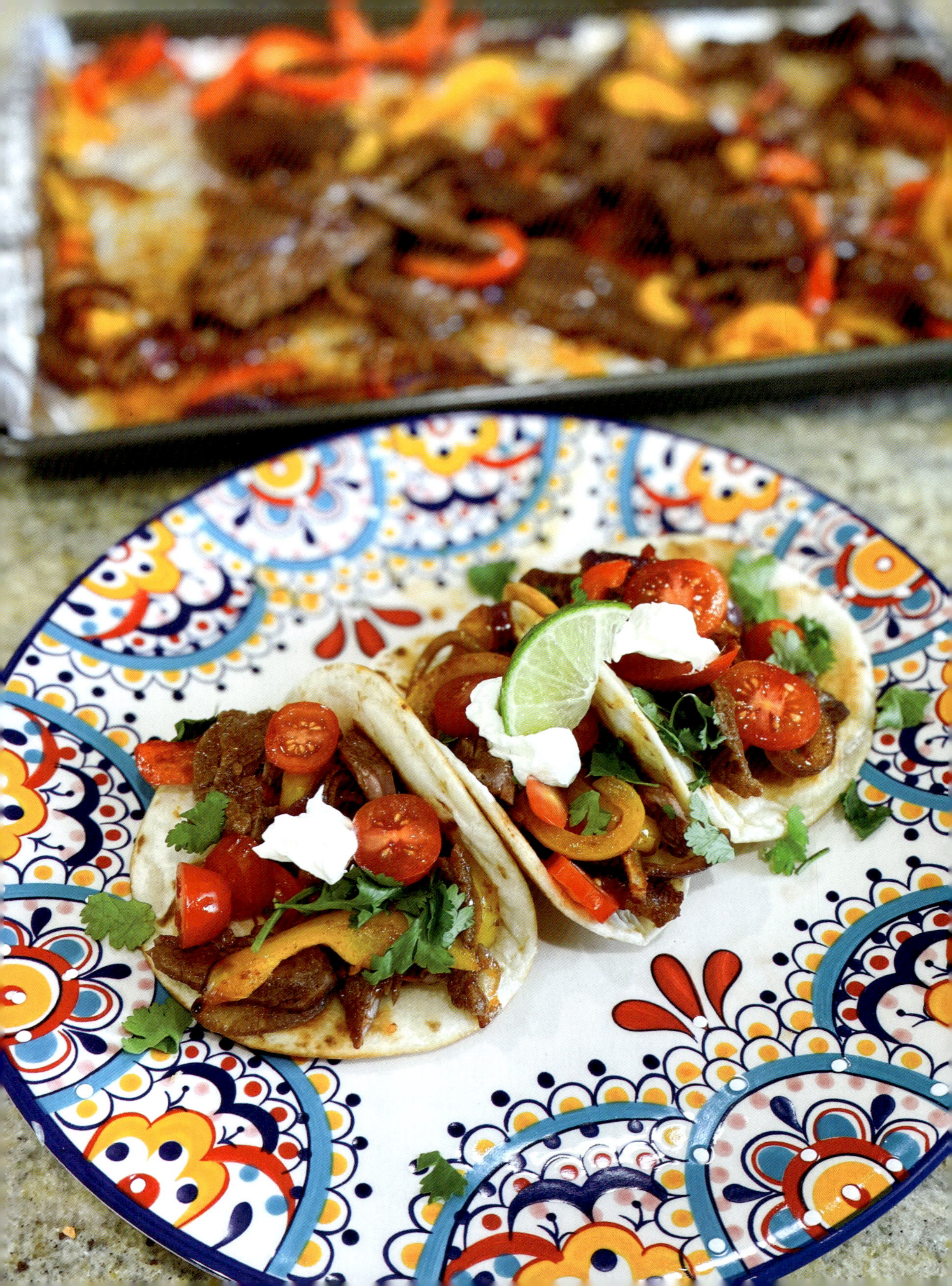

Sheet Pan Steak Fajitas

Flavorful, juicy steak and seasoned vegetables are topped with your favorite toppings and wrapped in warm tortillas. Make these Sheet Pan Steak Fajitas for a delicious and simple meal.

Prep time: 15 mins   **Cook time:** 15 mins   **Servings:** 4-5

INGREDIENTS

- 1 1/2 lbs flank steak, sliced thin against the grain
- 3 tbsp olive oil
- 1 yellow bell pepper, sliced thin
- 1 red bell pepper, sliced thin
- 1 red onion, sliced thin
- 2 tbsp fajita seasoning (or taco seasoning)
- 2 tbsp lime juice
- corn or flour tortillas

Toppings (optional)

- cheese, cilantro, diced avocado

DIRECTIONS

1. Set the oven to broil.
2. Spray a sheet pan with non-stick spray.
3. To a large bowl add the steak, oil, peppers, onion, seasoning, and lime juice. Stir to coat. Place the mixture on the sheet pan and spread out evenly.
4. Broil for 8 minutes, then remove from the oven and toss everything around. Place back in the oven for an additional 8 minutes, or until the steak is cooked to your liking.
5. Serve alongside warm tortillas and top with your favorite fajita toppings. Enjoy!

Sheet Pan Chicken Tenderloins

Sheet Pan Chicken Tenderloins are full of flavor and an essential part of a delicious meal for your entire family.

Prep time: 5 mins **Cook time:** 16 mins **Servings:** 4

INGREDIENTS

- 1 lb chicken tenderloins
- 2 tbsp mayonnaise
- 1/2 cup parmesan cheese
- 1/2 cup Italian seasoned breadcrumbs

DIRECTIONS

1. Preheat oven to 425°F.
2. In a bowl, add the chicken and the mayonnaise. Stir to coat the chicken in the mayonnaise.
3. In a large plastic bag, add the parmesan cheese and breadcrumbs. Shake to combine.
4. Grease a sheet pan with nonstick spray.
5. Place 2 chicken tenderloins in the plastic bag with the breadcrumb mixture. Shake to coat.
6. Place the tenders on the sheet pan in a single layer. Repeat with the rest of the tenders.
7. Bake for 8 minutes, then flip the tenders and continue to bake for an additional 8-10 minutes or until the chicken is cooked.

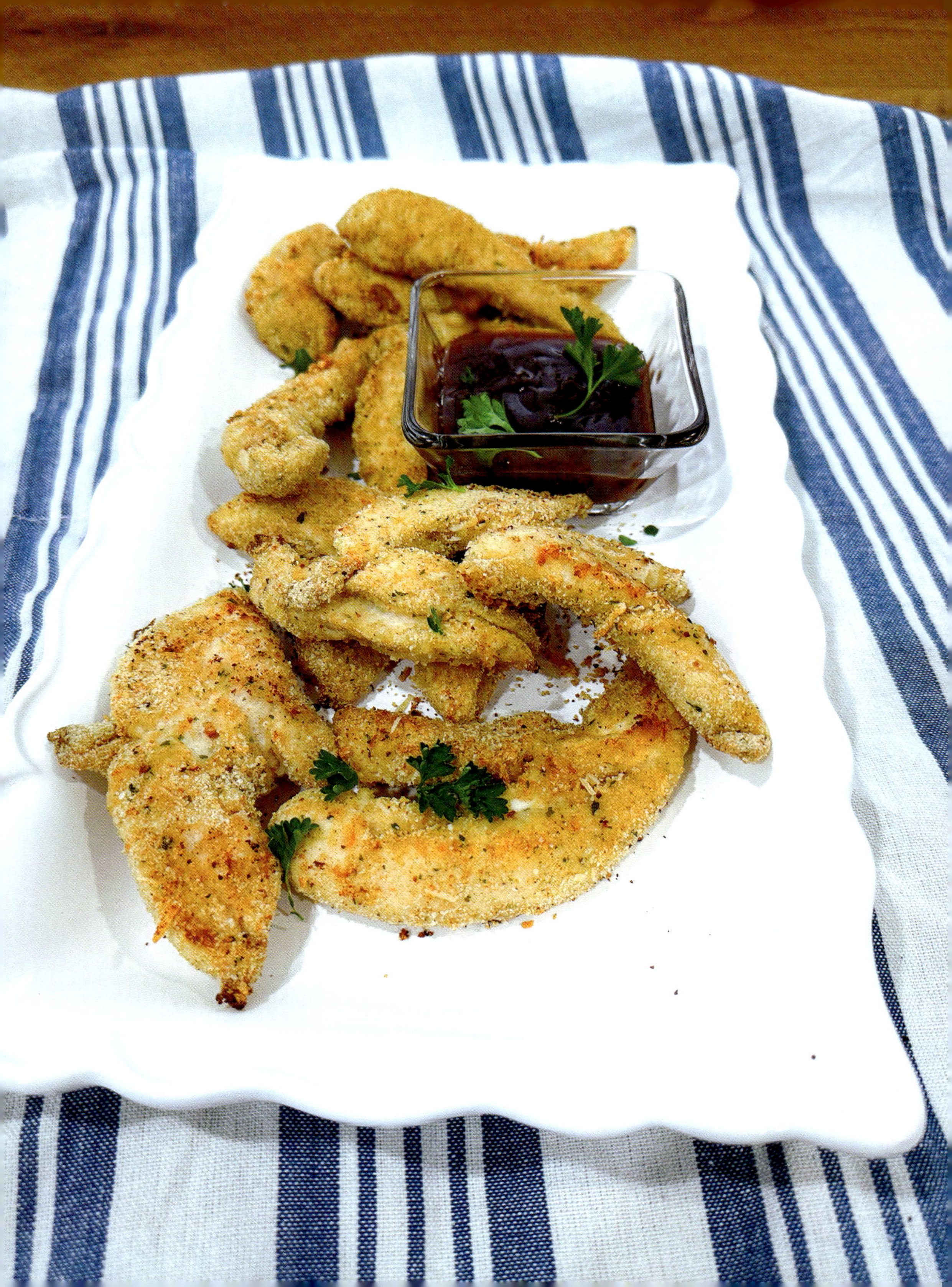

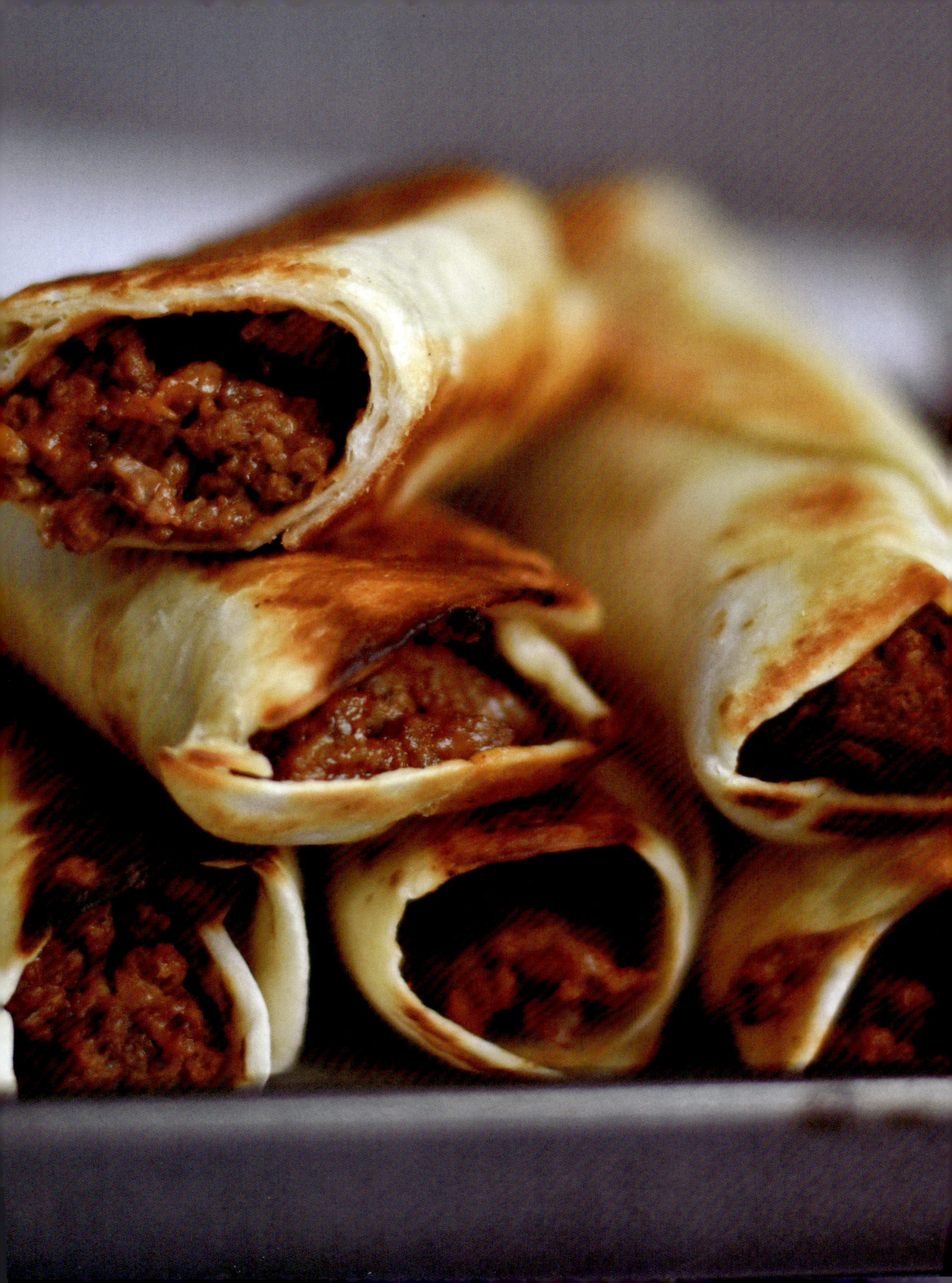

Beef Taquitos

Pan-fried Beef Taquitos are golden and crispy and stuffed with seasoned ground beef and gooey cheese.

Prep time: 15 mins **Cook time:** 15 mins **Servings:** 4-5

INGREDIENTS

- 1 lb ground beef
- 2 tbsp taco seasoning
- 1/4 cup water
- 1/3 cup Mexican-style cheese
- 4 tbsp olive oil
- 12 street taco-sized flour tortillas

Cornstarch Slurry

- 1/4 cup water
- 1 tbsp cornstarch

DIRECTIONS

1. Cook the ground beef in a skillet over medium heat. Once cooked through, remove any excess grease from the pan. Add the taco seasoning and 1/4 cup of water. Simmer for 5 minutes, stirring frequently. Stir in the cheese.
2. In a small bowl, whisk the cornstarch slurry ingredients together. Set aside.
3. Wrap the tortillas in a damp paper towel and microwave for about one minute. This will prevent the tortillas from cracking when rolling.
4. To assemble, put a small scoop of the ground beef mixture in the middle of a tortilla and roll it up part way. Brush a small amount of the cornstarch slurry on the edge of the tortilla and finish rolling it up. The cornstarch will act like glue and the tortillas won't come unrolled. Repeat for the remaining tortillas.
5. To a skillet on the stove over medium heat, add the olive oil. Once the oil is hot, add the taquitos and fry for about 30 seconds on each side or until golden brown. Work in batches to not overcrowd the pan. Once cooked, transfer the taquitos to a plate lined with a paper towel. Serve with your favorite toppings and enjoy!

NOTES

ONE POT MEALS

Some nights you just need a break from washing multiple pots, pans, bowls and utensils! The meals in this section are sure to please!

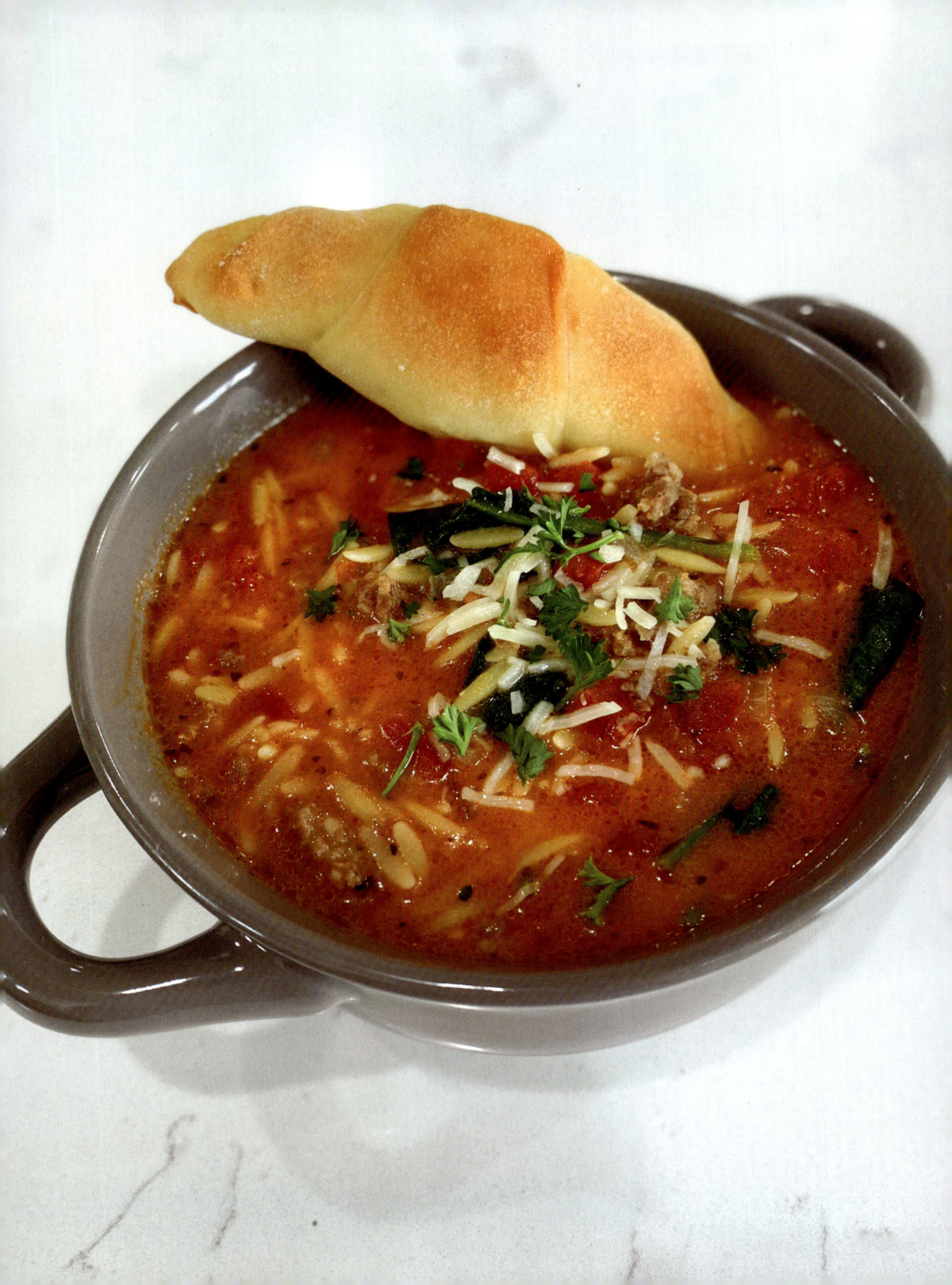

Sausage Orzo Soup

Pantry staple ingredients, orzo, and Italian sausage create a fantastic, tasty Sausage Orzo Soup that is simple to make.

Prep time: 10 mins   **Cook time:** 20 mins   **Servings:** 4-5

INGREDIENTS

- 1 tbsp olive oil
- 1 tbsp minced garlic
- 1 yellow onion, diced
- 1 lb Italian sausage
- 1/2 tsp pepper
- 2 tsp Italian seasoning
- 1 tsp salt
- 4 1/2 cups chicken broth
- 2 - 14.5 oz cans petite diced tomatoes
- 1 cup dry orzo pasta
- 3 cups fresh spinach, chopped
- 1/3 cup half and half
- 1/2 cup Parmesan cheese, for topping

DIRECTIONS

1. To a large pot or Dutch oven, add the oil, garlic, onion, and sausage. Break the sausage up and let it cook through. Once cooked, absorb any excess grease with a paper towel. Add in the pepper, Italian seasoning, salt, chicken broth, and diced tomatoes. Stir well and scrape all of the flavorful bits off the bottom of the pot.
2. Add in the orzo and stir well. Let simmer, covered, for 10 minutes, stirring occasionally, so the orzo doesn't stick to the bottom of the pot.
3. Once the orzo is tender, stir in the spinach and put the lid back on top. Let the spinach wilt down for about two minutes. Turn the heat off and stir in the half and half.
4. Ladle into bowls and top with Parmesan cheese. Enjoy!

Cheesy Chicken and Broccoli Pasta

Creamy, cheesy, and full of veggies, this Cheesy Chicken and Broccoli Pasta is so easy and a great way to add more greens to your dinner.

Prep time: 10 mins   **Cook time:** 20 mins   **Servings:** 4-5

INGREDIENTS

- 2 large carrots, chopped
- 1 yellow onion, chopped
- 1 large head of broccoli, chopped
- 2 tbsp olive oil
- 1 tbsp butter
- 1 lb chicken breast, cubed
- 1/2 tsp salt
- 1/2 tsp pepper
- 1 tsp oregano
- 1 tsp paprika
- 1 tsp onion powder
- 1 tsp garlic powder
- 1/2 tsp dried thyme
- 2 cups chicken broth
- 1 1/2 cups milk
- 3/4 lb medium shell pasta
- 1/4 cup Parmesan cheese
- 1 cup cheddar cheese, shredded

DIRECTIONS

1. To a large pot over medium heat, add the oil. Once hot, add the onions, carrots, and broccoli and cook for 2-3 minutes.
2. Add in the butter and the cubed chicken and season with all of the seasonings. Cook for 3 minutes. The chicken does not need to be completely cooked through at this point.
3. Stir in the broth and milk. Bring up to a simmer. Stir in the pasta and let simmer for 10-12 minutes, stirring frequently, until the pasta is tender. Once the pasta is cooked, stir in the Parmesan and cheddar cheese. Let the cheese melt and serve. Enjoy!

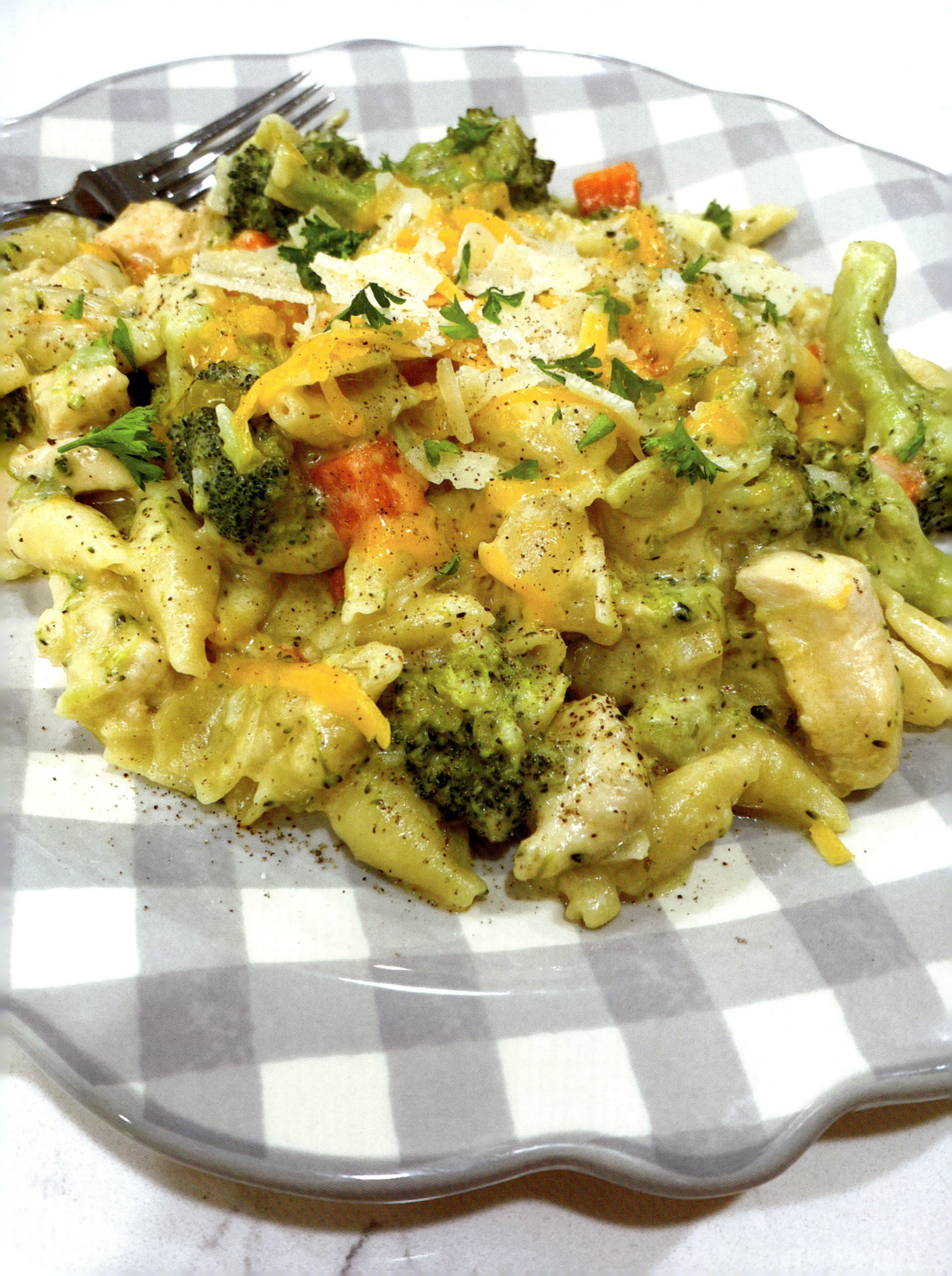

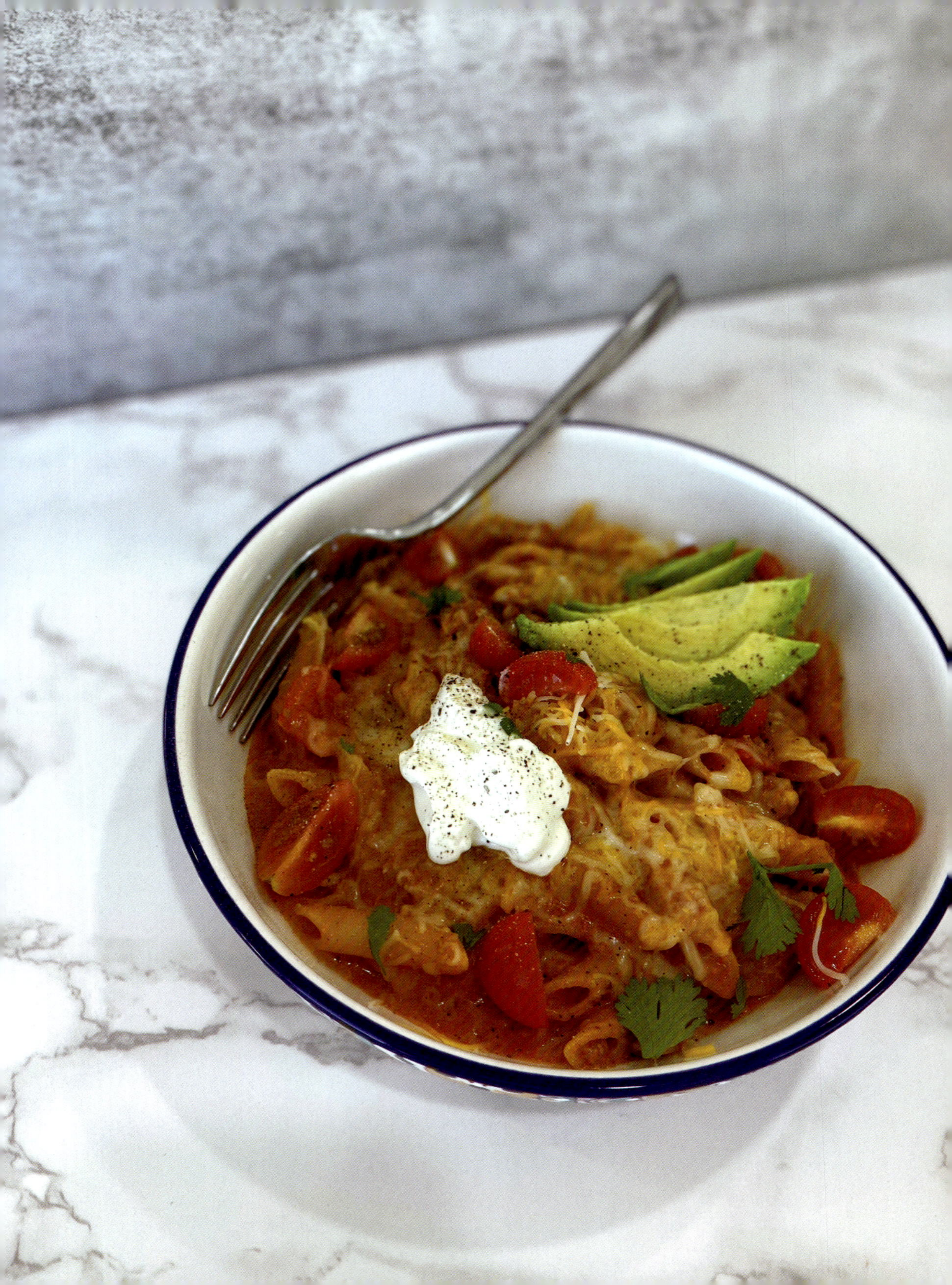

One-Pot Ground Turkey Pasta

This One-Pot Ground Turkey Pasta is cheesy and spicy with a creamy tomato sauce and fresh cilantro on top.

Prep time: 5 mins **Cook time:** 20 mins **Servings:** 4-5

INGREDIENTS

- 1 tbsp olive oil
- 1 pound ground turkey
- 1 medium yellow onion, diced
- 1 red bell pepper, diced
- 2 tbsp minced garlic
- 2 tsp chili powder
- 1/2 tsp paprika
- 1/2 tsp cumin
- 1 tsp salt
- 1/2 tsp pepper
- 15 oz tomato sauce
- 1 1/4 cup chicken stock
- 8 oz penne pasta
- 1/4 cup sour cream
- 1/2 cup shredded Mexican blend cheese
- 1/4 cup chopped cilantro
- sliced avocado, optional

DIRECTIONS

1. To a large pot, add the olive oil. Once hot, add turkey, onion, peppers, and garlic. Break up the turkey and cook through. Add in the chili powder, paprika, cumin, and salt and pepper.
2. Add in tomato sauce, broth, and pasta, then stir well. Simmer for 14 minutes, stirring occasionally, until tender.
3. Stir in sour cream and cheese until the cheese is melted and incorporated. Serve with cilantro and avocado on top and enjoy!

One-Pot Mexican Quinoa

This Mexican Quinoa one-pot dish is so easy to make and is a little different than what you're probably eating on a regular weeknight.

Prep time: 5 mins **Cook time:** 25 mins **Servings:** 4-5

INGREDIENTS

- 1 tbsp olive oil
- 2 tbsp minced garlic
- 1 jalapeño, diced
- 1 cup quinoa, rinsed
- 1 cup chicken or vegetable broth
- 15 oz can black beans, drained and rinsed
- 14.5 oz can fire-roasted diced tomatoes
- 14 oz can corn kernels
- 1 tsp chili powder
- 1/2 tsp cumin
- kosher salt and freshly ground black pepper, to taste
- juice of 1 lime
- shredded cheese, lettuce, avocado, sour cream, or salsa, for topping

DIRECTIONS

1. Add the oil to a large pot. Once hot, add the jalapeño and sauté for 2-3 minutes.
2. Add in garlic, quinoa, broth, beans, diced tomatoes, corn, chili powder, cumin, and salt and pepper, and stir well.
3. Let simmer, covered, for 18-22 minutes, stirring occasionally until tender. Stir in lime juice and serve with your favorite toppings. Enjoy!

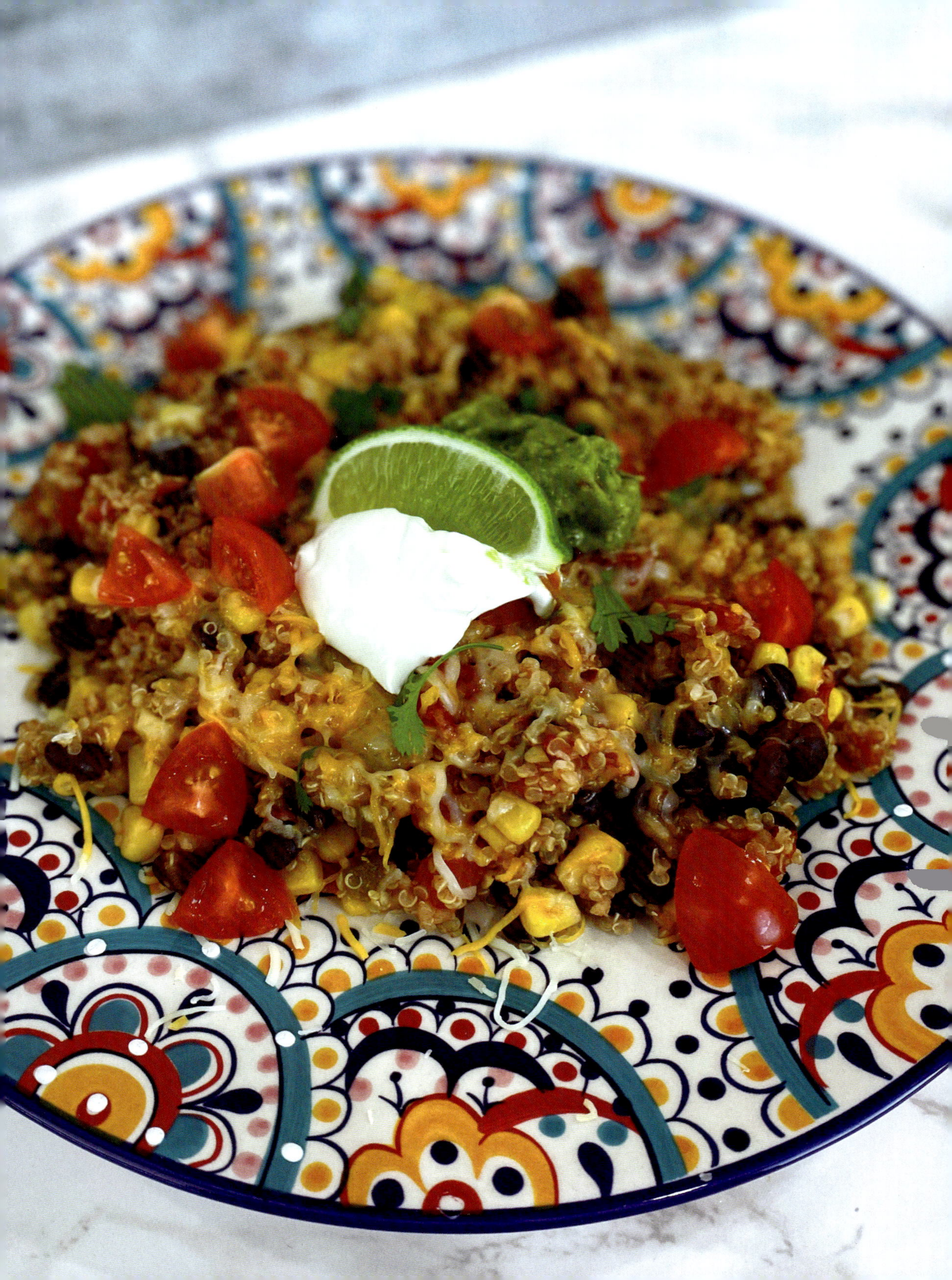

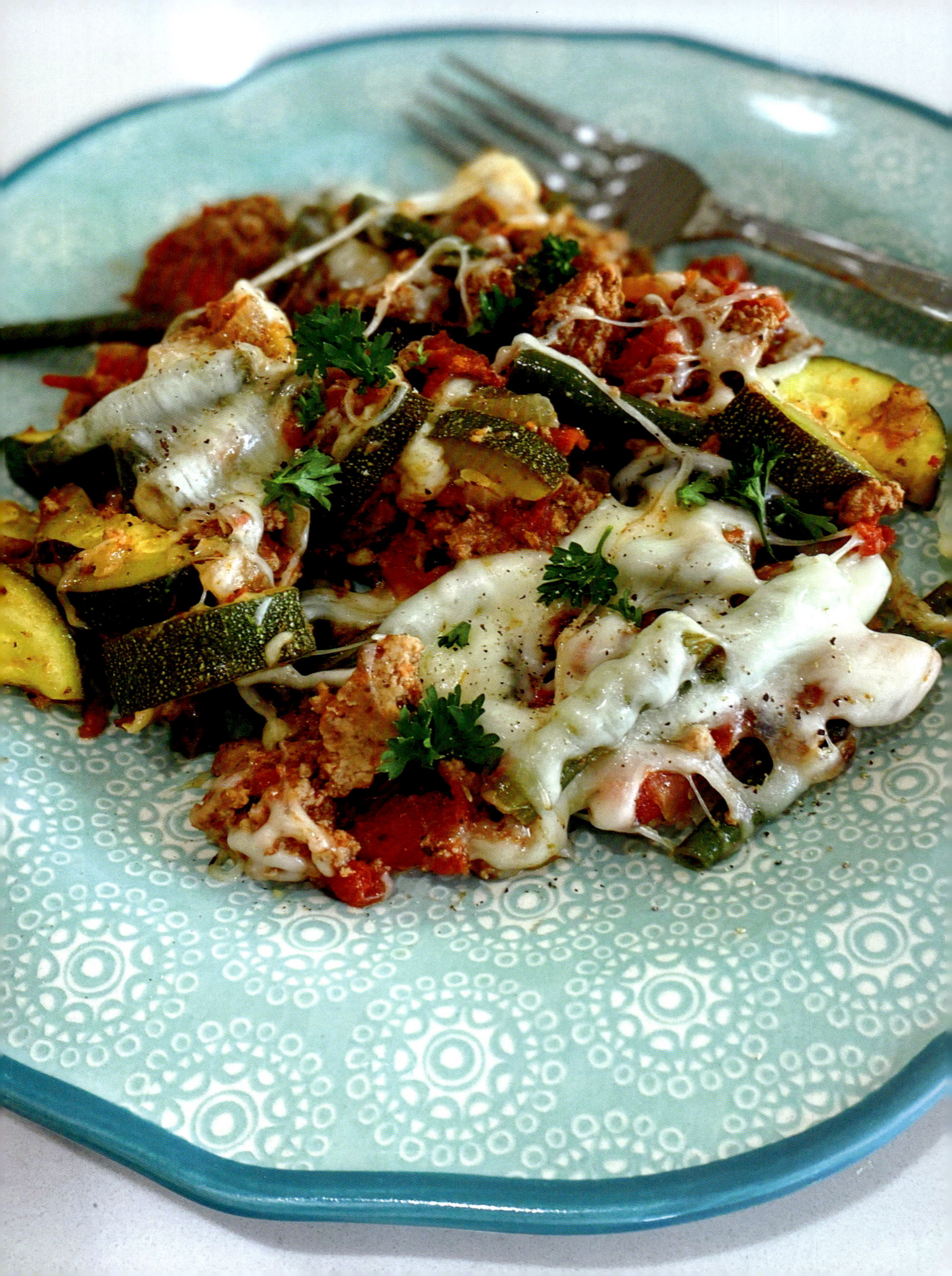

Low Carb Turkey Vegetable Skillet

Veggies and ground turkey simmer together with lots of spices and are topped with cheese for a yummy low-carb dinner.

Prep time: 15 mins   **Cook time:** 25 mins   **Servings:** 4-5

INGREDIENTS

- 1 yellow onion, diced
- 2 medium zucchinis, sliced
- 1 lb fresh green beans, trimmed and cut into bite-sized pieces
- 1 tbsp olive oil
- 1 lb ground turkey or ground beef
- 1 tbsp minced garlic
- 1/2 tsp salt
- 1/2 tsp pepper
- 1 tsp Italian seasoning
- 1/2 tsp dried oregano
- 1/2 tsp paprika
- 14 oz fire-roasted diced tomatoes
- 1/2 cup chicken broth
- 1 cup mozzarella cheese, shredded

DIRECTIONS

1. To a large skillet over medium heat add the oil. Once hot, add in the diced onion and turkey. Break the turkey up with a spatula and cook it through.
2. Once the turkey is cooked, add in the minced garlic and seasonings. Stir well.
3. Turn the heat to low and add in the diced tomatoes, green beans, zucchini, and chicken broth. Stir well and let simmer for about 10-15 minutes, stirring occasionally, until the vegetables are tender.
4. Sprinkle the cheese on top, then cover with a lid until the cheese is melted. Enjoy!

Sausage and Tomato Gnocchi

Pillowy gnocchi is served with a creamy tomato sauce and spicy sausage for a decadent, but simple, one-pot meal.

Prep time: 5 mins   **Cook time:** 25 mins   **Servings:** 4-5

INGREDIENTS

- 1 white onion, diced
- 1 lb Italian sausage
- 1 tsp Italian seasoning
- 1 tsp garlic powder
- 1/2 tsp pepper
- 1/2 tsp salt
- 1 tbsp minced garlic
- 3/4 cup heavy cream
- 14 oz can diced tomatoes
- 16 oz potato gnocchi
- 4 cups fresh spinach
- 1 cup mozzarella cheese

DIRECTIONS

1. To a large pot or Dutch oven over medium heat, add the onion, sausage, seasonings, and minced garlic. Break the sausage up and cook it through. Once cooked remove any grease from the pot.
2. Stir in the heavy cream, diced tomatoes, gnocchi, and spinach. Simmer for 12-15 minutes, stirring frequently.
3. Stir in the mozzarella cheese and let melt. Enjoy!

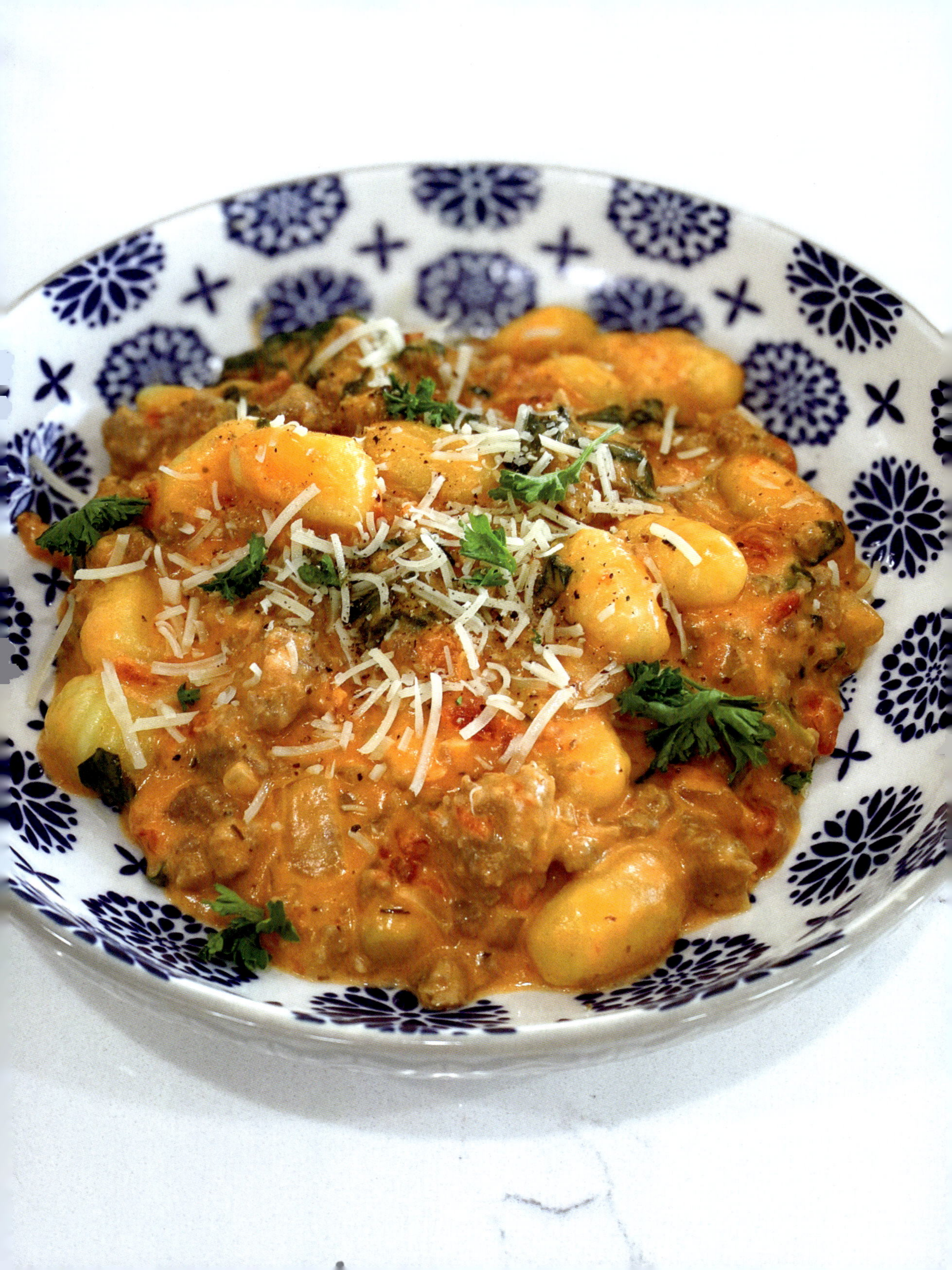

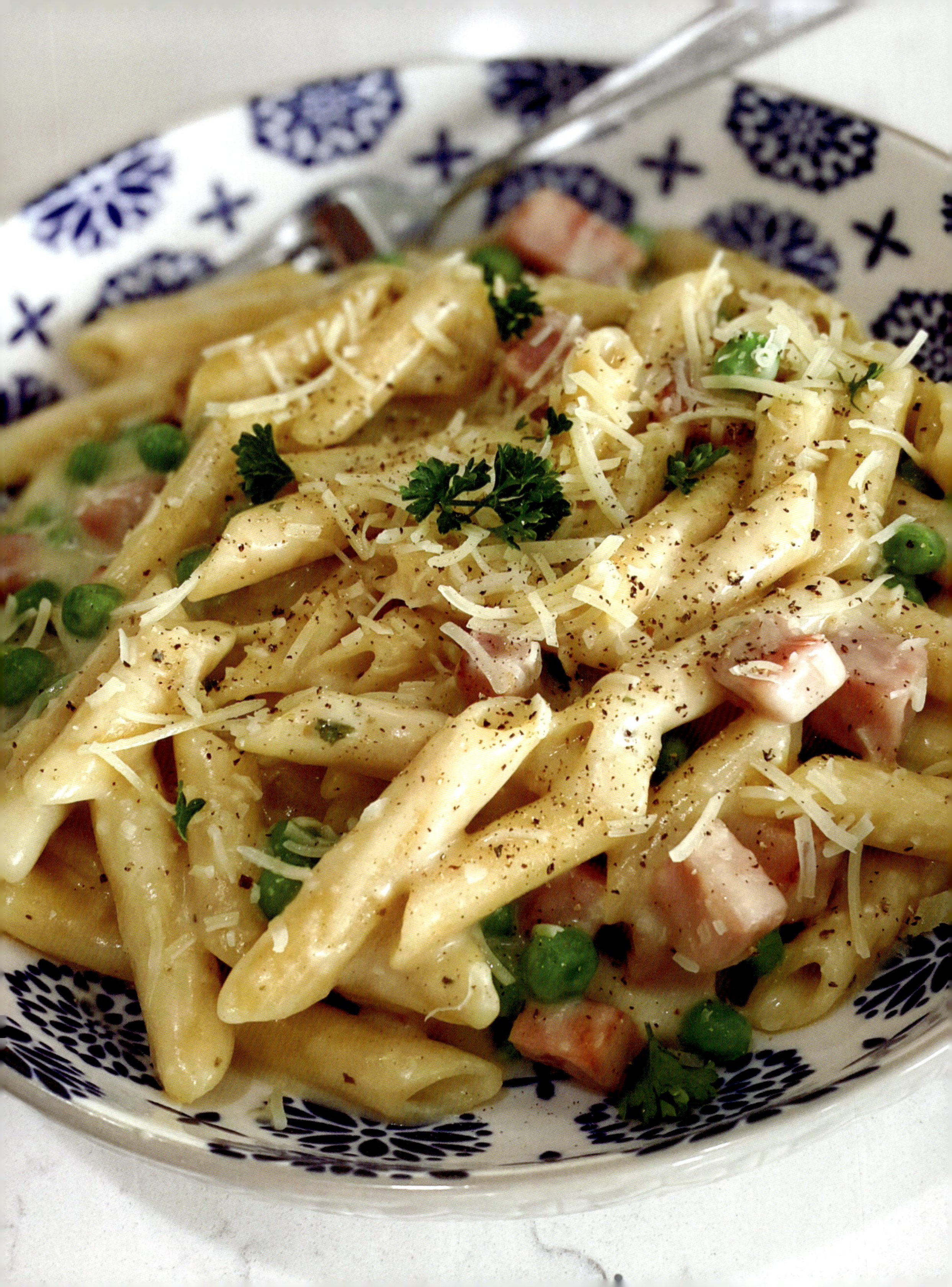

Ham and Noodle One Pot Meal

Creamy white sauce, Parmesan cheese, ham, and peas come together to create a rich and comforting dish.

Prep time: 10 mins   **Cook time:** 30 mins   **Servings:** 4-5

INGREDIENTS

- 2 tbsp olive oil
- 1 white onion, diced
- 1 lb precooked ham steak, diced
- 1 tbsp minced garlic
- 1/2 tsp salt
- 1/2 tsp pepper
- 1 tsp dried parsley
- 1 tsp dried basil
- 1/2 tsp oregano
- 1/4 cup all-purpose flour
- 4 cups chicken broth
- 2 cups milk
- 16 oz dry penne pasta
- 2 cups frozen sweet peas
- 1/2 cup Parmesan cheese

DIRECTIONS

1. To a large pot or Dutch oven over medium heat, add the oil. Once hot, add in the onion and ham and cook, stirring frequently, for 5-7 minutes, or until the ham is a nice golden color.

2. Stir in the minced garlic and all of the seasonings. Stir in the flour and cook for one minute, or until the flour turns a golden color. Slowly stir in the broth. Pour it in slowly so no clumps form. Stir in the milk.

3. Bring to a simmer, then add in the pasta. Simmer for 15-20 minutes, or until the pasta is cooked. If the liquid gets too low, add 1/2 cup water at a time until the pasta is tender.

4. Stir in the frozen peas and let them simmer in the pot for 2-3 minutes. Stir in the Parmesan cheese. Enjoy!

Alfredo Chicken Broccoli Skillet Lasagna

There's no better duo than Alfredo sauce and pasta! This Alfredo Chicken Broccoli Skillet Lasagna is a unique and delicious take on classic pasta dishes.

Prep time: 10 mins   **Cook time:** 25 mins   **Servings:** 4-5

INGREDIENTS

- 2 tbsp olive oil
- 1 tbsp minced garlic
- 2 1/2 cups chicken broth
- 1 1/2 cups heavy cream
- 1 tsp salt
- 1/2 tsp pepper
- 1 tsp Italian seasoning
- 10 lasagna noodles, broken into bite-sized pieces
- 3 cups rotisserie chicken, shredded
- 12 oz frozen broccoli florets
- 1 cup mozzarella cheese, shredded

DIRECTIONS

1. To a large skillet over medium heat, add the oil. Once hot, add in the garlic and stir for about 20 seconds, or until it's fragrant.
2. Stir in the broth, heavy cream, seasonings, broken lasagna noodles, and rotisserie chicken. Bring up to a simmer and let cook, stirring frequently, for 15 minutes. If the liquid gets too low, add in 1/2 cup of water at a time.
3. Stir in the frozen broccoli and continue to simmer for 5-7 more minutes, or until the pasta is tender. Stir in the mozzarella cheese. Once melted, serve and enjoy!

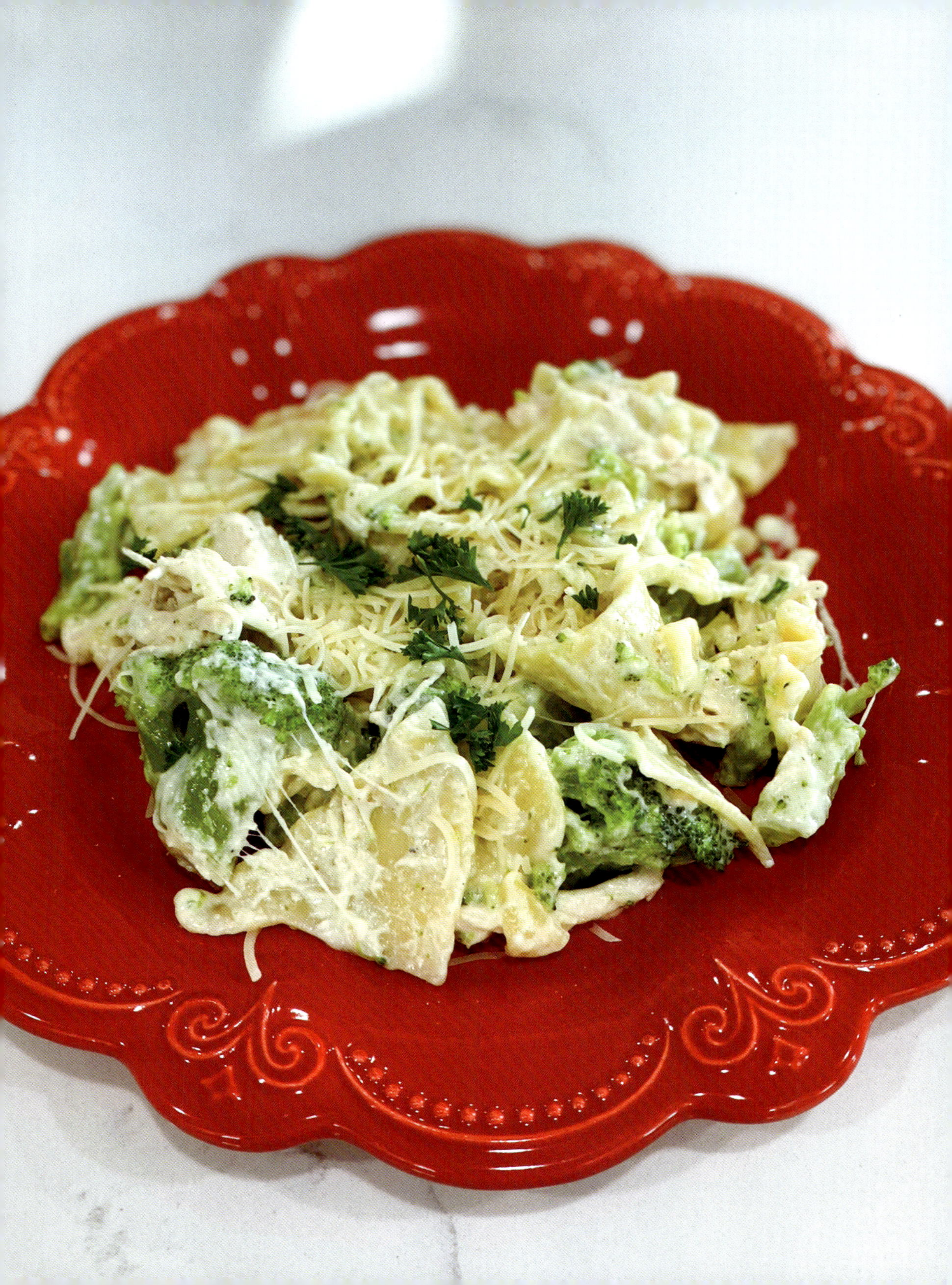

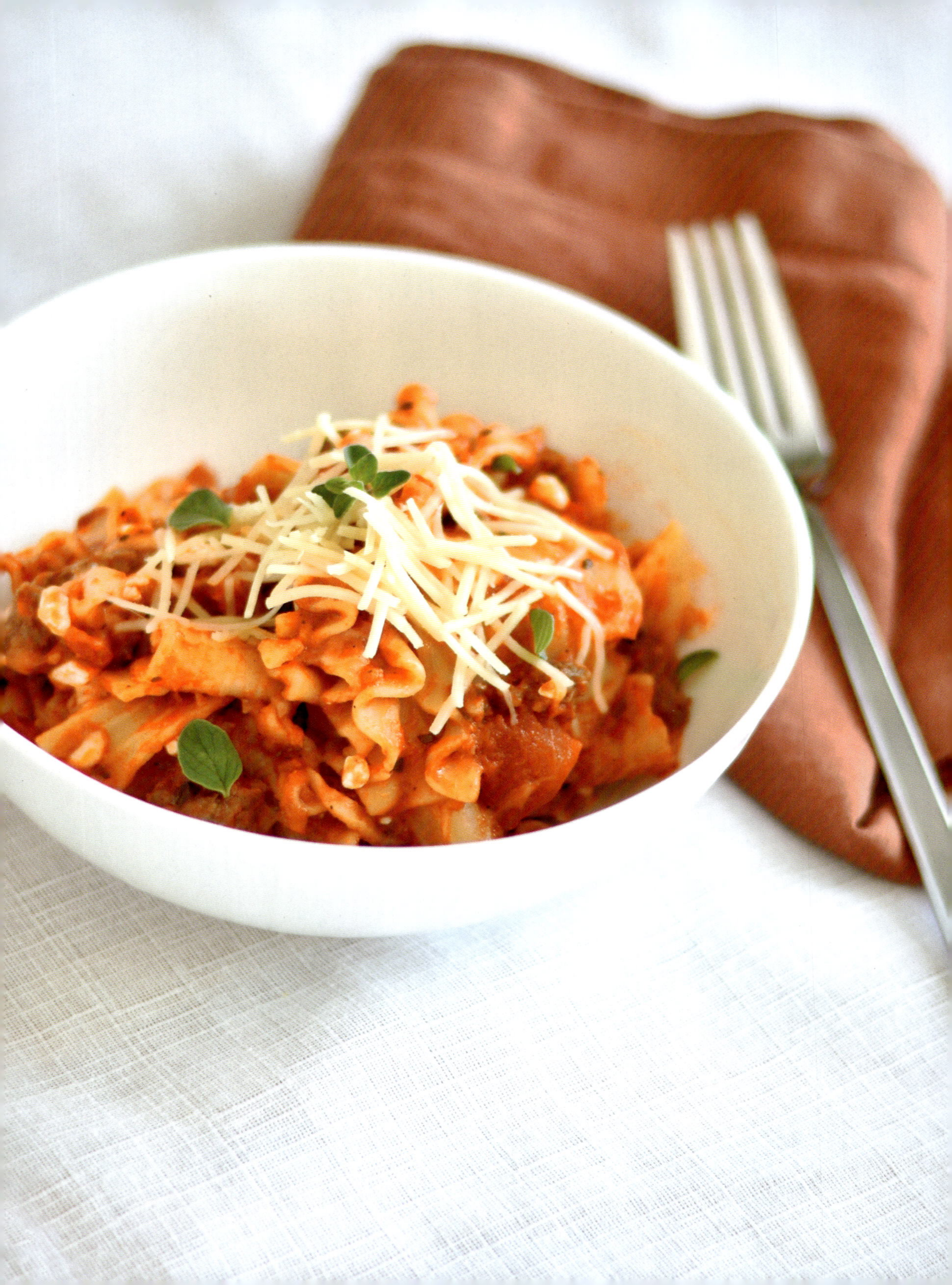

Skillet Lasagna One-Pot

Get all the flavors of lasagna doing a fraction of the work with this Skillet Lasagna. Perfect for a busy weeknight dinner.

Prep time: 5 mins   **Cook time:** 30 mins   **Servings:** 4-5

INGREDIENTS

- 1 lb Italian sausage
- 1/2 tsp onion powder
- 1/2 tsp garlic powder
- 1/2 tsp Italian seasoning
- dash of salt and pepper
- 24 oz marinara sauce, any brand
- 2 cups chicken broth, plus extra if needed
- 14 oz diced tomatoes
- 3/4 lb lasagna noodles, broken into bite-sized pieces

Cheesy Mixture

- 1/3 cup cottage cheese or ricotta cheese
- 1/4 cup Parmesan cheese
- 1 cup mozzarella cheese

DIRECTIONS

1. Add the sausage to a large skillet and cook through. Once cooked, remove any excess grease.
2. Stir in the seasonings. Add the marinara sauce, broth, diced tomatoes, and lasagna noodles, then bring to a simmer. Cover and let simmer for 20 minutes, or until the noodles are cooked, stirring frequently so the noodles don't stick. You might need to add more broth in if the liquid gets too low while simmering.
3. Add the ingredients for the cheesy mixture to a small bowl and stir well.
4. Once the noodles are tender, turn the heat off and stir in the cheesy mixture. Let the cheese melt and serve. Enjoy!

Sun-Dried Tomato Tortellini

Sun-Dried Tomato Tortellini is a burst of sunshine and comfort. All it takes is one pot and 30 minutes to create this sent-from-heaven dish.

Prep time: 10 mins   **Cook time:** 15 mins   **Servings:** 4-5

INGREDIENTS

- 1 tbsp olive oil
- 1 lb chicken breast, cubed
- 1/2 tsp salt
- 1/2 tsp pepper
- 1 tsp Italian seasoning
- 1/2 tsp dried basil
- 1/2 tsp garlic powder
- 1/4 cup water
- 2 tsp cornstarch
- 1 tbsp minced garlic
- 14 oz can Italian-style petite diced tomatoes
- 1/3 cup sun-dried tomatoes, chopped
- 1/2 cup chicken broth
- 1/2 cup heavy cream
- 3 1/2 cups frozen cheese tortellini
- 2 cups fresh spinach, chopped
- 1 cup mozzarella cheese
- 1/4 cup Parmesan cheese

DIRECTIONS

1. To a large pot, add the oil and heat over medium heat. Once hot, add in the chicken and the seasonings. Cook the chicken for 3 to 4 minutes. The chicken does not need to be completely cooked through at this point.
2. While the chicken is cooking, make the cornstarch slurry. Add the water and cornstarch to a small bowl. Whisk well together to create a slurry.
3. To the pot, add in the minced garlic, diced tomatoes, sun-dried tomatoes, broth, heavy cream, and cornstarch slurry. Stir well and bring up to a simmer.
4. Once simmering, add in the tortellini and let simmer for 5-8 minutes, or until the chicken is cooked through and the tortellini is tender. Stir in the spinach, mozzarella, and Parmesan. Let cook for 2 minutes to wilt the spinach and melt the cheese. Enjoy!

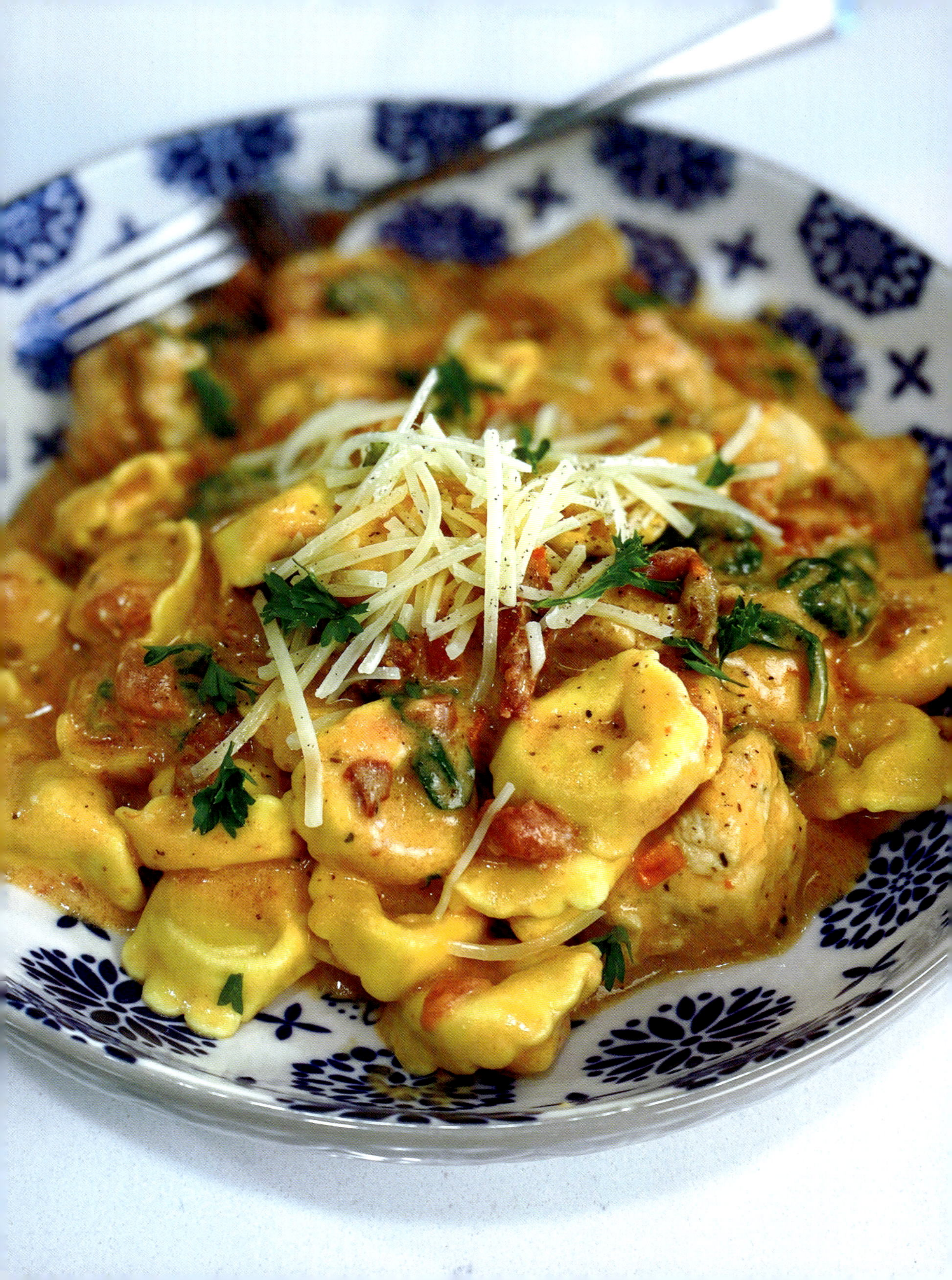

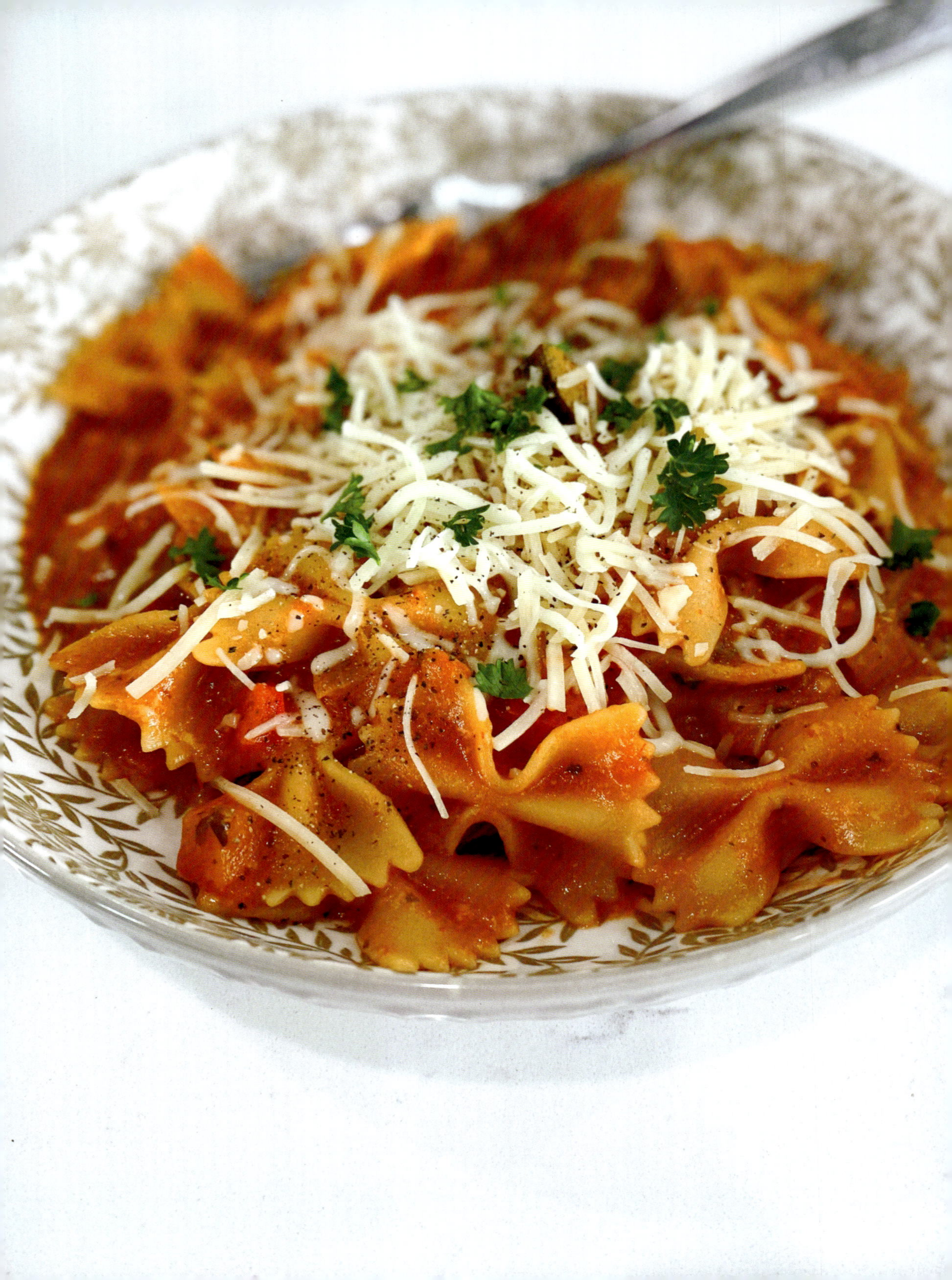

Italian Vegetable Pasta One-Pot Dinner

Full of vegetables and rich Italian flavor, Italian Vegetable Pasta is healthy and mouthwateringly delicious.

Prep time: 10 mins   **Cook time:** 20 mins   **Servings:** 4-5

INGREDIENTS

- 2 tbsp olive oil
- 1 tbsp minced garlic
- 1 yellow bell pepper, diced
- 1 red bell pepper, diced
- 1 medium zucchini, cut into bite-sized pieces
- 8 oz white mushrooms, sliced
- 3 tbsp tomato paste
- 2 tsp Italian seasoning
- 2 1/3 cups vegetable broth
- 2 cups marinara sauce
- 1/2 lb uncooked bow-tie pasta (or similar pasta)
- 1/2 cup mozzarella cheese (optional)

DIRECTIONS

1. To a large Dutch oven or pot over medium heat, add the oil. Once hot, add in the minced garlic, bell peppers, and onion. Cook for 3-4 minutes to start to soften the vegetables. Add in the zucchini and sliced mushrooms and cook for an additional 3 minutes, stirring occasionally.

2. Add in the tomato paste, Italian seasoning, broth, marinara sauce, and pasta. Stir and bring to a simmer and cover.

3. Turn heat to low and let simmer, stirring occasionally, for 12-15 minutes, or until the pasta is tender. If too much liquid boils out, you can add 1/3 cup of water. Once the pasta is tender, stir in the cheese, let melt, and serve. Enjoy!

Beef Stew

Perfectly seasoned, melt-in-your-mouth tender beef and hearty vegetables make this Beef Stew the perfect comfort meal.

Prep time: 10 mins **Cook time:** 1 hour 15 mins **Servings:** 4-5

INGREDIENTS

- 2 tbsp olive oil
- 1.5 lbs beef stew meat, cubed
- 2 1/2 tbsp all-purpose flour
- 1.5 oz packet beef stew seasoning mix
- 3 cups water
- 1 onion, diced
- 2 Russet potatoes, peeled and cubed
- 2 sticks celery, sliced
- 2 large carrots, sliced

DIRECTIONS

1. In a medium-sized bowl, combine the beef and the flour. Stir to coat the beef in the flour.
2. In a Dutch oven or large pot over medium heat, add the oil. Once hot, add in the beef and sear on all sides.
3. Add in the seasoning packet and 3 cups of water. Scrape the bits off the bottom of the pan. Bring to a boil, drop to a simmer, and let simmer, covered, for 45 minutes. Stir occasionally.
4. Add the chopped vegetables to the pot and stir well. Simmer, covered, for an additional 30 minutes, or until the vegetables and meat are tender. Enjoy!

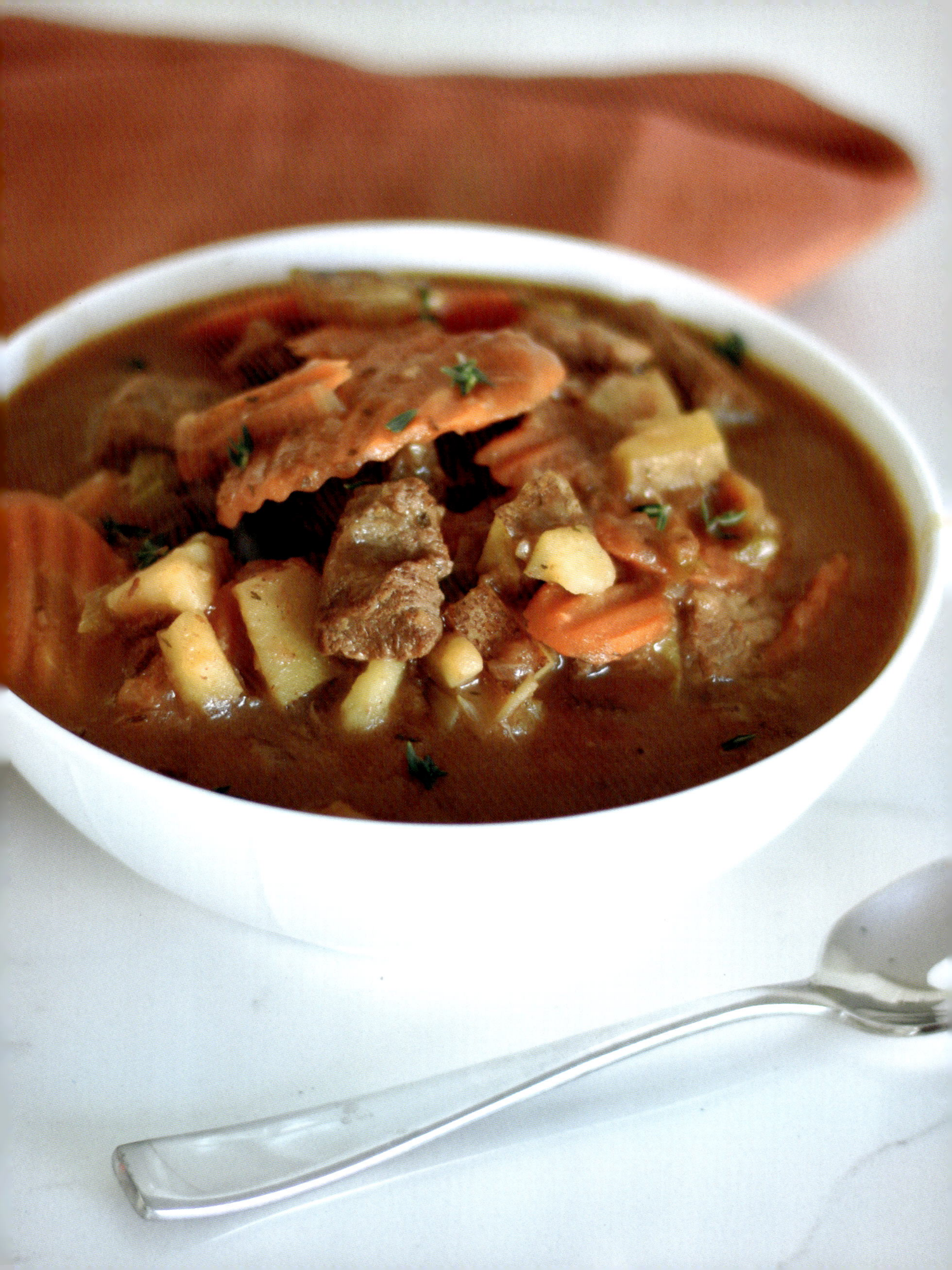

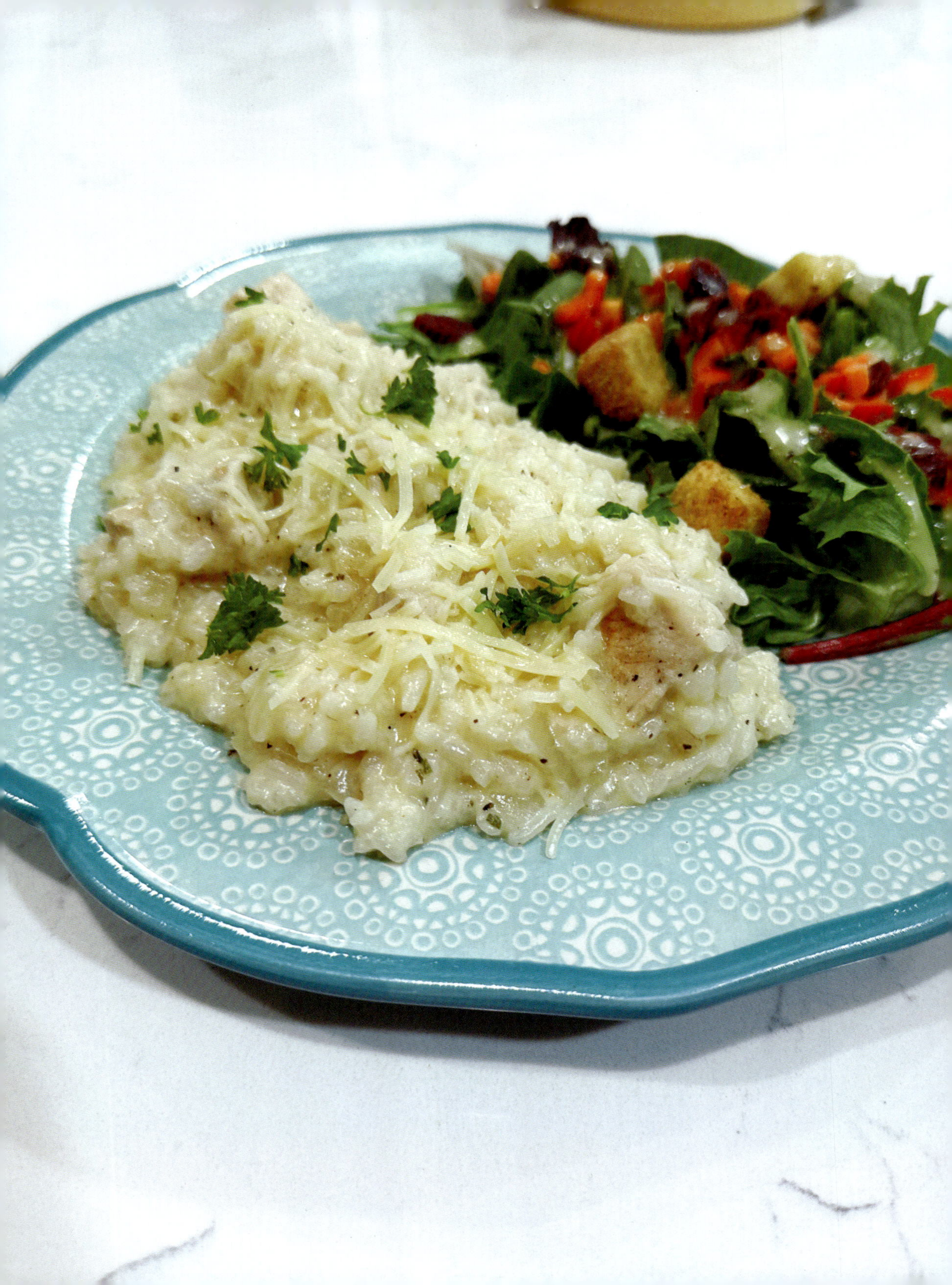

Italian Chicken and Rice

This Italian Chicken and Rice dish feels more dressed up than your average chicken and rice dish but doesn't require much effort at all.

Prep time: 10 mins **Cook time:** 25 mins **Servings:** 4-5

INGREDIENTS

- 1 tbsp olive oil
- 1 tbsp butter
- 1 lb chicken breast, cubed
- 2 tsp paprika
- 2 tsp Italian seasoning
- 1 tsp salt
- 1/2 tsp pepper
- 1 yellow onion, diced
- 1 tbsp minced garlic
- 2 1/2 cups chicken broth
- 1 cup uncooked jasmine rice OR white rice
- 1/2 cup heavy cream
- 1/3 cup Parmesan cheese

DIRECTIONS

1. To a large Dutch oven or pot over medium-high heat, add the oil and butter. Once the oil is hot and the butter is melted, add in the chicken, seasonings, onion, and garlic. Let cook together for 5-6 minutes, stirring occasionally.

2. Add in the chicken broth and rice and stir well. Let simmer, covered, for 17-20 minutes, stirring occasionally, so the rice doesn't stick to the bottom of the pot. Once the rice is tender, turn the heat off and stir in the heavy cream and Parmesan cheese. Let the cheese melt and serve. Enjoy!

Minestrone Soup

Minestrone soup is cozy, hearty, and very nutritious. It's perfect to eat when the weather starts to cool down!

Prep time: 10 mins   **Cook time:** 35 mins   **Servings:** 6

INGREDIENTS

- 1 zucchini, diced
- 2 stocks of celery, sliced
- 2 medium carrots, sliced
- 1 white onion, diced
- 2 tbsp olive oil
- dash of salt and pepper
- 28 oz can crushed tomatoes
- 14 oz can tomato sauce
- 14 oz can kidney beans, drained and rinsed
- 5 1/2 cups vegetable broth
- 1 tbsp dried basil
- 2 tsp dried parsley
- 1 tsp oregano
- 1 1/2 cups small pasta
- 2 cups fresh chopped spinach
- Parmesan cheese, for topping

DIRECTIONS

1. In a large pot or Dutch oven, heat the oil and add in the celery, carrots, and onion.
2. Season with a dash of salt and pepper and cook until the vegetables soften, about 5-9 minutes.
3. Add the crushed tomatoes, tomato sauce, kidney beans, vegetable broth, and seasonings. Let simmer, covered for 15 minutes.
4. Add the pasta in and let simmer for an additional 10 mins.
5. Once the pasta is tender, stir in the spinach and let it wilt down. Serve the soup with lots of Parmesan cheese on top. Enjoy!

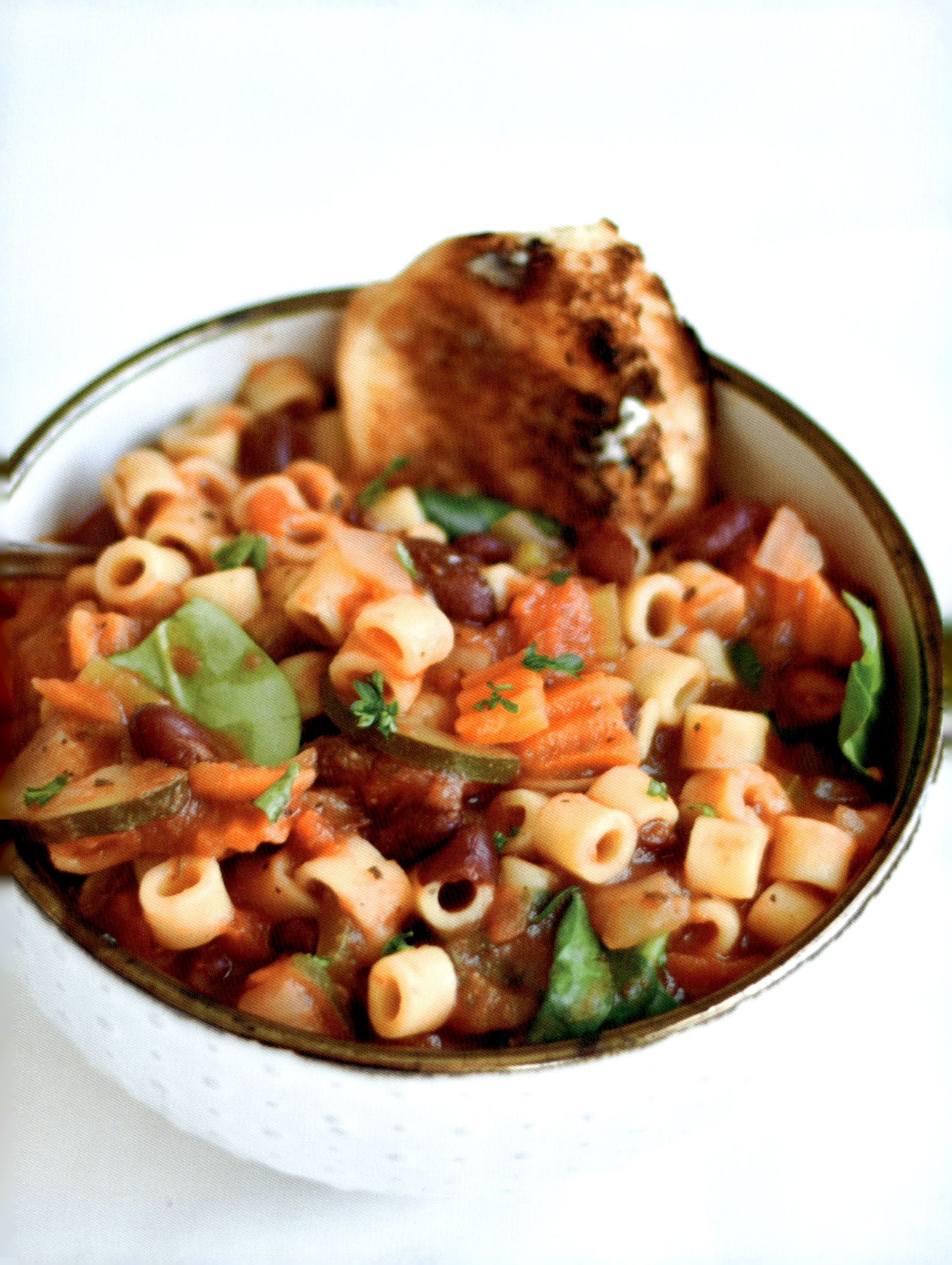

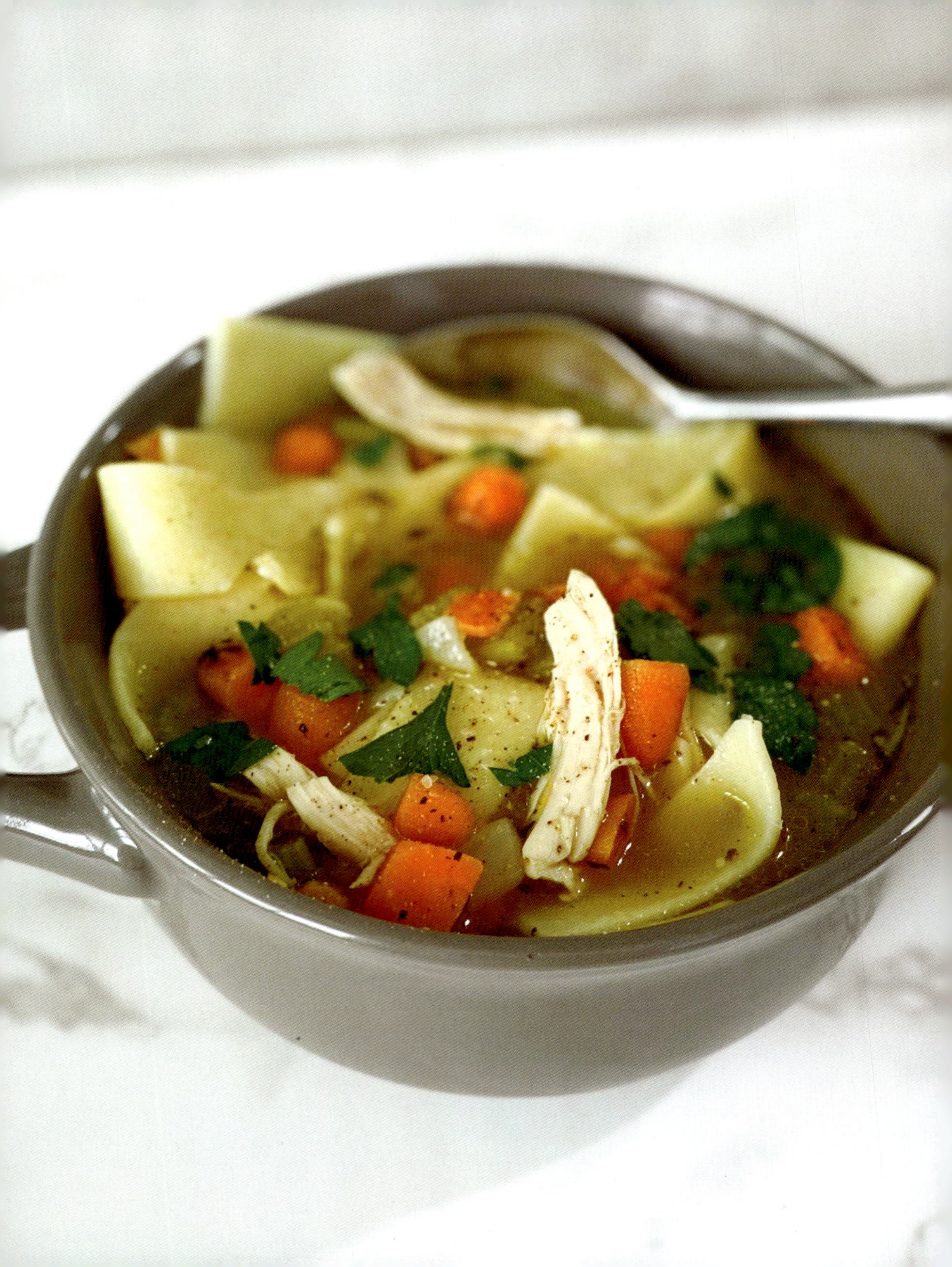

Easy Chicken Noodle Soup

This homemade chicken noodle soup is warm, comforting, and so easy to make!

Prep time: 5 mins   **Cook time:** 30 mins   **Servings:** 4

INGREDIENTS

- 1 tbsp butter
- 1 tbsp olive oil
- 1 1/2 cups sliced carrots
- 1 cup sliced celery
- 1 yellow onion, diced
- 1 Tbsp minced garlic
- 1 tsp dried thyme
- 1/2 tsp dried sage
- 2 bay leaves
- 1 tsp pepper
- 1 tsp salt, or more to taste
- 1 tsp garlic powder
- 9 cups chicken broth
- 8 oz thick old fashioned Amish or country wide egg noodles
- 2 cups cooked shredded chicken

DIRECTIONS

1. To a large pot, add the butter and oil.
2. Add the carrots, celery, and onion and sauté for 5-7 minutes.
3. Stir in minced garlic and all the seasonings and cook until garlic is fragrant.
4. Add in the broth and bring to a simmer.
5. Stir in pasta and cook for 18 minutes or until pasta is tender.
6. Remove bay leaves and stir in chicken. Let it cook for 1-2 minutes, or until the chicken is warmed through and serve. Enjoy!

White Chicken Chili

This White Chicken Chili is creamy, hearty, and bursting with flavor, thanks to loads of spices and green chiles.

Prep time: 10 mins   **Cook time:** 20 mins   **Servings:** 4-5

INGREDIENTS

- 3 tbsp olive oil
- 1 large onion, chopped
- 2 garlic cloves, minced
- 2 tsp chili powder
- 1 1/2 tsp cumin
- 1 tsp oregano
- 3-15 oz cans Great Northern white beans, drained and rinsed
- 3-4 chicken breasts, cooked and diced
- 1 cup corn kernels (optional)
- 1 can diced green chilies
- 4 cups chicken broth
- 1/4 tsp salt
- 2 tbsp butter, softened
- 1 1/2 tbsp flour
- pepper, to taste
- 1/4 cup whipping cream
- shredded cheddar cheese, cilantro, or lime juice, for topping

DIRECTIONS

1. Warm the oil in a large, heavy saucepan over medium heat.
2. Add the onion and garlic and sauté, stirring often, for 7 minutes.
3. Stir in the chili powder, cumin, and oregano, and sauté for another minute. Stir in the white beans, chicken, corn, green chilies, chicken broth, and salt. Bring the mixture to a gentle simmer and allow it to continue simmering, partially covered, for 10 minutes.
4. In a small bowl, blend the butter and flour. Add the mixture to the chili and stir until it thickens, about a minute. Add more salt and pepper to taste. Add more broth to thin the chili, if desired.
5. Stir in the cream. Serve hot, topped with cheese, cilantro, and lime juice, and enjoy!

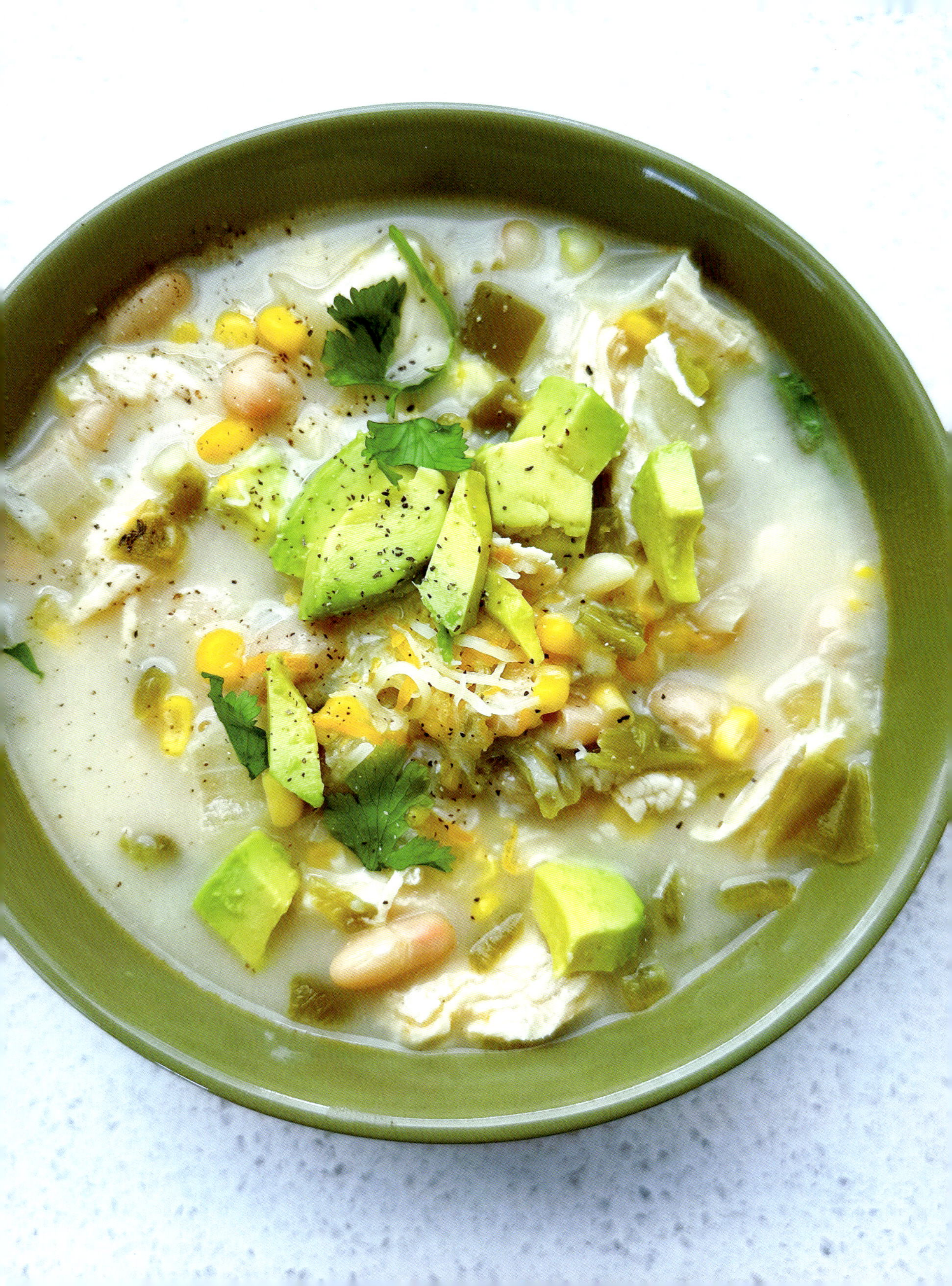

NOTES

SLOW COOKER

I cannot say enough about the slow cooker! When I first got married, I quickly realized how almost foolproof it was to create incredible meals hours ahead of time for a relatively low cost. I hope you enjoy some of my family's favorite slow cooker meals!

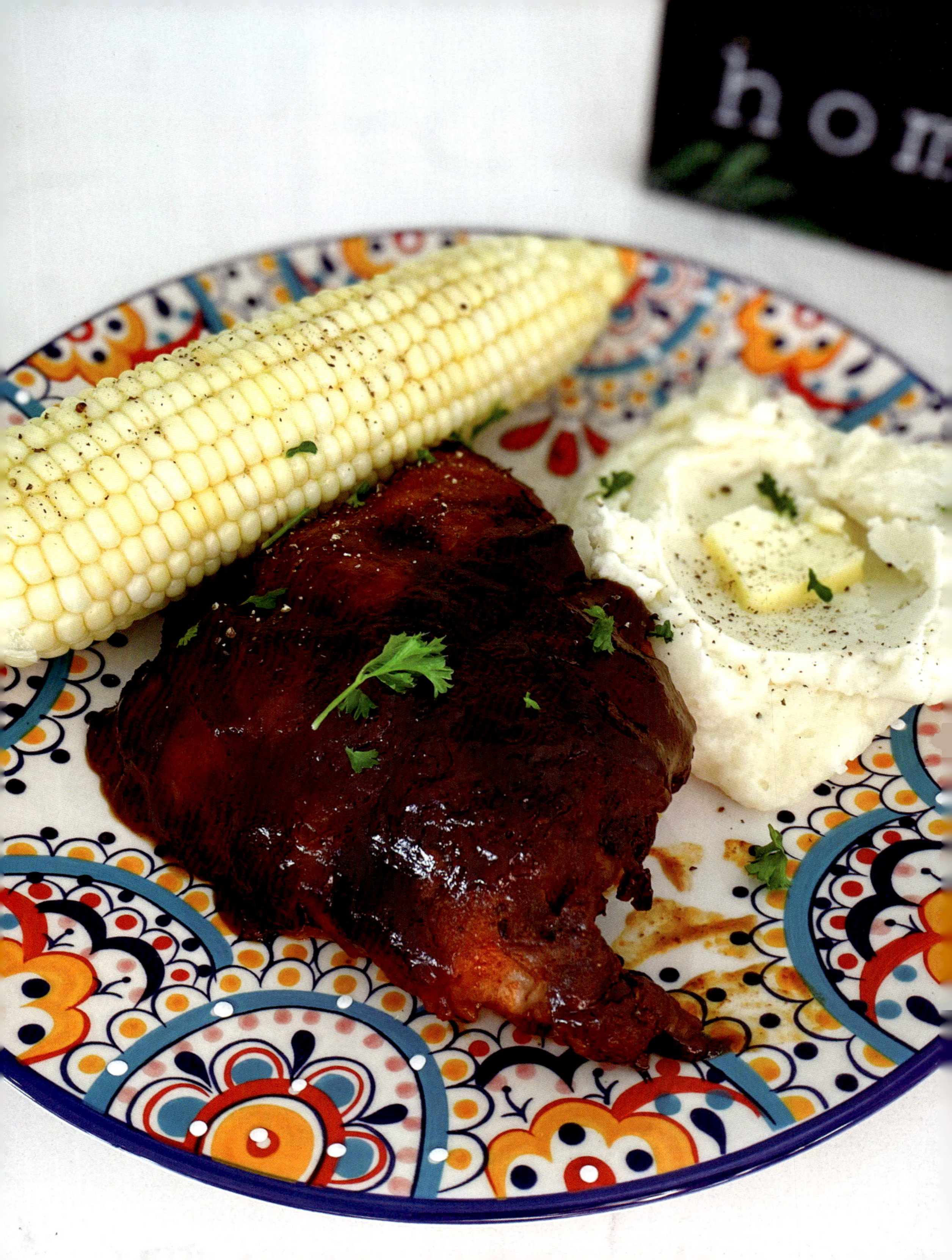
hom

Slow Cooker Barbecue Ribs

Slow Cooker Barbecue Ribs end up juicy and tender enough to fall off the bone. They're so simple to make and always taste amazing.

Prep time: 10 mins   **Cook time:** 6 hours   **Servings:** 4-5

INGREDIENTS

- 3 tbsp paprika
- 1 tbsp salt
- 1/2 tbsp pepper
- 3 tbsp brown sugar
- 4-5 pounds pork back ribs
- 18 oz barbecue sauce
- 1/4 cup apple cider vinegar

DIRECTIONS

1. Add the paprika, salt, pepper, and brown sugar to a small bowl. Whisk to combine.
2. Rub the seasoning mixture on both sides of the ribs. Brush 1 1/4 cups of the barbecue sauce all over the ribs.
3. Place ribs into the slow cooker standing upright with the meaty side against the inside wall of the slow cooker. Pour the remaining barbecue sauce over the top. Pour the apple cider vinegar over everything.
4. Place lid on top and cook on LOW for 6-7 hours, or until the ribs are fall-apart tender. Do not open the slow cooker while cooking. Brush more barbecue sauce on at the end serve and enjoy!

Slow Cooker Chicken Tortilla Soup

This Chicken Tortilla Soup will make your kitchen smell amazing all day long and will taste even better. All you have to do is throw the ingredients in the slow cooker!

Prep time: 5 mins   **Cook time:** 6-8 hours   **Servings:** 4-5

INGREDIENTS

- 1 lb chicken breast
- 15 oz chicken broth
- 1 cup water
- 15 oz can corn
- 10 oz can Diced Tomatoes and Green Chiles
- 1 yellow onion, diced
- 1 tbsp minced garlic
- 10 oz enchilada sauce
- 2 tbsp taco seasoning
- 1 tsp chili powder
- 1 tsp salt
- 1/2 tsp pepper

Toppings (optional)

- tortilla strips
- shredded cheese
- sour cream
- chopped cilantro

DIRECTIONS

1. To a slow cooker, add all of the ingredients except the toppings. Cook on LOW for 7-8 hours or HIGH for 6 hours, until the chicken is cooked.
2. Remove the cooked chicken from the slow cooker and shred. Place back into slow cooker and stir. Serve and top with toppings of your choice. Enjoy!

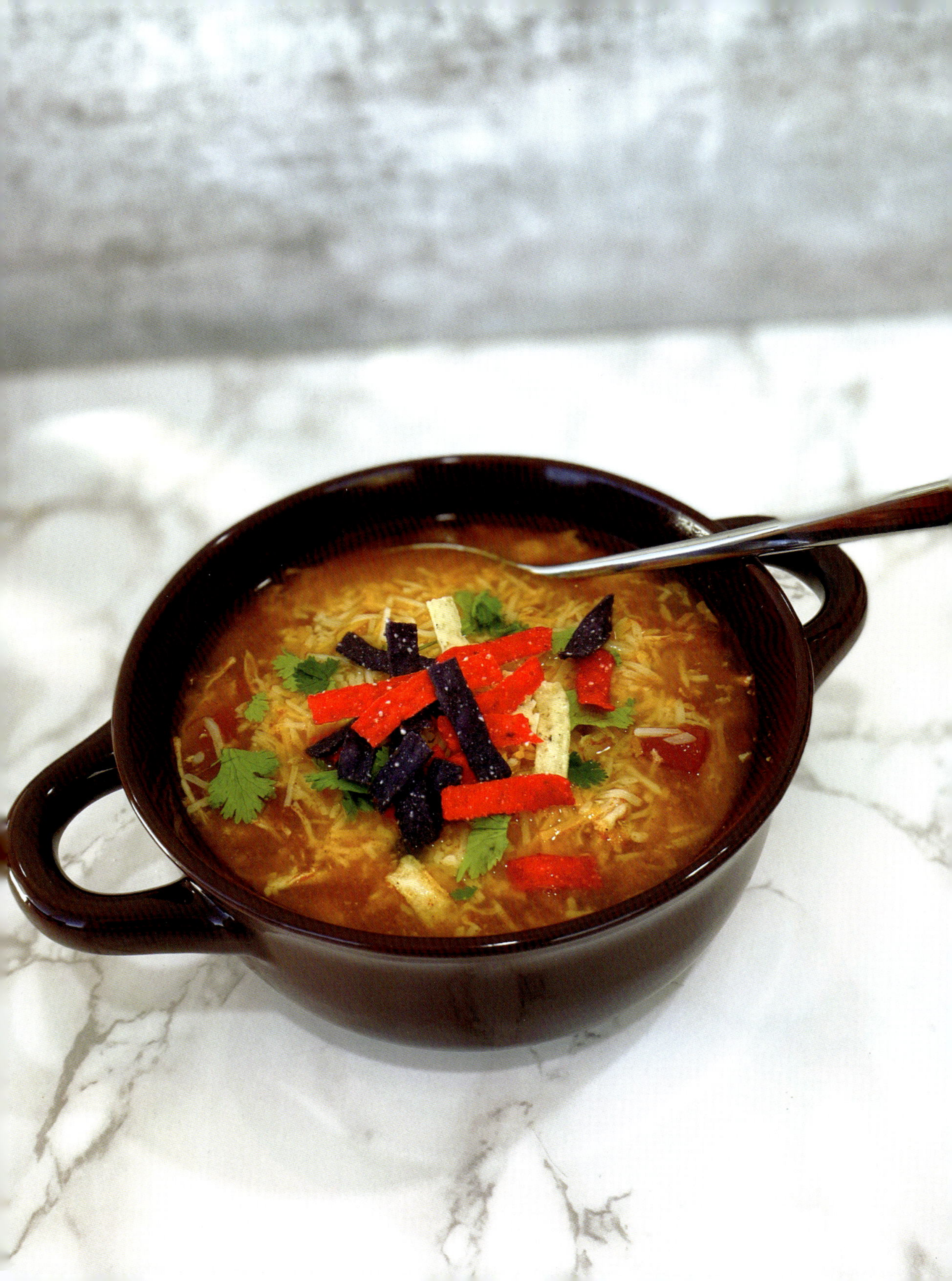

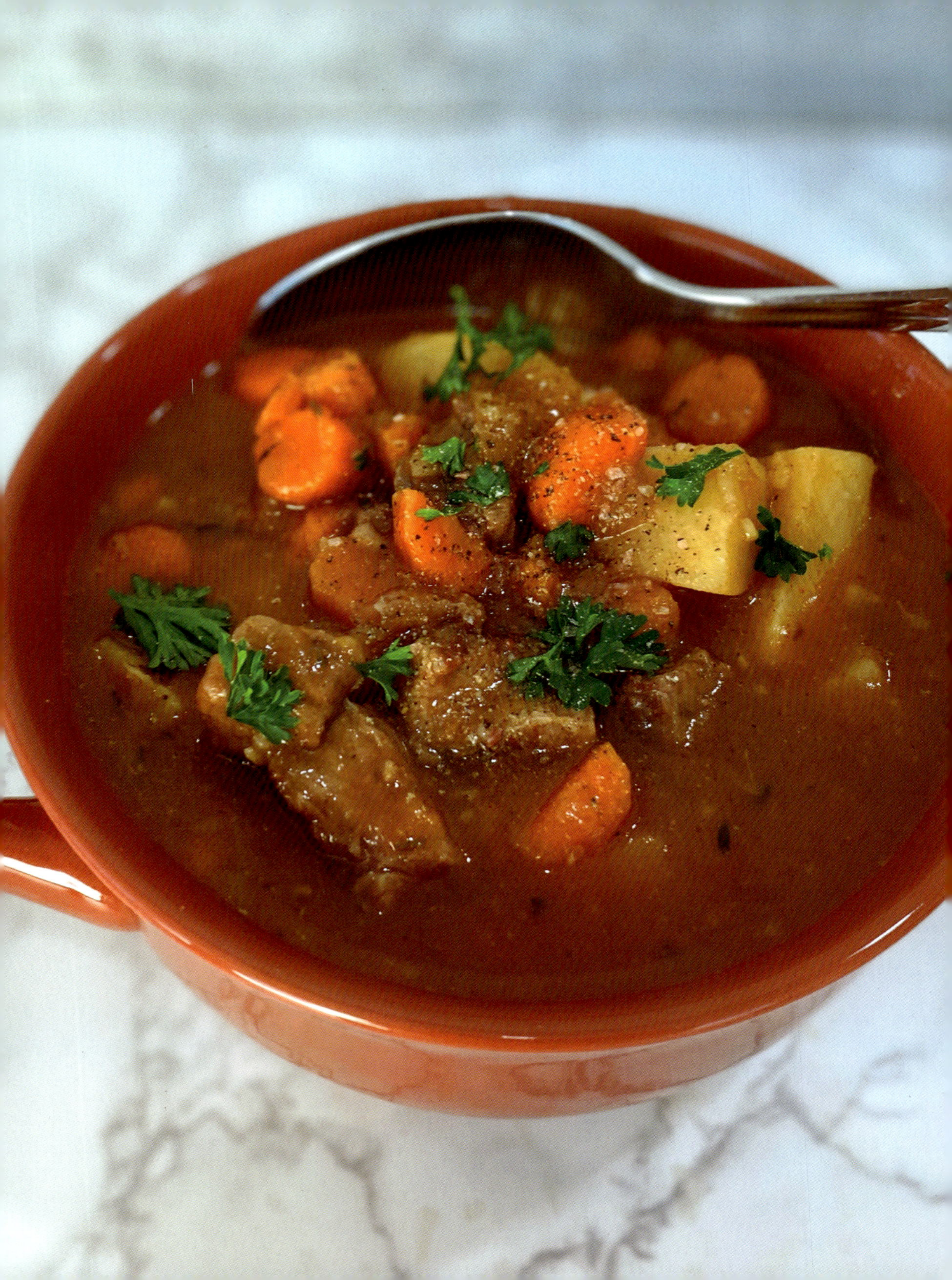

Easy Slow Cooker Beef Stew

This Easy Slow Cooker Beef Stew is a nostalgic and hearty meal that will warm you from the inside out and fulfill your comfort food needs.

Prep time: 15 mins   **Cook time:** 6-8 hours   **Servings:** 4-5

INGREDIENTS

- 3 tbsp olive oil
- 1.5 lbs beef stew meat
- 2 tsp salt, divided
- 1 tsp pepper, divided
- 3-4 medium Russet potatoes, peeled and cut into bite-sized pieces
- 5 large carrots, cut into bite-sized pieces
- 1 yellow onion, diced
- 3 1/2 cups beef broth
- 8 oz tomato sauce
- 2 tbsp Worcestershire sauce
- 2 tsp dried thyme
- 2 tsp dried rosemary
- 1 tsp paprika
- 2 bay leaves
- 1/4 cup all-purpose flour

DIRECTIONS

1. Season stew meat with 1 tsp salt and 1/2 tsp pepper. Add the oil to a skillet over high heat. Once hot, add the stew meat and sear on each side to form a golden brown crust. This will caramelize the natural sugars in the meat and create a delicious crust that locks in all the juices and flavor.
2. Remove stew meat from the skillet and place into the slow cooker with the rest of the ingredients except for the flour.
3. Stir and let cook on LOW for 7-8 hours or HIGH for 5-6 hours.
4. Twenty minutes before cooking time has elapsed, remove 3/4 cup of the liquid from the slow cooker and pour into a small bowl with the flour. Whisk until smooth. Pour this mixture into the slow cooker and stir well. This will help thicken the stew. Let cook for an additional 20 minutes.
5. Serve over noodles, mashed potatoes, or on its own. Enjoy!

Slow Cooker Shredded Chicken Tacos

Slow Cooker Shredded Chicken Tacos require only 4 ingredients (and that includes the tortillas!) and 5 minutes of prep time!

Prep time: 5 mins   **Cook time:** 5-7 hours   **Servings:** 4-5

INGREDIENTS

- 2 lbs chicken breast
- 3 tbsp taco seasoning
- 16 oz tomato salsa (any brand will work)
- tortillas

Toppings

- sour cream
- shredded lettuce
- diced tomatoes
- guacamole
- shredded cheese

DIRECTIONS

1. Place chicken into slow cooker, sprinkle with taco seasoning, then pour the salsa over the top. Cook on LOW for 7 hours or HIGH for 5 hours.
2. Shred the chicken in the slow cooker then serve in tortillas with your favorite taco toppings. Enjoy!

Freezer Meal Directions

1. Add the chicken (can be frozen or fresh), salsa, and taco seasoning into a gallon-sized freezer bag. Release any air in the bag, seal the bag, and place in the freezer for up to three months.
2. Before cooking, thaw in the refrigerator overnight. Place into the slow cooker and follow the cooking instructions above.

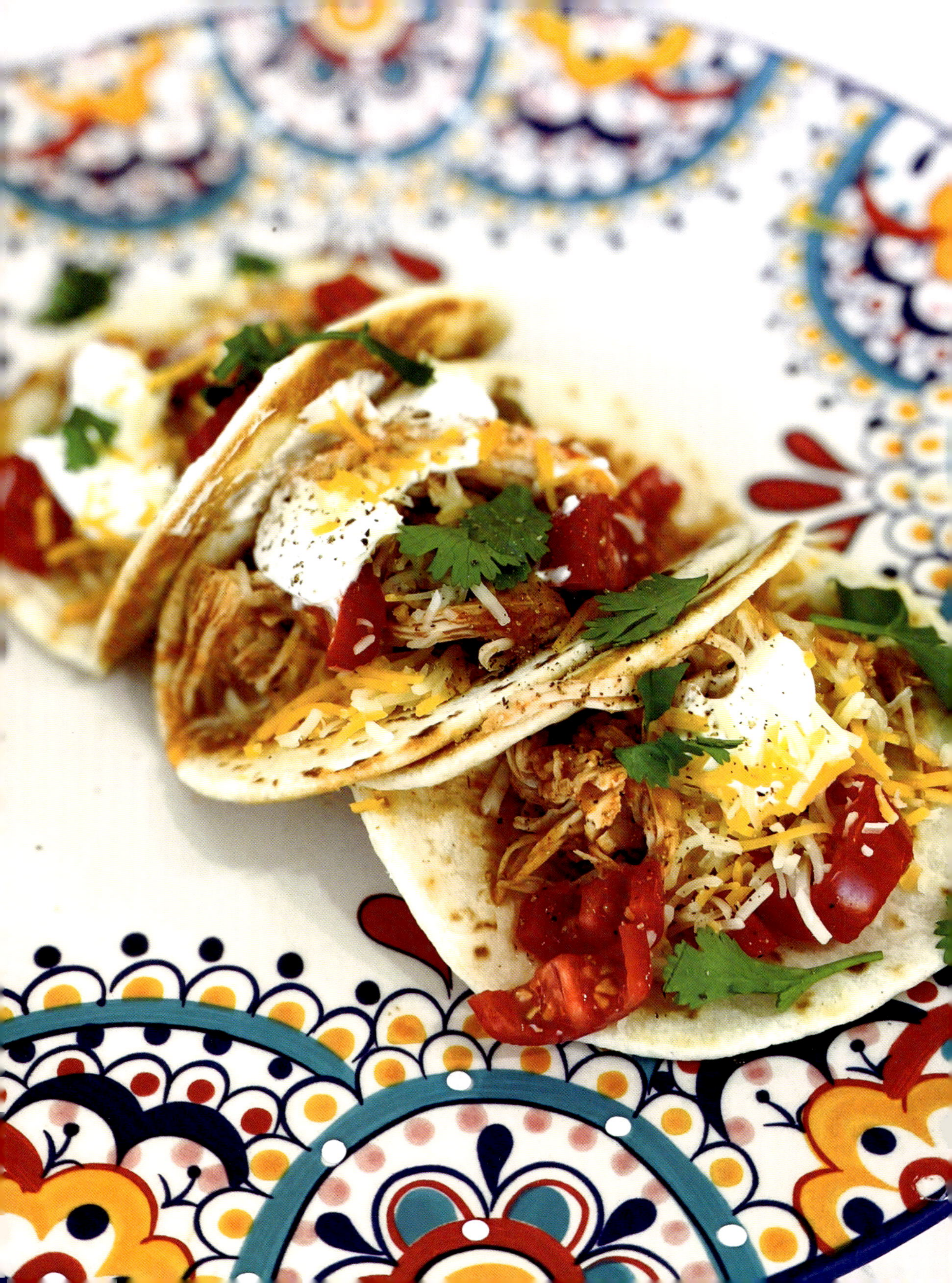

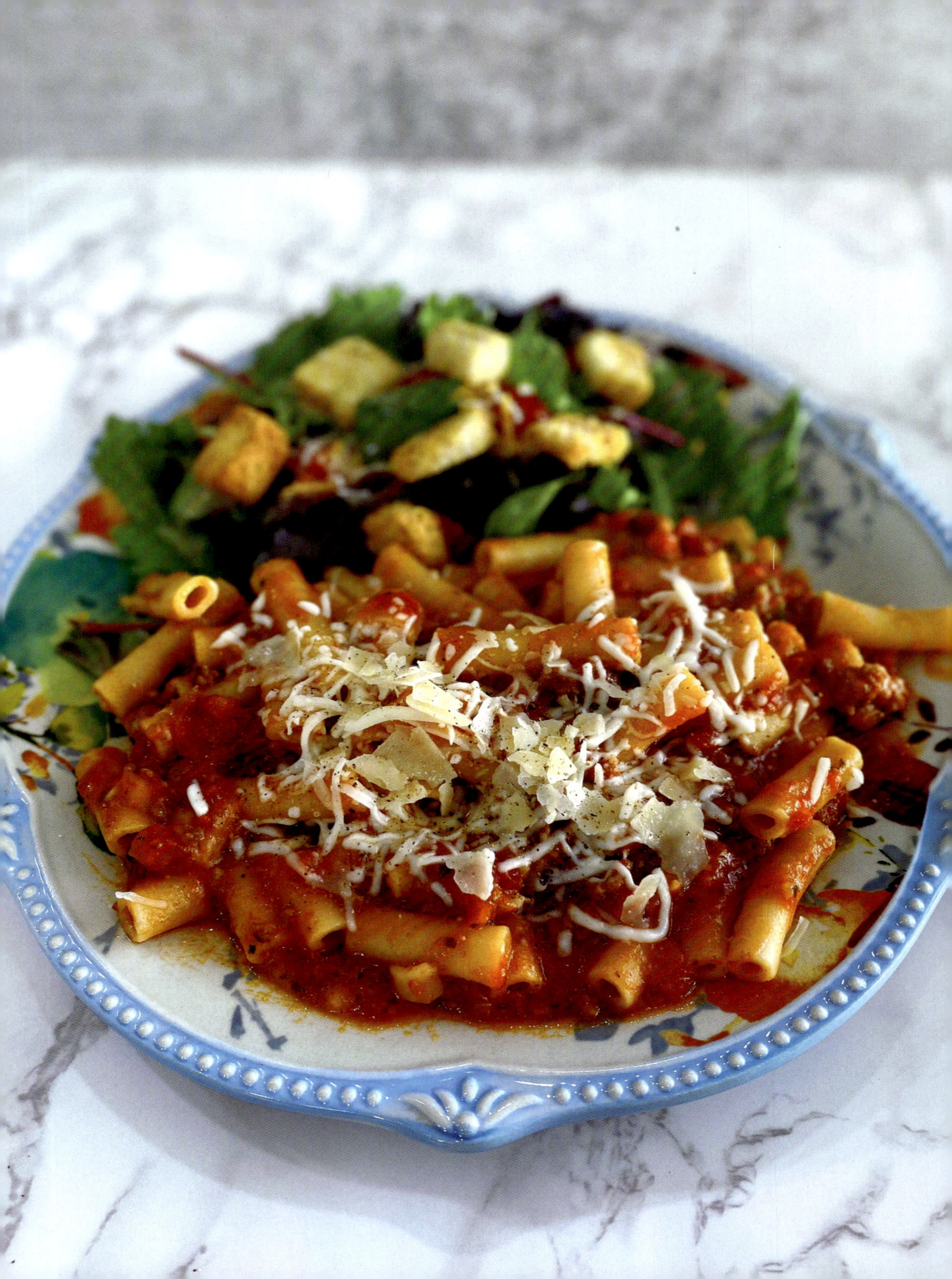

Slow Cooker Baked Ziti

Slow Cooker Baked Ziti is easy, cheesy and perfect for a cool night in. It cooks in your slow cooker (not the oven) all day and tastes great.

Prep time: 15 mins **Cook time:** 4-7 hours **Servings:** 6

INGREDIENTS

- 1 lb Italian sausage
- 1 onion, diced
- 2 tbsp minced garlic
- 1 tsp salt
- 1/2 tsp pepper
- 1 tsp dried basil
- 28 oz can Italian-style diced tomatoes
- 24 oz marinara sauce
- 2 1/2 cups water or chicken broth
- 13 oz ziti pasta
- 1 cup shredded mozzarella cheese

DIRECTIONS

1. Add the sausage to a large skillet over medium heat and brown. Once cooked through, remove any grease from the pan.
2. Add the sausage to a large slow cooker along with the diced onion, minced garlic, diced tomatoes, seasonings, marinara sauce, and water. Stir well.
3. Cook on LOW for 7 hours or HIGH for 4 hours.
4. Turn slow cooker to high and stir in the uncooked pasta. Let cook for an additional 16-35 minutes or until the pasta is cooked. This may vary depending on your slow cooker. Sprinkle the cheese on top and stir in once melted. Serve and enjoy!

Slow Cooker Chicken Enchilada Pasta

The Slow Cooker Chicken Enchilada Pasta is cheesy, spicy, and unexpectedly delicious. Prep it in the morning and it will be ready come dinner time.

Prep time: 15 mins   **Cook time:** 4-6 hours   **Servings:** 4-5

INGREDIENTS

- 1 lb chicken breast
- 1 tsp salt
- 1/2 tsp pepper
- 1 tsp chili powder
- 1 tsp cumin
- 1 tsp oregano
- 28 oz red enchilada sauce
- 4 oz can green chiles
- 16 oz pasta
- 1 cup cheddar cheese
- 3/4 cup sour cream
- toppings like cheese, sour cream, shredded lettuce, avocado, and diced tomatoes

DIRECTIONS

1. To a slow cooker, add the chicken, seasonings, enchilada sauce, and green chiles. Cover and cook on LOW for 6 hours or HIGH for 4 hours, or until chicken is cooked.
2. Once the chicken is almost cooked through, bring a large pot of water to a boil over the stove and cook the pasta according to the box instructions. Strain and set aside.
3. Shred the cooked chicken into small pieces with two forks, then stir in the cheese and sour cream. Stir in the pasta and serve with your favorite taco toppings. Enjoy!

Freezer Meal Directions

1. Place the chicken, seasonings, enchilada sauce, and green chiles into a large freezer bag, release any air, and seal the bag. Can be frozen for up to 3 months.
2. Thaw in the refrigerator overnight before cooking. Place into the slow cooker and follow the cooking instructions above. Make sure to add the cheese and sour cream in at the end and serve over cooked pasta.

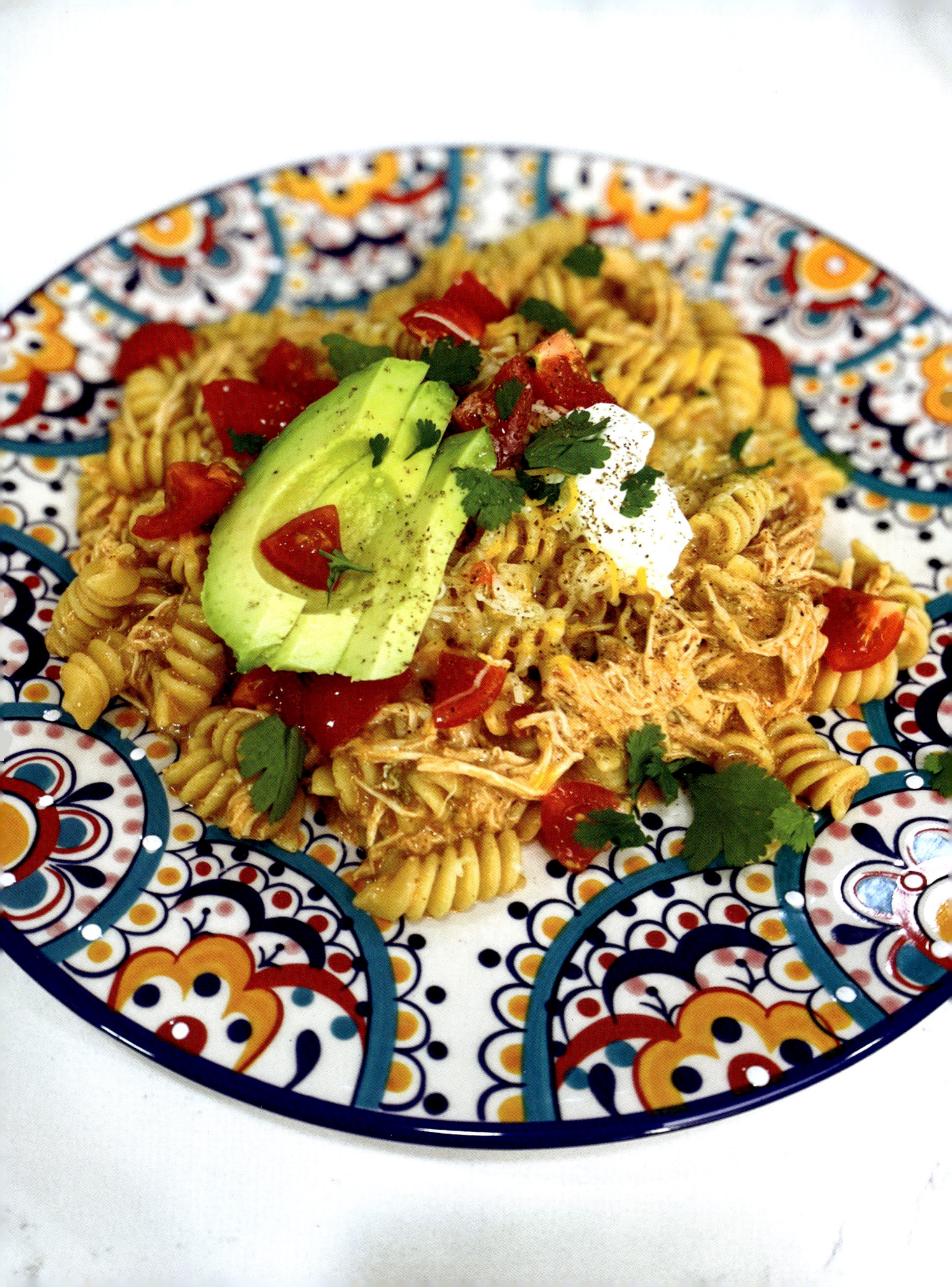

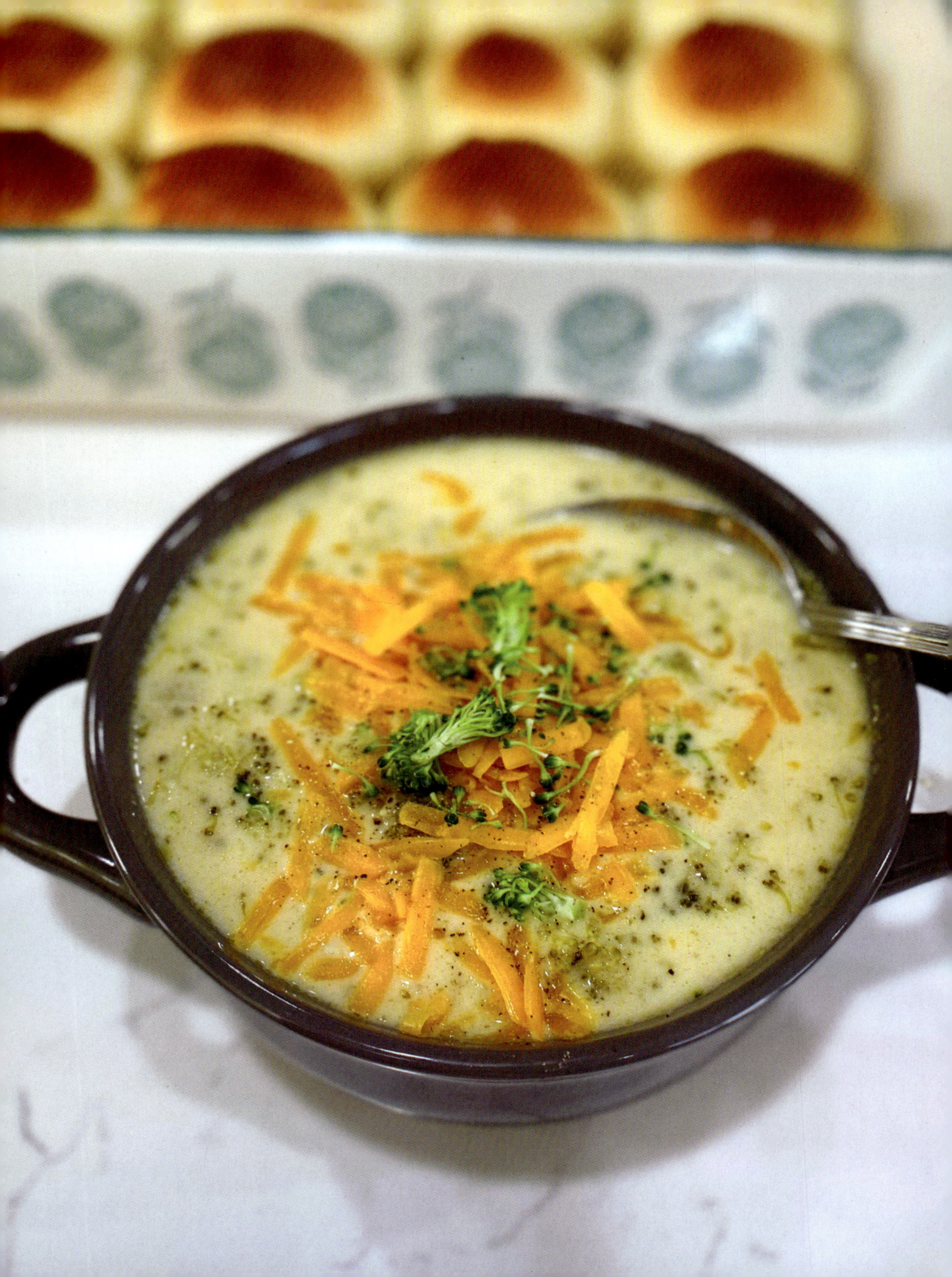

Slow Cooker Broccoli Cheese Soup

Slow Cooker Broccoli Cheese Soup simmers away in the slow cooker all day, and is so delicious you're going to want to make it all the time.

Prep time: 5 mins   **Cook time:** 6-7 hours   **Servings:** 4-5

INGREDIENTS

- 6 cups fresh broccoli florets, chopped small
- 2 large carrots, sliced
- 1 yellow onion, diced
- 2 tbsp butter
- 1 tbsp minced garlic
- 2 tsp salt
- 1 tsp pepper
- 1/3 cup cornstarch
- 6 cups vegetable broth
- 5 cups sharp cheddar cheese, shredded
- 1-2 cups heavy cream

DIRECTIONS

1. To a large slow cooker, add the broccoli, carrots, onion, butter, garlic, and salt and pepper.
2. To a small bowl, add in 1 cup of the broth and the cornstarch and whisk together well so the broth isn't clumpy. Add this cornstarch slurry into the slow cooker with the remaining broth. Cook on LOW for 6-7 hours.
3. Once cooked, add in cheese and heavy cream, stir well, put the lid on top, and cook on HIGH for 30-40 minutes until the cheese is melted and everything is warmed through. Serve and enjoy!

Slow Cooker Barbeque Chicken

This Slow Cooker BBQ Chicken has three ingredients and is bursting with flavor. Serve on hamburger buns for delicious and simple pulled chicken sandwiches.

Prep time: 5 mins **Cook time:** 4-6 hours **Servings:** 4-5

INGREDIENTS

- 1.5 lbs chicken breast
- 1/2 cup barbecue sauce
- 1/3 cup Italian dressing
- hamburger buns

DIRECTIONS

1. To a greased slow cooker add the chicken, barbecue sauce, and Italian dressing. Cover with the lid and cook on HIGH for 4 hours or LOW for 6 hours, or until the chicken is cooked.
2. Shred with two forks in the slow cooker. Serve on buns and with coleslaw, if desired, and enjoy.

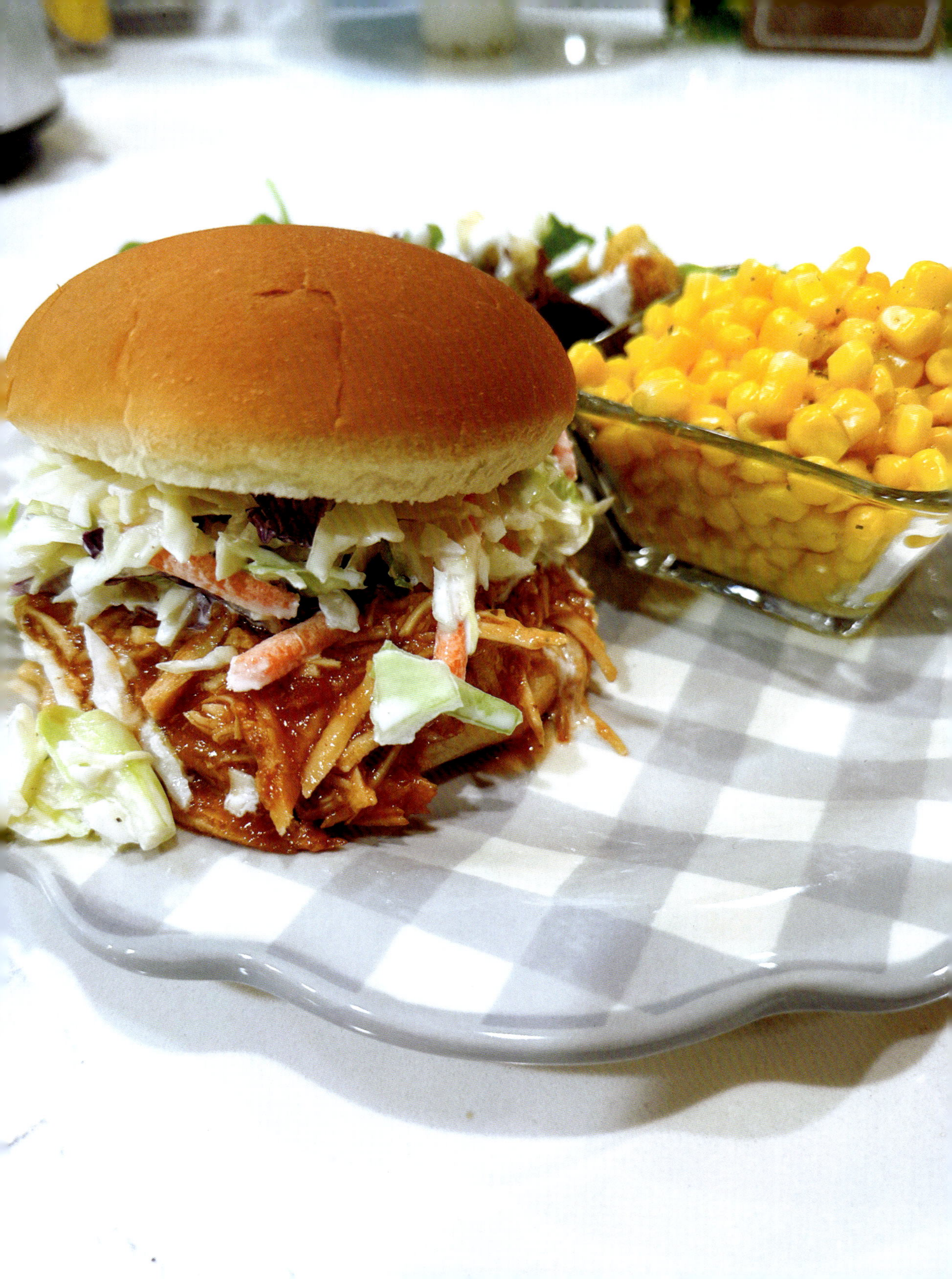

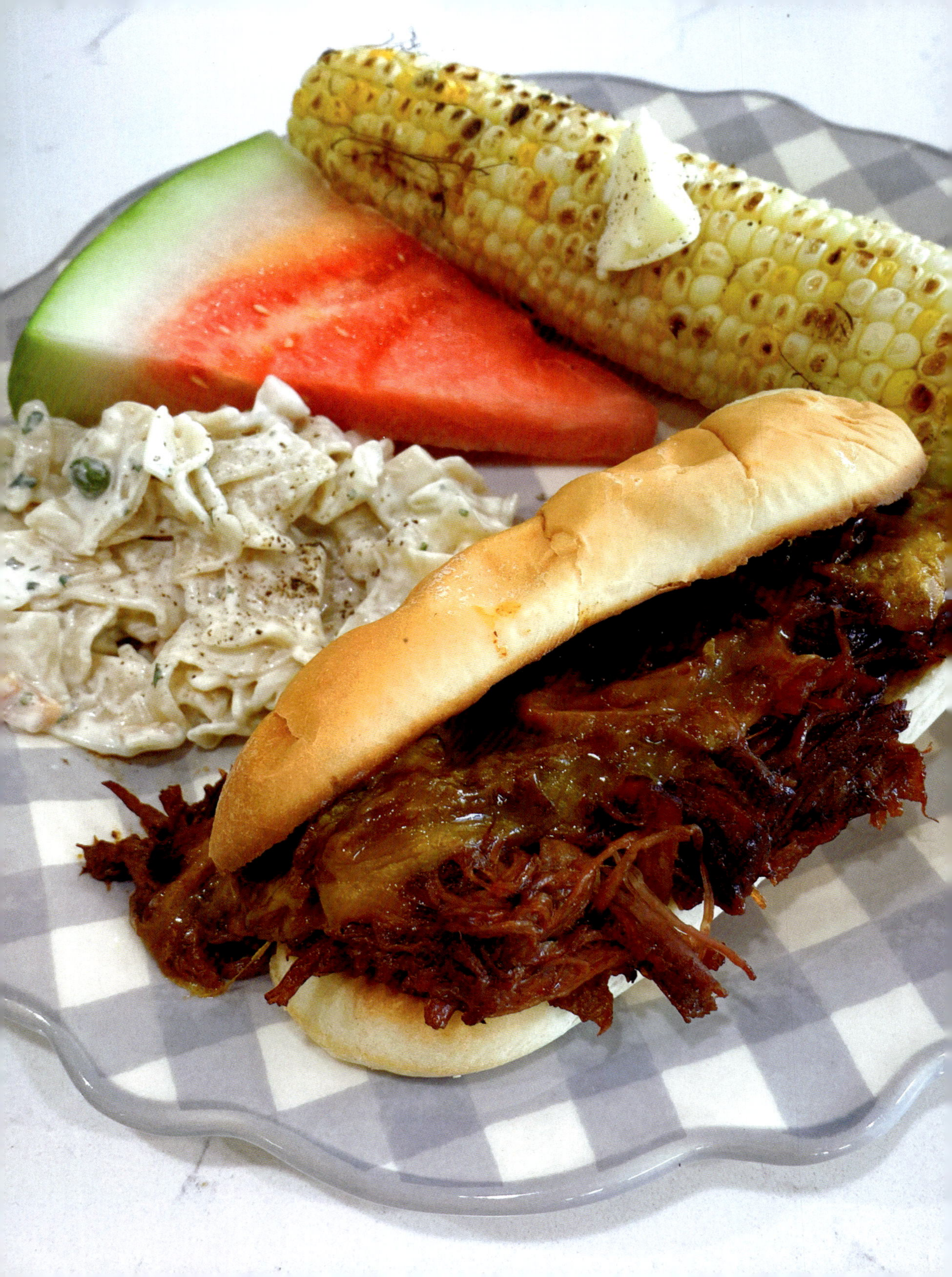

Slow Cooker Pulled Beef Sandwiches

Melt-in-your-mouth pulled beef is slathered in BBQ sauce and sandwiched between melty cheese and toasty rolls. These Slow Cooker Pulled Beef Sandwiches are to-die-for good.

Prep time: 10 mins   **Cook time:** 8 hours   **Servings:** 4-5

INGREDIENTS

- 1 tbsp brown sugar
- 1 tsp salt
- 1/2 tsp pepper
- 1 tbsp paprika
- 1 tsp chili powder
- 1 tsp onion powder
- 1 tsp garlic powder
- 6-10 lb chuck roast
- 2 cups barbecue sauce
- hoagie rolls
- sliced cheddar cheese

DIRECTIONS

1. To a small bowl add all of the seasonings and stir to combine. Rub the seasoning mixture all over the chuck roast. Place the chuck roast into a greased slow cooker and cook on LOW for 8-9 hours, or until cooked through and very tender.
2. Remove the roast from the slow cooker and shred, removing any excess fat from the meat. Discard the liquid in the slow cooker. Place the shredded beef back into the slow cooker, add in the barbecue sauce, and stir well. Cook on LOW for an additional 30-45 minutes.
3. Slice the hoagie rolls and place them on a sheet pan. Broil for 2-3 minutes, or until golden brown. Remove from the oven and place slices of cheese and some of the BBQ beef on the bottom half of each roll. Broil for an additional 2-3 minutes, or until the cheese is melty. Enjoy!

Slow Cooker Marry Me Chicken

One of my very favorite slow cooker dishes of all time, this Marry Me Chicken Recipe is easy and extremely indulgent! Sun-dried tomatoes and a creamy sauce make this dish so amazing.

Prep time: 5 mins   **Cook time:** 4-7 hours   **Servings:** 4-5

INGREDIENTS

- 1 1/2 lbs chicken breast
- 1 1/2 cups chicken broth
- 3 tbsp corn starch
- 1 cup heavy cream
- 1 tbsp minced garlic
- 1/2 tsp salt
- 1 tsp pepper
- 1 tsp Italian seasoning
- 1/2 tsp paprika
- 2 tbsp butter, sliced thin
- 1/3 cup sun-dried tomatoes (drained)

DIRECTIONS

1. To a medium-sized bowl, add the chicken broth then slowly whisk in the cornstarch. Whisk slowly to avoid lumps.
2. Add this mixture to a slow cooker along with the cream, minced garlic, and seasonings. Place the chicken into the slow cooker and top with butter slices and sun dried tomatoes.
3. Cook on LOW for 6-7 hours or HIGH for 4 hours.
4. Once cooked, shred the chicken and serve with pasta, mashed potatoes, or rice. Enjoy!

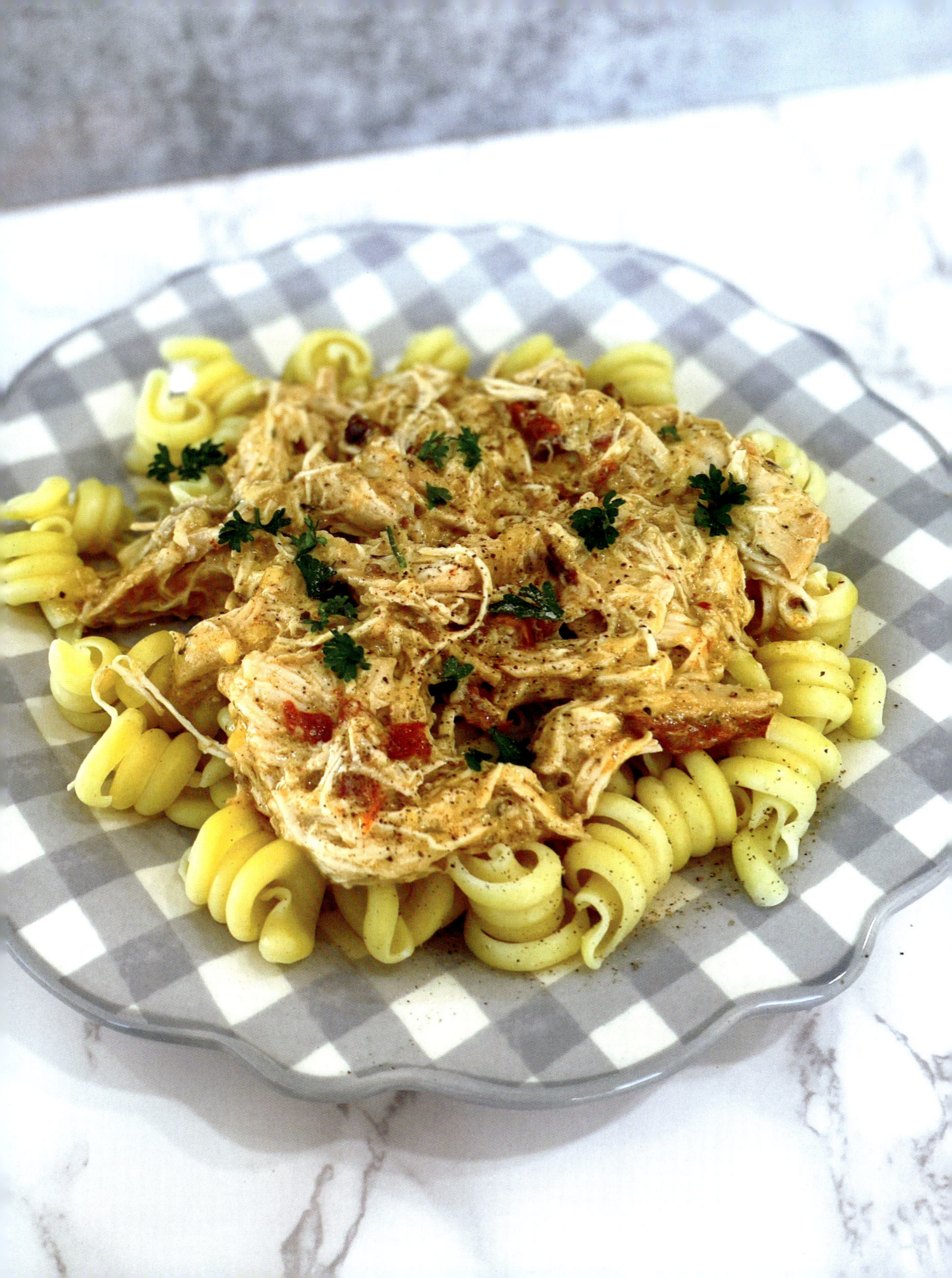

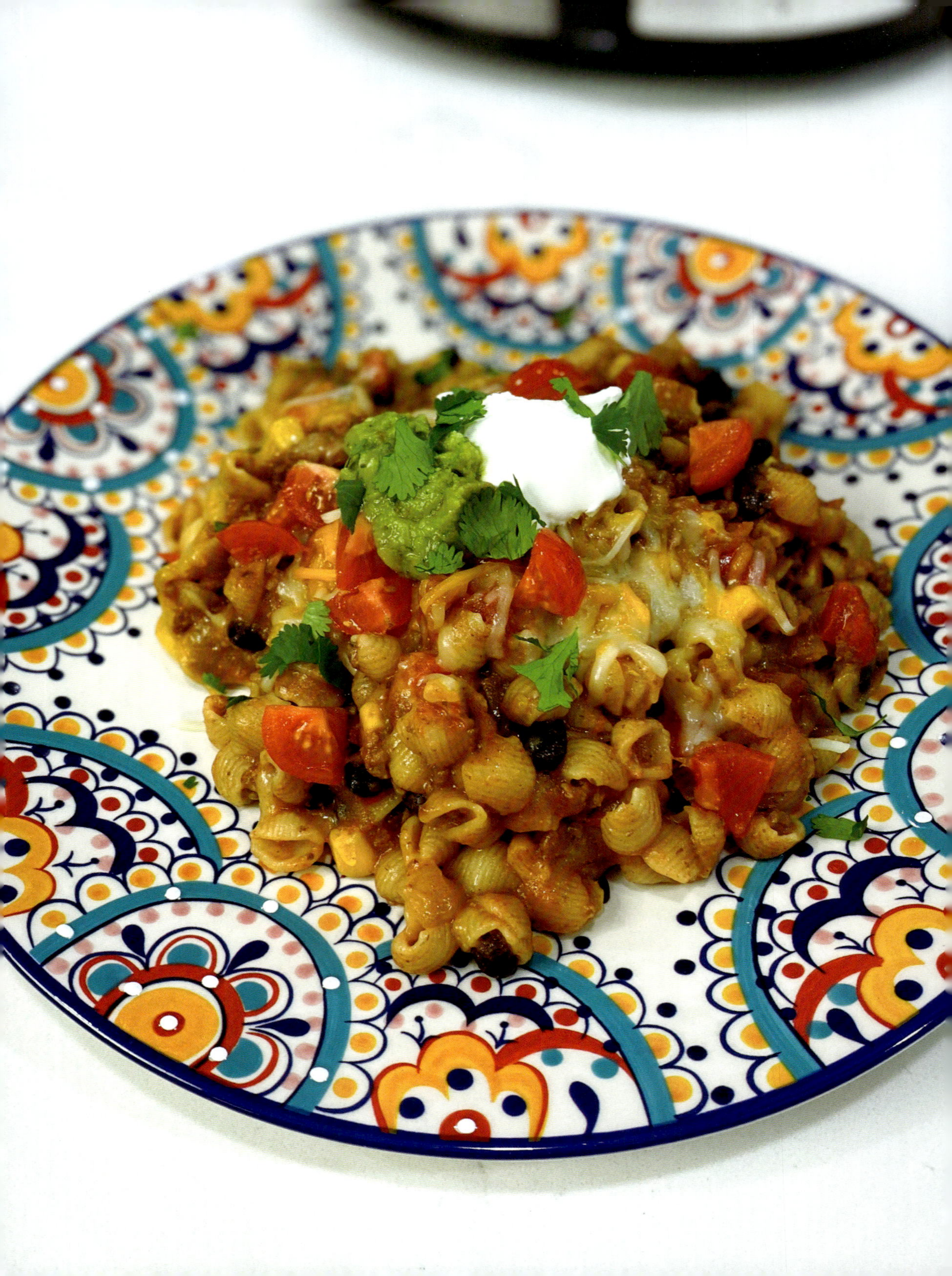

Slow Cooker Mexican Pasta

All the flavors of Mexican food wrapped up in cheesy pasta and made in the slow cooker with almost no prep? That's Slow Cooker Mexican Pasta!

Prep time: 15 mins **Cook time:** 4-6 hours **Servings:** 4-5

INGREDIENTS

- 1 lb ground beef
- 1 yellow onion, diced
- 1 red bell pepper, diced
- 1 tsp oregano
- 1 tsp chili powder
- 1 tsp onion powder
- 1 tsp garlic powder
- 16 oz tomato sauce
- 10 oz can Tomatoes and Diced Green Chiles
- 15 oz can corn, drained
- 15 oz can black beans, drained and rinsed
- 2 3/4 cup beef broth
- 1 1/2 cups Mexican style cheese
- 16 oz small pasta shells

Toppings (optional)

- sour cream
- cheese
- shredded lettuce
- diced Tomatoes
- avocado

DIRECTIONS

1. To a large skillet over medium-high heat, add the ground beef and brown until it is cooked through. Remove any grease from the pan. Add the beef to the slow cooker. Add in all the remaining ingredients except for the cheese and the pasta.
2. Stir well and cook on LOW for 6 hours or HIGH for 4 hours. After the cooking time elapses, stir in the cheese and the dry pasta. Cook on high for 30 minutes, checking every 15 minutes and stirring until the pasta is tender.
3. Serve with your favorite toppings and enjoy!

Slow Cooker Fiesta Chicken

My Fiesta Chicken is tender shredded chicken cloaked in creamy, flavorful, and spicy sauce. Serve over chips or stuff into tortillas.

Prep time: 5 mins   **Cook time:** 6 hours   **Servings:** 5

INGREDIENTS

- 2 large chicken breasts
- 2 tbsp taco seasoning
- 1 can sweet corn, undrained
- 1 can Diced Tomatoes & Green Chiles
- 1 can cannellini beans, drained and rinsed
- 8 oz cream cheese, cubed
- chips or tortillas, for serving

Toppings (optional)

- guacamole
- shredded cheese
- lettuce
- sour cream
- lime wedges
- diced tomatoes

DIRECTIONS

1. Add the chicken to the bottom of a greased slow cooker. Pour all the ingredients in except for the cream cheese. Place the block of cream cheese on top of everything.
2. Cook on LOW for 6 hours, or until chicken is cooked.
3. Once cooked, shred the chicken and mix everything together.
4. Serve over a bed of chips and topped with guacamole, cheese, tomato, lime, lettuce, and sour cream, or make tacos or burritos. Enjoy!

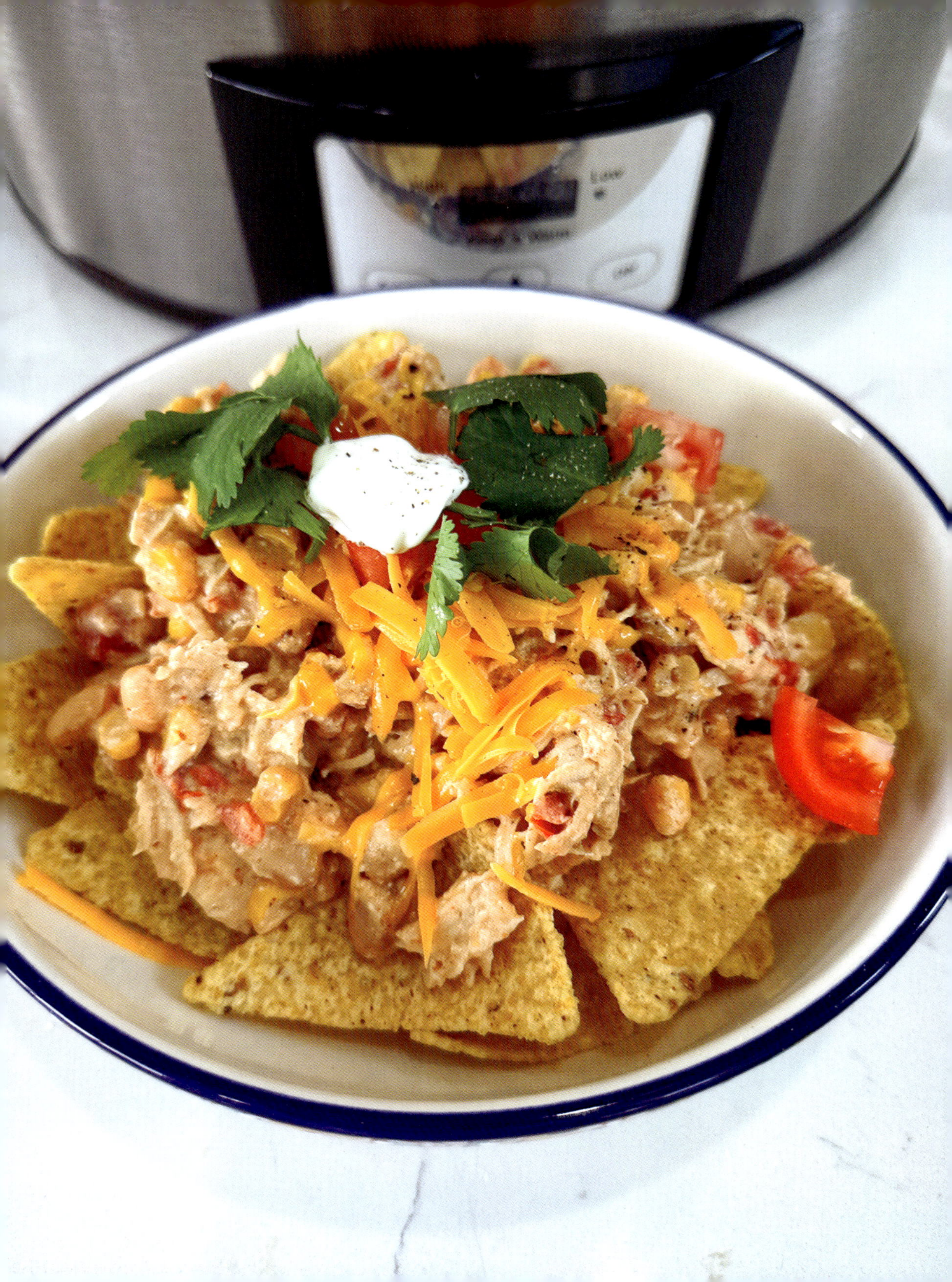
Low

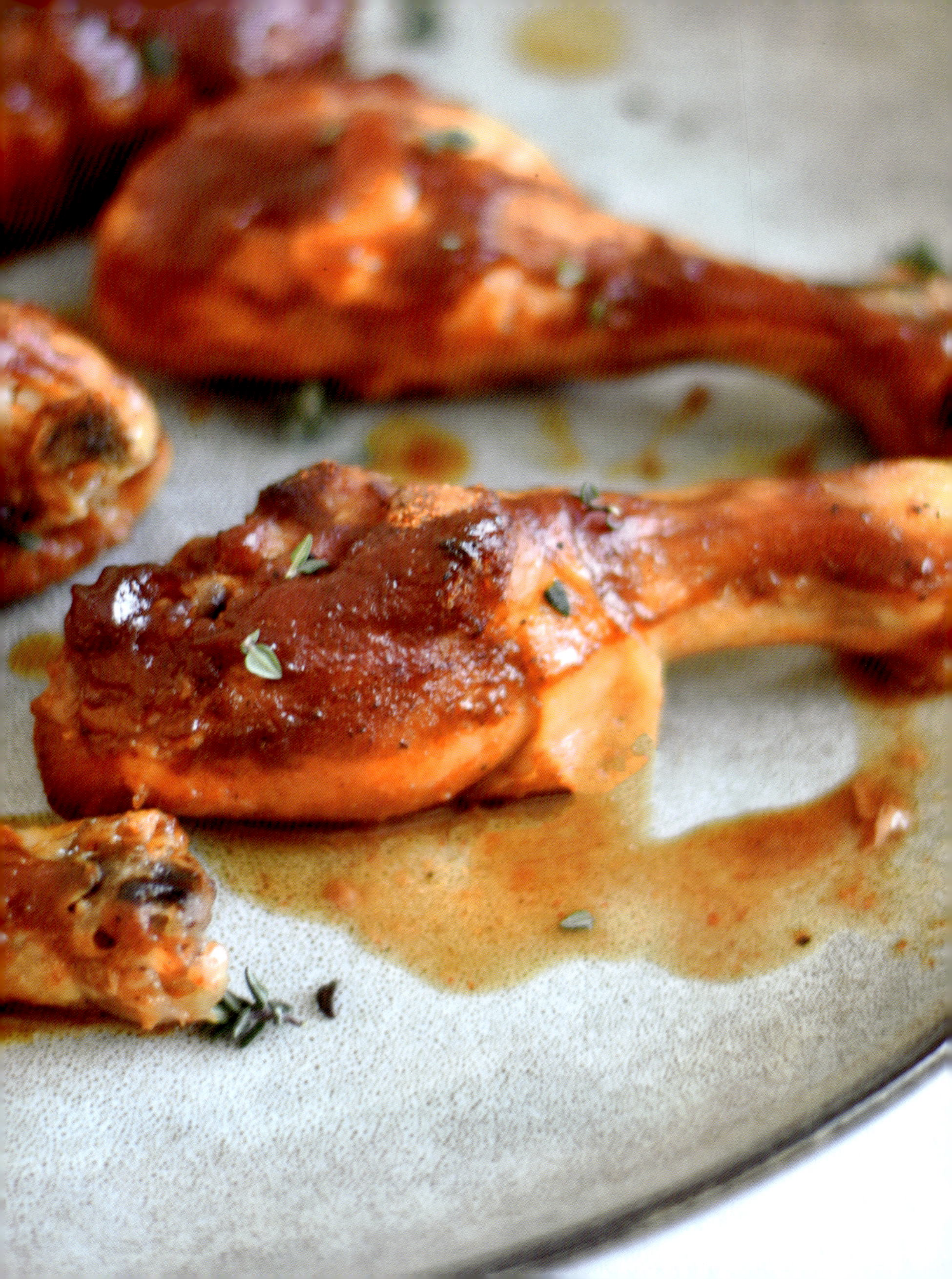

Slow Cooker BBQ Chicken Drumsticks

BBQ Slow Cooker Chicken Drumsticks are perfect for a BBQ with the family or on game day. Dry rub adds so much amazing flavor.

Prep time: 5 mins   **Cook time:** 6-7 hours   **Servings:** 4-5

INGREDIENTS

Dry Rub
- 1/4 cup brown sugar
- 1 tbsp paprika
- 1/2 tsp pepper
- 1/2 tsp salt
- 1/2 tbsp garlic powder
- 1/2 tbsp onion powder
- 1/2 tsp mustard
- dash of cayenne pepper

Drumsticks
- 1 1/4 cups BBQ sauce
- 6 chicken drumsticks

DIRECTIONS

1. In a small bowl, mix the dry rub together.
2. In a greased slow cooker, add the drumsticks and the dry rub. Coat the drumsticks evenly with the rub and work it in with your hands.
3. Add in 1 cup of the BBQ sauce and cook on LOW for 6-7 hours.
4. Once the 6-7 hours is up, remove from the slow cooker and place on a sheet pan. Add 1/4 cup more BBQ sauce on top and brush all over the drumsticks. Place under the broiler for about 2 minutes, or until the sauce thickens and turns into a glaze. Enjoy!

Creamy Chicken Pasta

Thanks to the Italian dressing mix, Creamy Chicken Pasta has some unexpected flavors and the creamiest sauce. It only takes 5 ingredients to make this tasty chicken pasta.

Prep time: 10 mins   **Cook time:** 6 hours   **Servings:** 5

INGREDIENTS

- 2 medium chicken breasts
- 1 packet Italian dressing mix
- 8 oz block of cream cheese
- 10.5 oz can cream of chicken soup
- 1/2 lb pasta of your choice

DIRECTIONS

1. To a greased slow cooker, add the chicken, Italian dressing mix, cream cheese, and cream of chicken soup. Cover and cook on LOW for 6 hours, or until chicken is cooked.
2. When the chicken is almost done, cook the pasta according to the package instructions.
3. Once the chicken is cooked, shred it and add the cooked pasta to the slow cooker. Stir to combine. Serve with shredded cheese on top and enjoy!

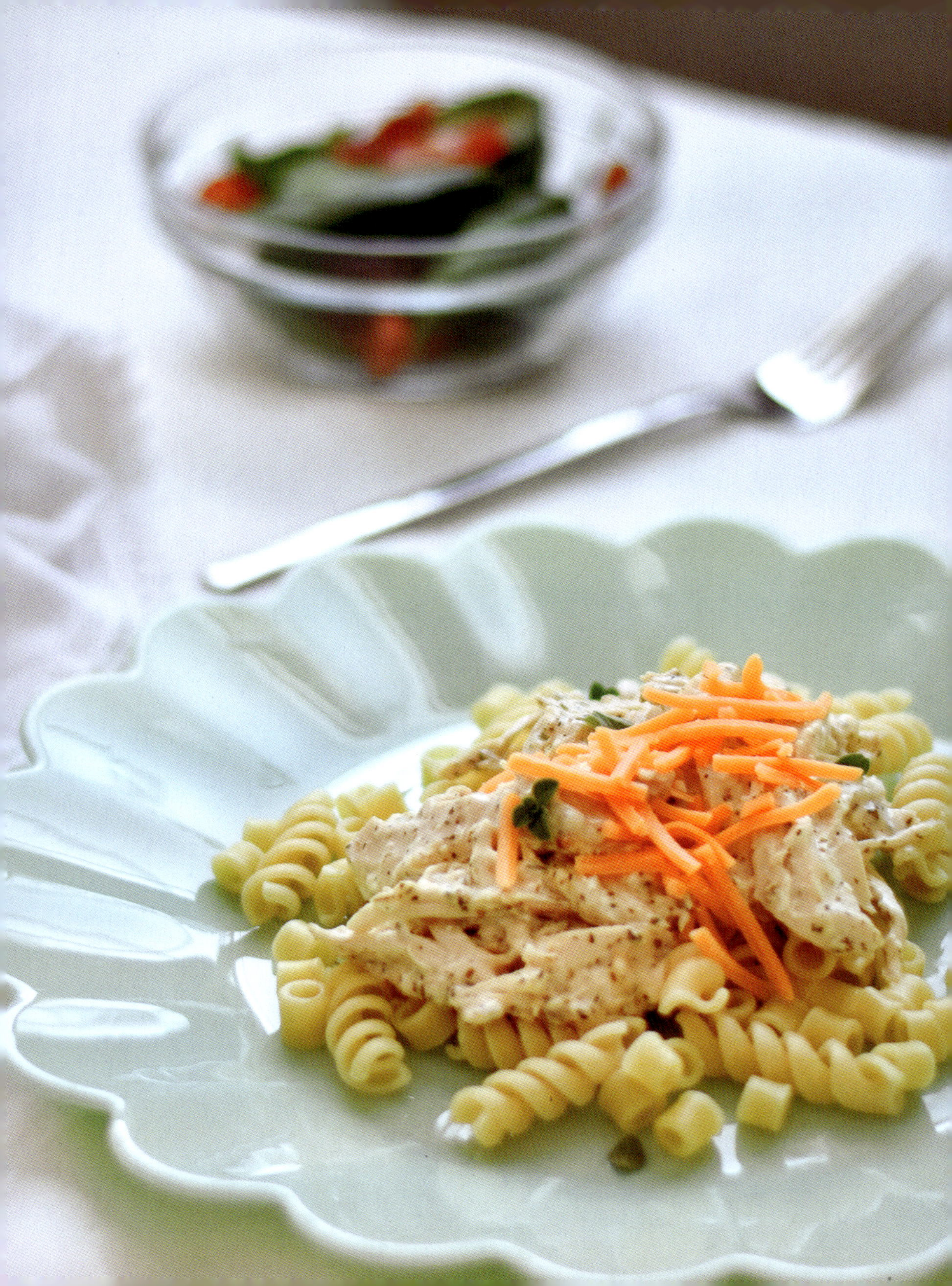

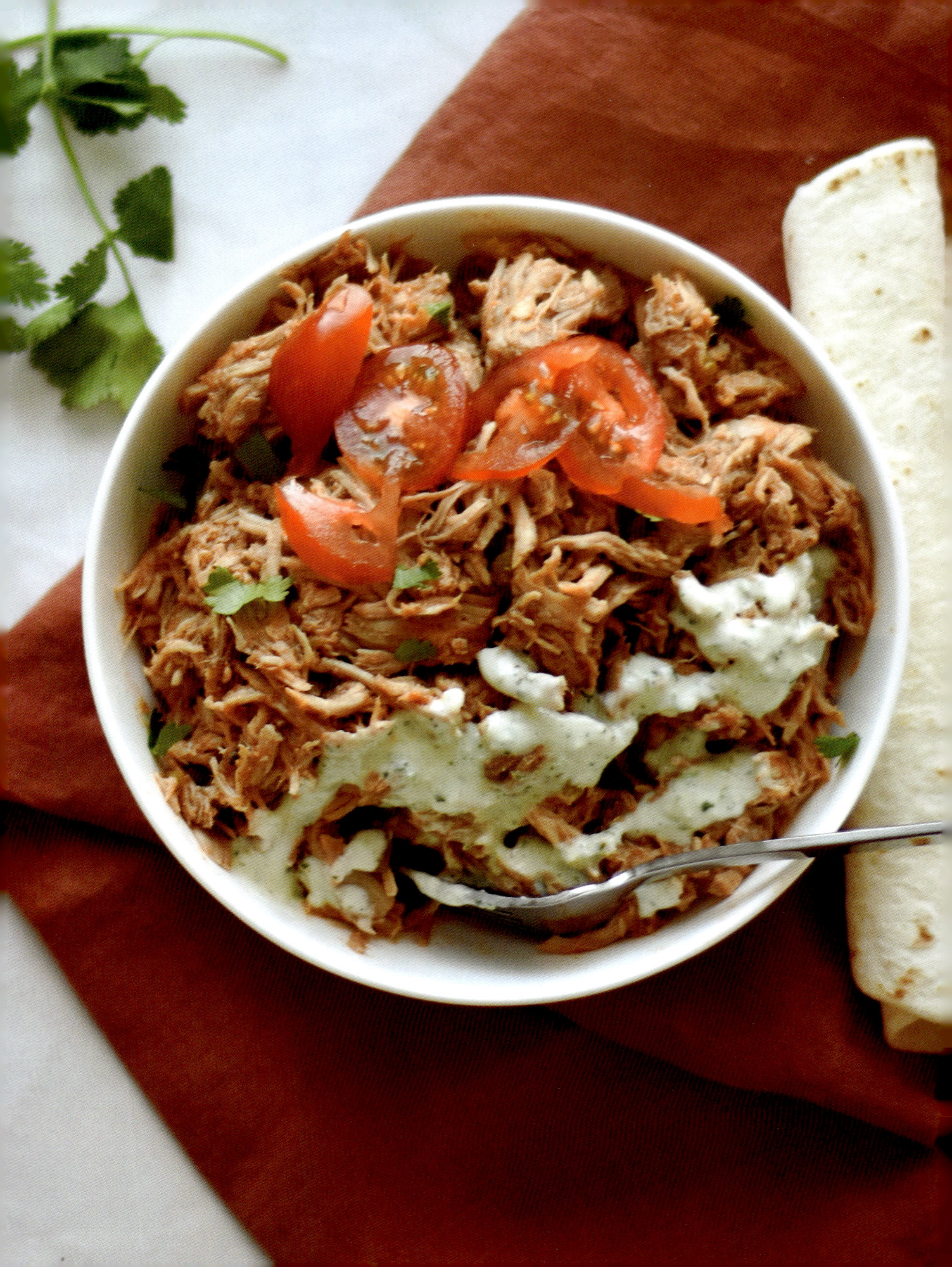

Sweet Pork Burritos

Juicy Sweet Pork is smothered with a creamy and flavorful dressing and stuffed into tortillas. These are the best burritos that you can make at home.

Prep time: 15 mins	**Cook time:** 7 hours	**Servings:** 5

INGREDIENTS

Sweet Pork
- 3 lb pork tenderloin, pork shoulder, or pork butt
- 2 cups cola soda
- 2/3 cup brown sugar, divided
- 10 oz can red enchilada sauce
- 4 oz can diced green chiles
- 1 tbsp minced garlic

Creamy Tomatillo Dressing
- 3 tomatillos, outside leafy layer removed
- 1 jalapeño
- 1 tbsp minced garlic
- 1 handful cilantro
- 2 limes, juice
- 2 cups milk
- 2 cups mayonnaise
- 3 1/2 tbsp ranch dressing mix

Burritos
- tortillas
- black beans
- shredded lettuce
- diced tomatoes
- lime wedges
- shredded Mexican-style cheese

DIRECTIONS

1. In a bowl whisk 1/3 cup of the brown sugar and 1 1/2 cups of the cola soda together. Add the pork to the bottom of a slow cooker and pour the coca cola mixture on top. Cook on LOW for 6 hours or HIGH for 4-5 hours.

2. While the pork is cooking, add all of the ingredients for the dressing into a food processor or blender for 1-2 minutes or until smooth. Pour into an air-tight container and refrigerate for at least an hour. This does make a lot of dressing, so half the recipe if you don't want extra.

3. After the cooking time is up, discard the liquid in the slow cooker and remove any excess fat on the pork. Shred the pork in the slow cooker with two forks, a hand mixer, or a meat masher. Add the enchilada sauce, garlic, 1/3 cup of brown sugar, 1/2 cup of soda, and the can of green chiles. Stir everything to combine. Cook on HIGH for 30 minutes-1 hour.

4. Once the cooking time is up, assemble the burritos. We like to serve our sweet pork in a tortilla with shredded Mexican-style cheese, lettuce, tomato, lime, black beans, and of course plenty of the yummy Creamy Tomatillo Dressing. Enjoy!

Slow Cooker Barbecue Ranch Pork Chops

Gone are the days of dry, flavorless pork chops. These pork chops are incredibly juicy and flavorful and are coated in ranch-seasoned barbecue sauce.

Prep time: 5 mins **Cook time:** 4-5 hours **Servings:** 4

INGREDIENTS

- 2 lbs boneless skinless pork chops
- 1 3/4 cups chicken broth
- 2 cups barbecue sauce
- 3 tbsp ranch dressing mix

DIRECTIONS

1. Place pork chops in the bottom of a greased slow cooker and pour the broth over top. Cover and cook on LOW for about 4 hours. Drain juices from the slow cooker.
2. In a small bowl, mix together the ranch seasoning and barbecue sauce. Pour the barbecue sauce mixture over the pork chops. Cook on LOW for 20 minutes. Serve and enjoy!

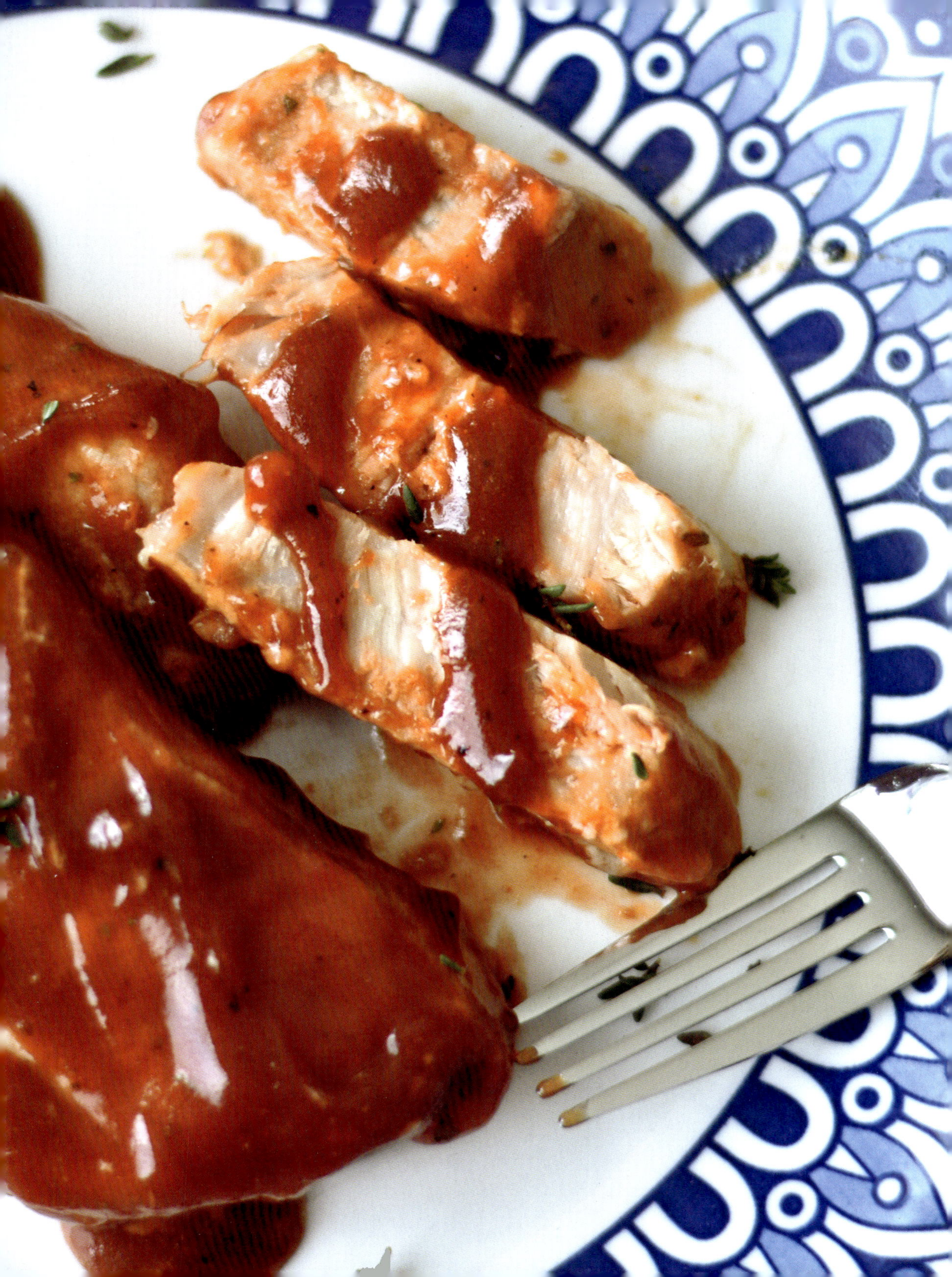

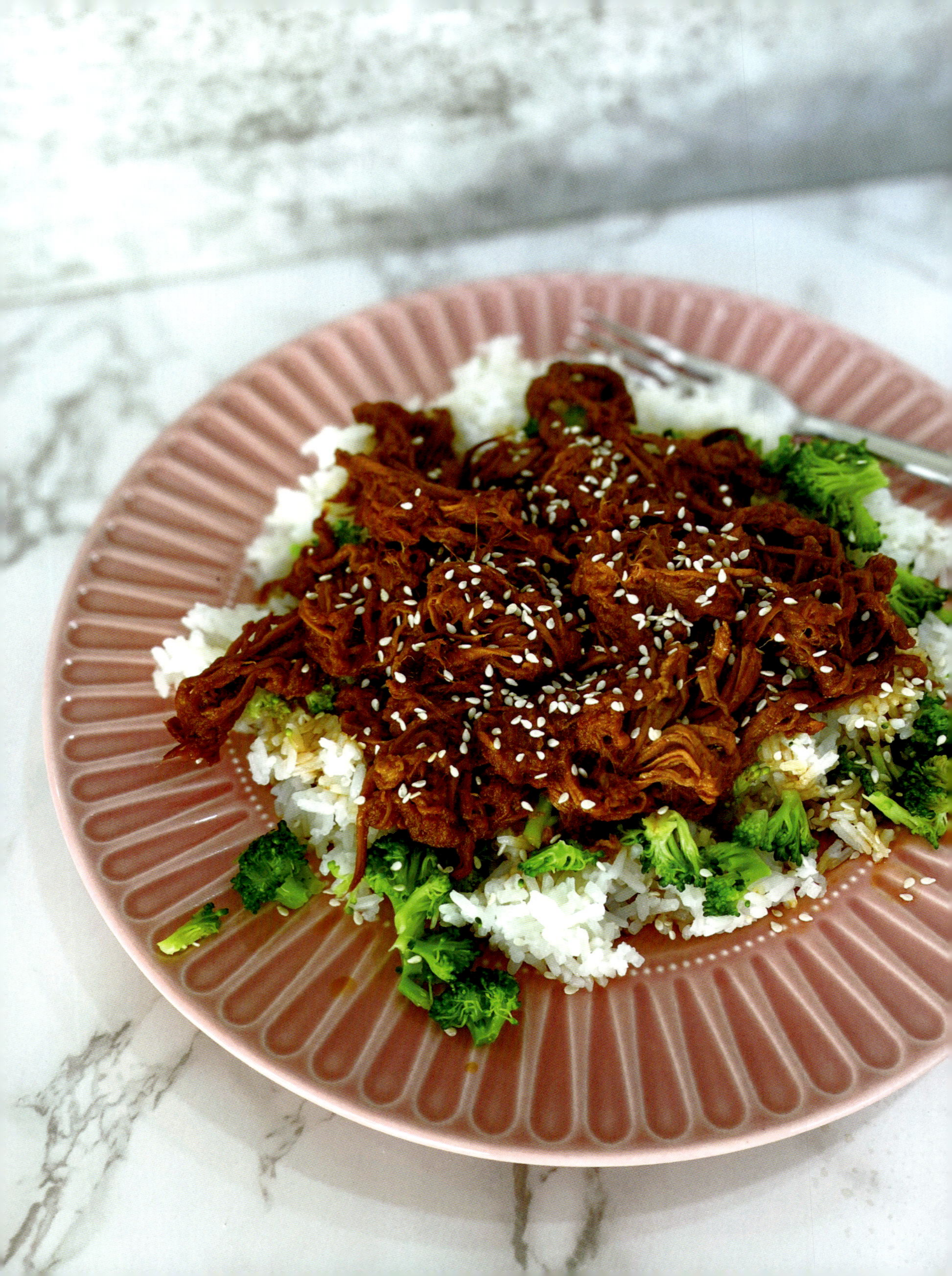

Slow Cooker Honey Garlic Pork Tenderloin

Slow Cooker Honey Garlic Pork Tenderloin is a little savory, a little sweet, and a whole lot DELICIOUS! Try it for dinner.

Prep time: 10 mins **Cook time:** 5-6 hours **Servings:** 4-5

INGREDIENTS

- 1 1/2 cups honey
- 3/4 cup ketchup
- 3/4 cup low sodium soy sauce
- 2 tbsp minced garlic
- 2 tbsp yellow mustard
- 2-4 lb pork tenderloin

DIRECTIONS

1. To a saucepan, add the honey, ketchup, soy sauce, garlic, and mustard, and bring to a boil. Simmer, stirring frequently, until the sauce starts to thicken, about 10 minutes.
2. Add the pork tenderloin to a greased slow cooker and pour the sauce over the top. Cook on LOW for 5-6 hours, or until pork is cooked through.
3. Shred pork in the slow cooker and stir well to coat with the sauce. Serve with rice or mashed potatoes. Enjoy!

NOTES

SUPER QUICK DINNERS

I created this section for those nights when you are running behind and need a quick meal. You can make these tasty recipes in about 20 minutes!

20-Minute Spaghetti Bolognese

This hearty meat sauce tastes like it spent hours simmering on the stove, but you can have it on the table in 20 minutes.

Prep time: 5 mins   **Cook time:** 20 mins   **Servings:** 4-5

INGREDIENTS

- 2 tbsp olive oil
- 1 white onion, diced
- 2 large carrots, diced
- 1 lb ground beef
- 1 tbsp minced garlic
- 1/3 cup beef broth
- 2 tbsp tomato paste
- 1 tbsp Worcestershire sauce
- 28 oz can crushed tomatoes
- 2 tsp dried oregano
- 2 tsp dried basil
- 1 tsp salt
- 1 tbsp brown sugar
- 10 oz spaghetti

DIRECTIONS

1. To a large Dutch oven or pot over medium heat, add the oil. Once hot, add the onion, carrots, and ground beef. Break the ground beef up and cook it through.
2. Once cooked, remove any excess grease from the pot. Sir in the garlic and cook for 20 seconds. Add in the broth and let it simmer for 2 minutes. Add in the tomato paste, Worcestershire sauce, crushed tomatoes, seasonings, and brown sugar. Simmer for at least 15 minutes, stirring occasionally.
3. Cook the spaghetti according to the package instructions. Drain and serve the sauce on top. Enjoy!

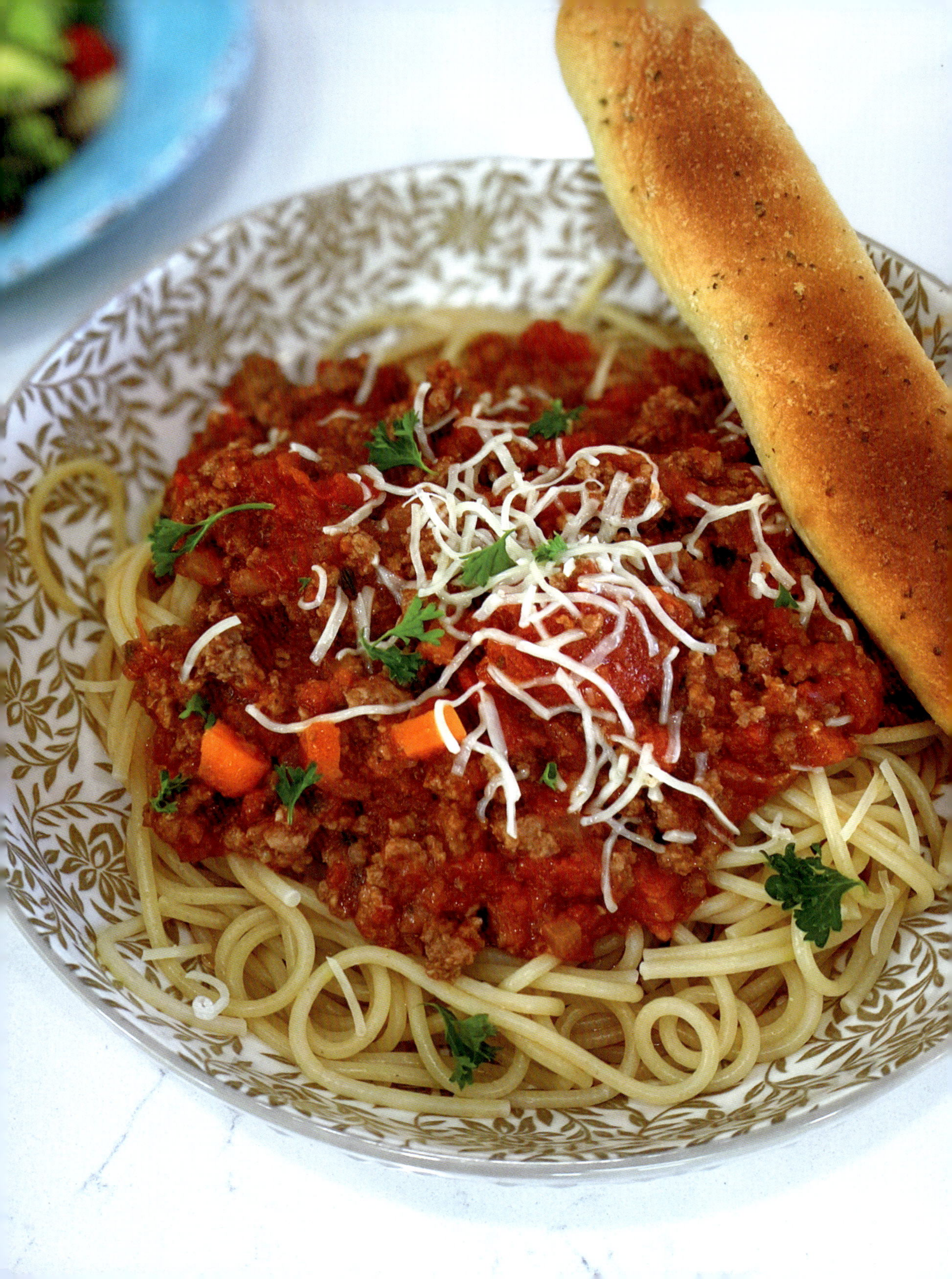

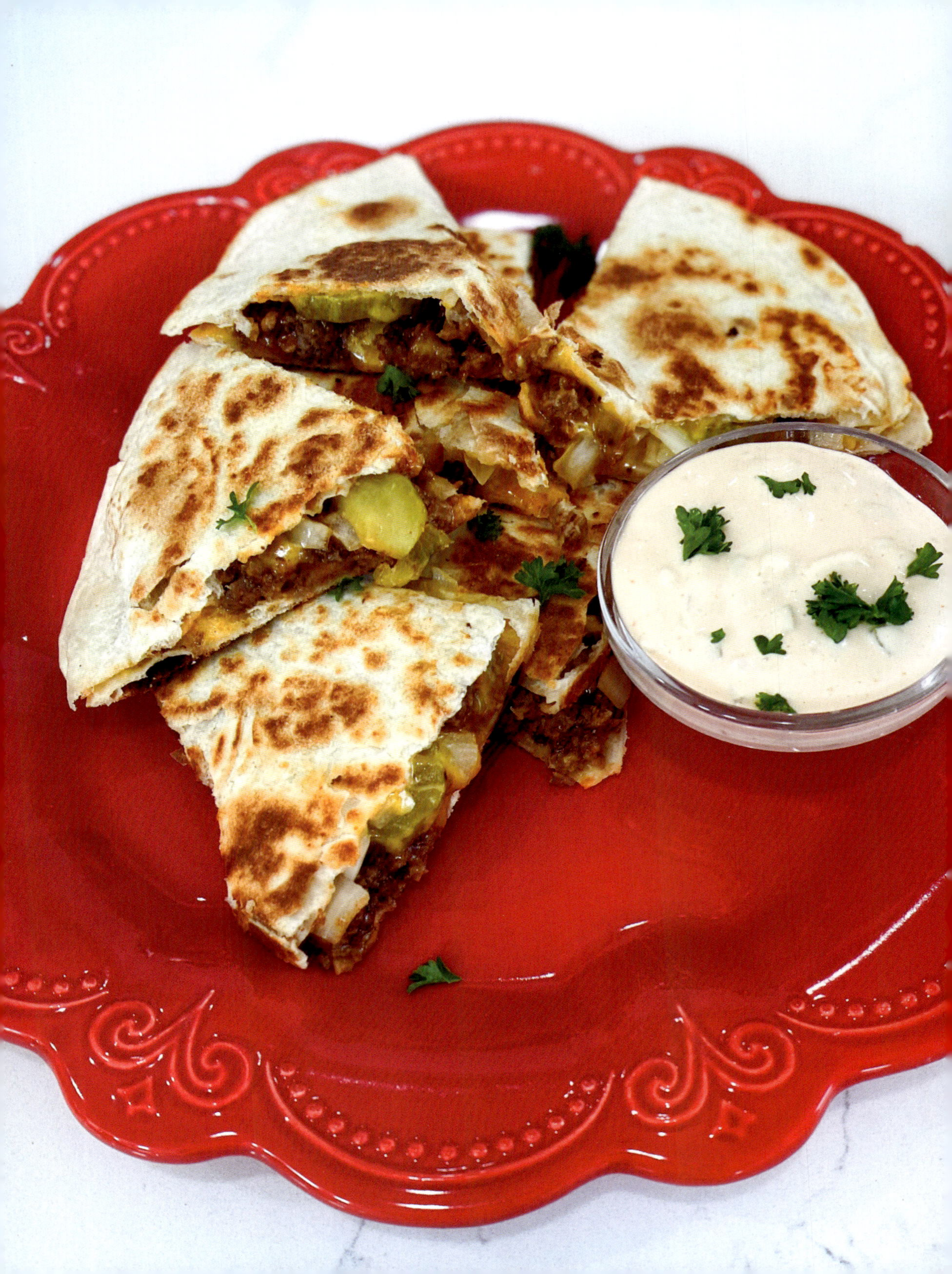

20-Minute Cheeseburger Quesadillas

Get all of the flavors of your favorite American classic wrapped up in a tortilla and smothered with a creamy, zingy sauce.

Prep time: 5 mins **Cook time:** 15 mins **Servings:** 4-5

INGREDIENTS

Special Sauce

- 1/2 cup mayonnaise
- 2 tbsp minced white onion
- 2 tbsp minced dill pickle
- 4 tbsp ketchup
- 2 tsp white vinegar

Quesadillas

- 1 lb ground beef
- 3-4 tbsp ketchup
- 2-3 tbsp yellow mustard
- 8 medium-sized tortillas
- 1 1/2 cups shredded cheddar cheese
- 1/2 cup sliced dill pickles
- 1/2 white onion, diced
- any other hamburger toppings you love

DIRECTIONS

1. To a small bowl add all of the sauce ingredients. Whisk well and store in the fridge.
2. To a skillet over medium-high heat, add the ground beef, break it up, and cook it through. Remove any excess grease from the pan. Stir in the ketchup and mustard.
3. To a clean greased skillet over medium-low heat, place a tortilla down and sprinkle it with cheese, the ground beef mixture, pickles, onion, more cheese, and any other hamburger toppings you enjoy. Place a second tortilla over the top and spray with oil spray. Cook on medium-low for about 4 minutes on each side, or until the tortilla is crispy and the cheese is melty. Repeat for all of your quesadillas.
4. Serve the quesadillas with the special sauce and enjoy!

20-Minute Honey Garlic Chicken

A sweet and savory sauce coats juicy and flavorful chicken. With just a few steps and minimal ingredients, this dish comes together in about 20 minutes.

Prep time: 5 mins   **Cook time:** 20 mins   **Servings:** 4-5

INGREDIENTS

- 1 lb chicken tenderloins or chicken breast
- 1/2 tsp salt
- 1/2 tsp pepper
- 2 tbsp olive oil
- 1 tbsp butter
- 1 tbsp minced garlic

Honey Garlic Sauce

- 1/3 cup chicken broth
- 1/3 cup honey
- 1 tbsp rice vinegar
- 2 tbsp low sodium soy sauce

DIRECTIONS

1. Season the chicken on both sides with salt and pepper.
2. To a skillet over medium heat, add the oil. Once the oil is hot, add the chicken tenderloins and cook for 4 minutes on each side.
3. While the chicken is cooking, add all of the ingredients for the Honey Garlic sauce to a small bowl. Whisk well.
4. Add the butter and garlic to the pan with the chicken and stir well until the butter melts and the garlic becomes fragrant. Stir in the sauce and let simmer for 4-6 minutes, or until the sauce thickens.
5. Serve over a bed of rice and a side of steamed vegetables. Enjoy!

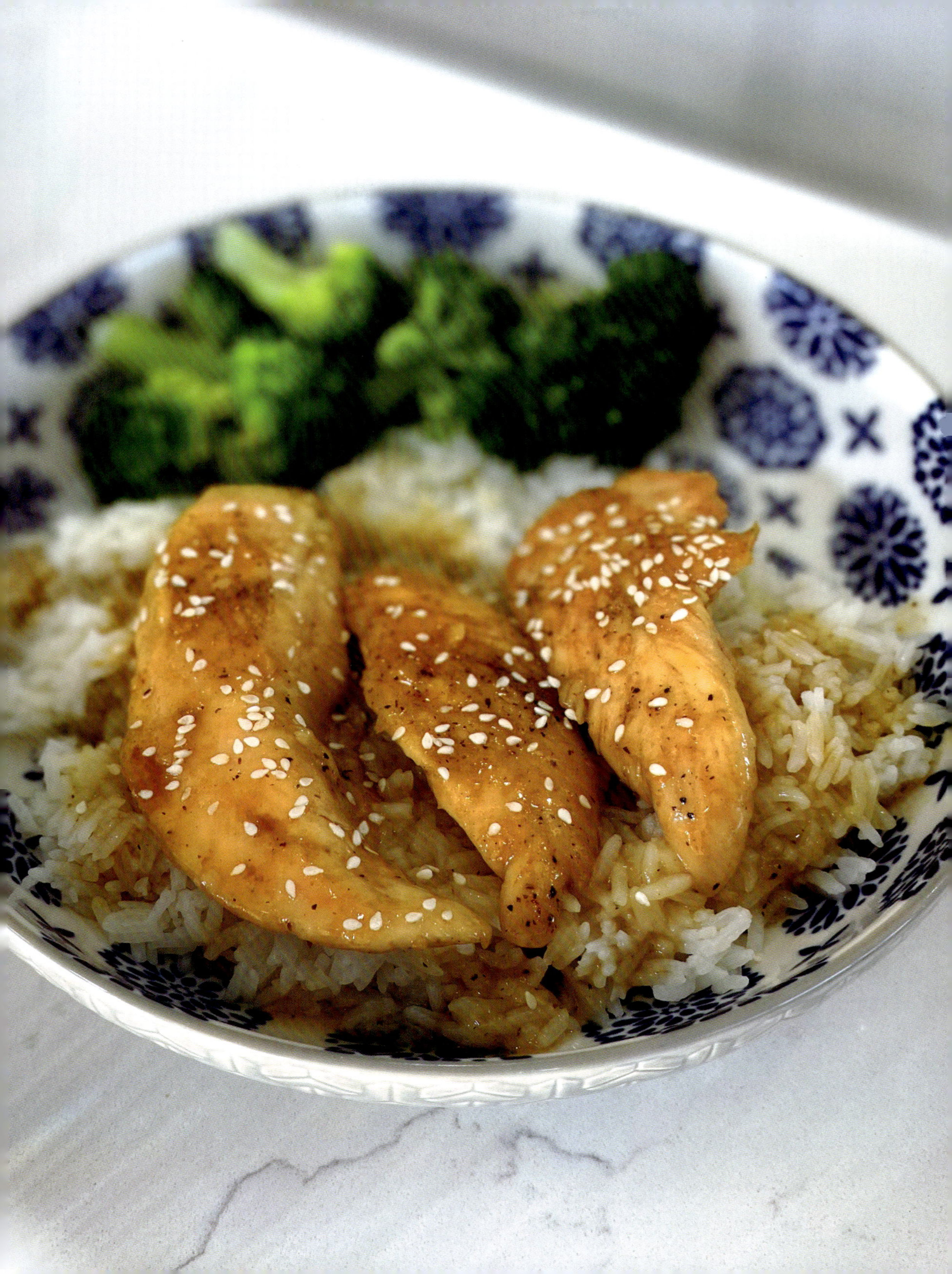

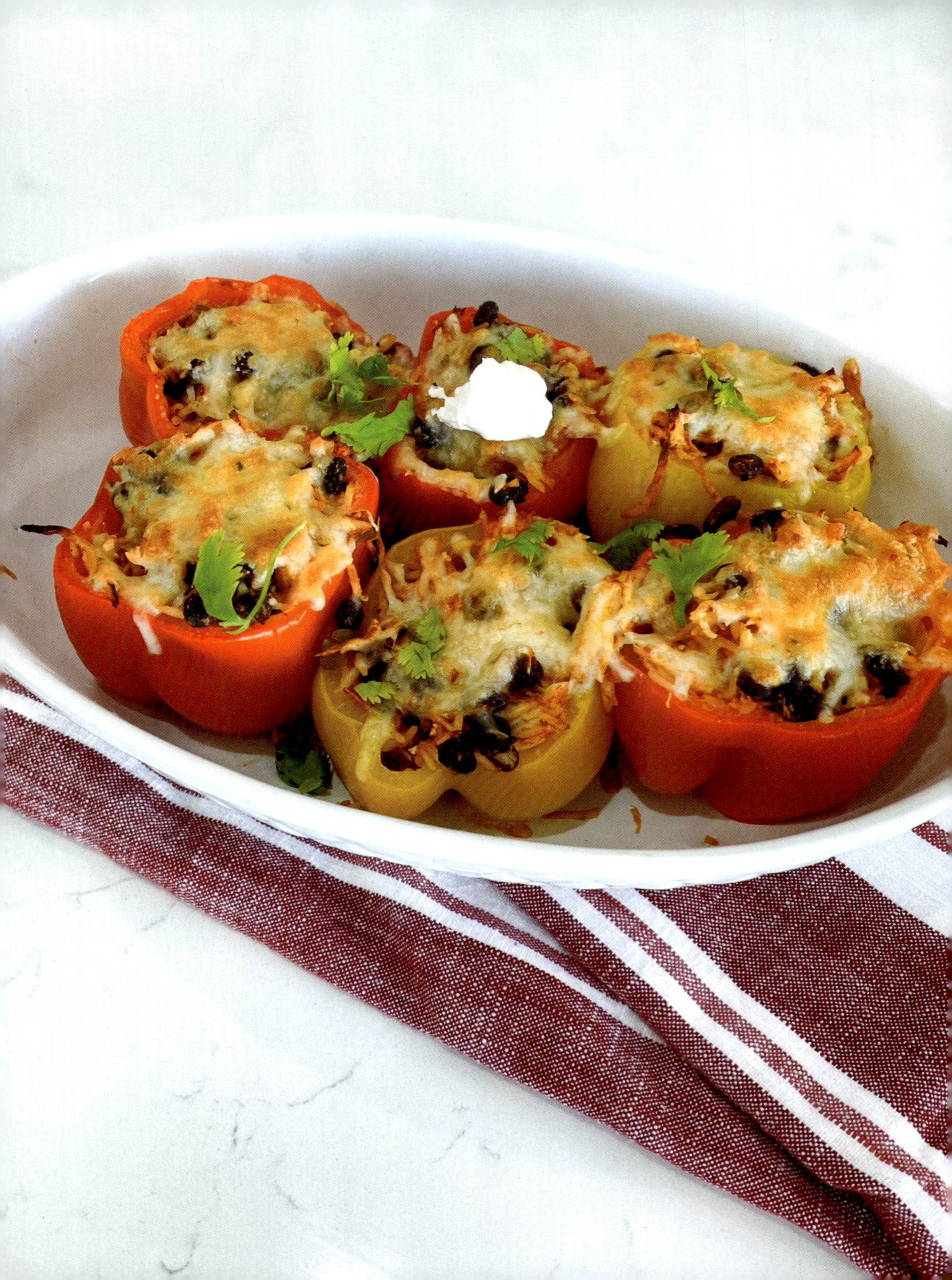

Taco Rice Stuffed Peppers

Bell peppers are stuffed with rice, chicken, salsa, and black beans then topped with melty pepper jack cheese for a hearty meal that's super fun to eat.

Prep time: 20 mins	**Cook time:** 20 mins	**Servings:** 4

INGREDIENTS

- 6 medium-sized bell peppers
- 2 cups cooked shredded chicken
- 1 cup black beans, drained and rinsed
- 1 cup cooked white or brown rice
- 1 cup salsa
- 2 tbsp taco seasoning
- 1/2 cup pepper jack cheese

DIRECTIONS

1. Preheat oven to 400°F.
2. Slice the tops off the bell peppers and remove the insides. Bring a large pot of water to a boil add the bell peppers. Boil for 7 minutes to soften the peppers. Drain the water and add the peppers to a large baking dish.
3. To a large bowl, add the chicken, beans, rice, salsa, and taco seasoning and stir well. Generously fill the peppers with the filling mixture and sprinkle the tops with cheese.
4. Bake for 20 minutes. Top with your favorite taco toppings like sour cream, diced tomatoes, or cilantro, and enjoy!

Baked Chicken Ranch Flautas

Baked Flautas make a perfect grab-and-go meal for those busy weeknights. These have a creamy ranch chicken filling that is so delicious.

Prep time: 15 mins | **Cook time:** 22 mins | **Servings:** 5

INGREDIENTS

- 3 cups cooked, shredded chicken
- 6 oz cream cheese, softened
- 4 green onions, sliced
- 3/4 cup Monterey Jack cheese
- 2 tbsp ranch seasoning
- 7-9 medium flour tortillas

DIRECTIONS

1. Preheat oven to 425°F. Line a sheet pan with parchment paper and set aside.
2. To a medium-sized bowl, add the chicken, cream cheese, green onions, cheese, and ranch seasoning and stir to combine.
3. Place 3 tablespoons of the chicken mixture on each tortilla, then roll it up tightly and place seam side down on the sheet pan. Bake for 22 minutes, or until the tops are golden, and serve with your favorite toppings like shredded cheese, sour cream, sliced avocado, or salsa. Enjoy!

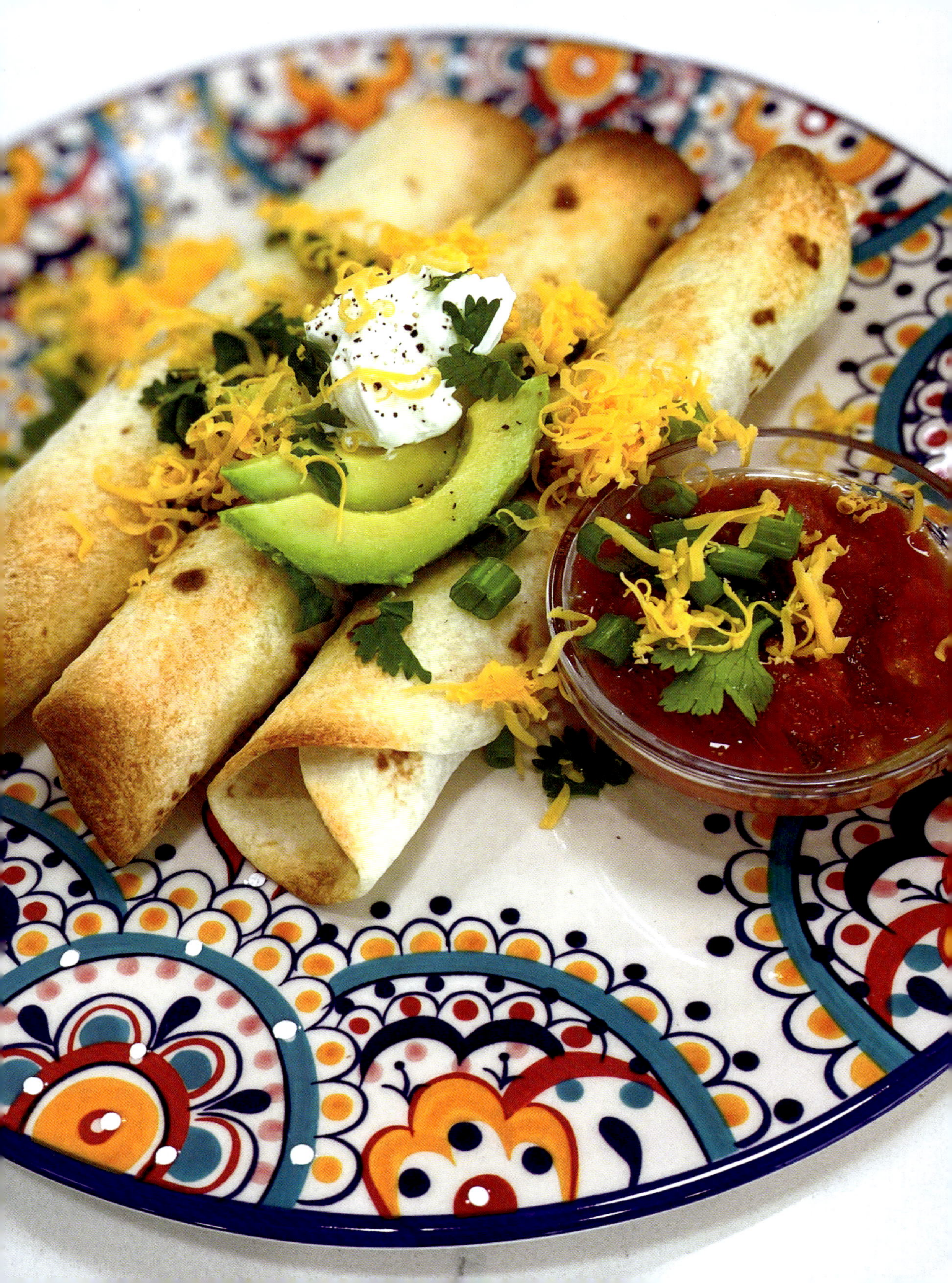

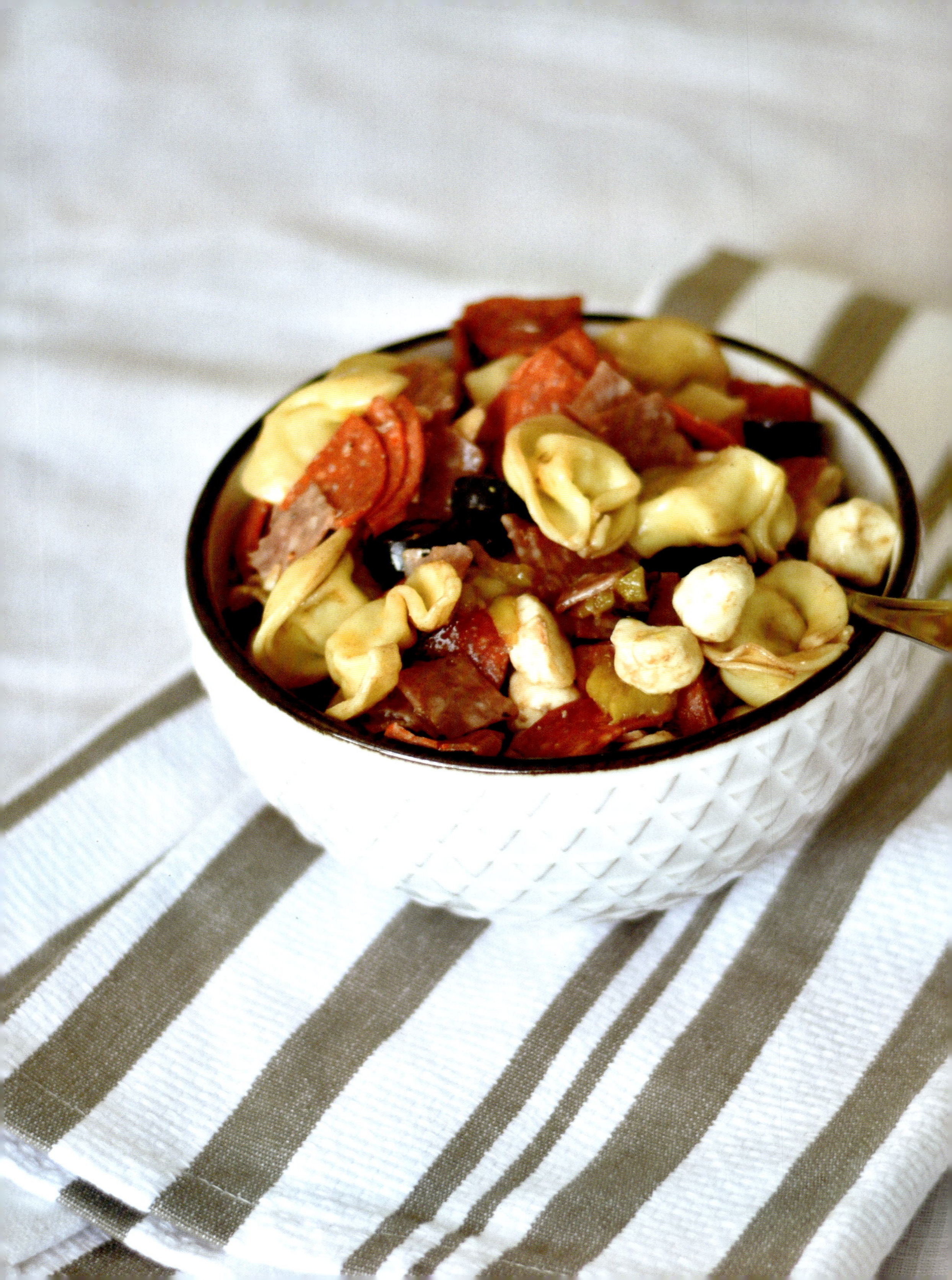

Antipasto Salad

With spicy peppers, charcuterie, and mozzarella cheese, Antipasto salad is a perfect side dish for a potluck or a summer cookout.

Prep time: 15 mins   **Cook time:** 10 mins   **Servings:** 6

INGREDIENTS

- 19 oz cheese tortellini
- 1/4 cup sliced black olives
- 1 cup sliced pepperoni, cut into small pieces
- 1 cup sliced salami, cut into small pieces
- 8 oz cubed mozzarella cheese
- 1/4 cup sliced peperoncini peppers

Dressing

- 1/4 cup olive oil
- 2 tbsp red wine vinegar
- 1/2 tbsp minced garlic
- 1/4 tsp Italian seasoning
- 1/4 tsp salt

DIRECTIONS

1. Cook the tortellini according to the package instructions. Drain and rinse with cold water to let the tortellini completely cool down.
2. In a large bowl, combine all of the dressing ingredients and whisk well.
3. To the bowl with the dressing, add the tortellini, black olives, pepperoni, salami, mozzarella cheese, and peperoncino peppers and stir to combine. Refrigerate for at least 1 hour. Enjoy!

Meatballs

This is the only Meatball recipe that you'll ever need. It's so delicious that my family always begs me to make this for family dinners.

Prep time: 10 mins   **Cook time:** 25 mins   **Servings:** 5

INGREDIENTS

- 1 lb ground beef
- 1 small onion, finely chopped
- dash of salt and pepper
- 3 tbsp milk
- 1 tbsp minced garlic
- 1/4 cup Parmesan cheese
- 1/4 cup ricotta cheese
- 1/2 cup breadcrumbs
- 3 tbsp fresh parsley

DIRECTIONS

1. Preheat oven to 425°F.
2. Add all the ingredients to a bowl and mix them together. Roll the meatballs into golf ball-sized rounds and place them on a baking sheet.
3. Bake for 20-25 mins. Serve over cooked pasta with your favorite pasta sauce. Enjoy!

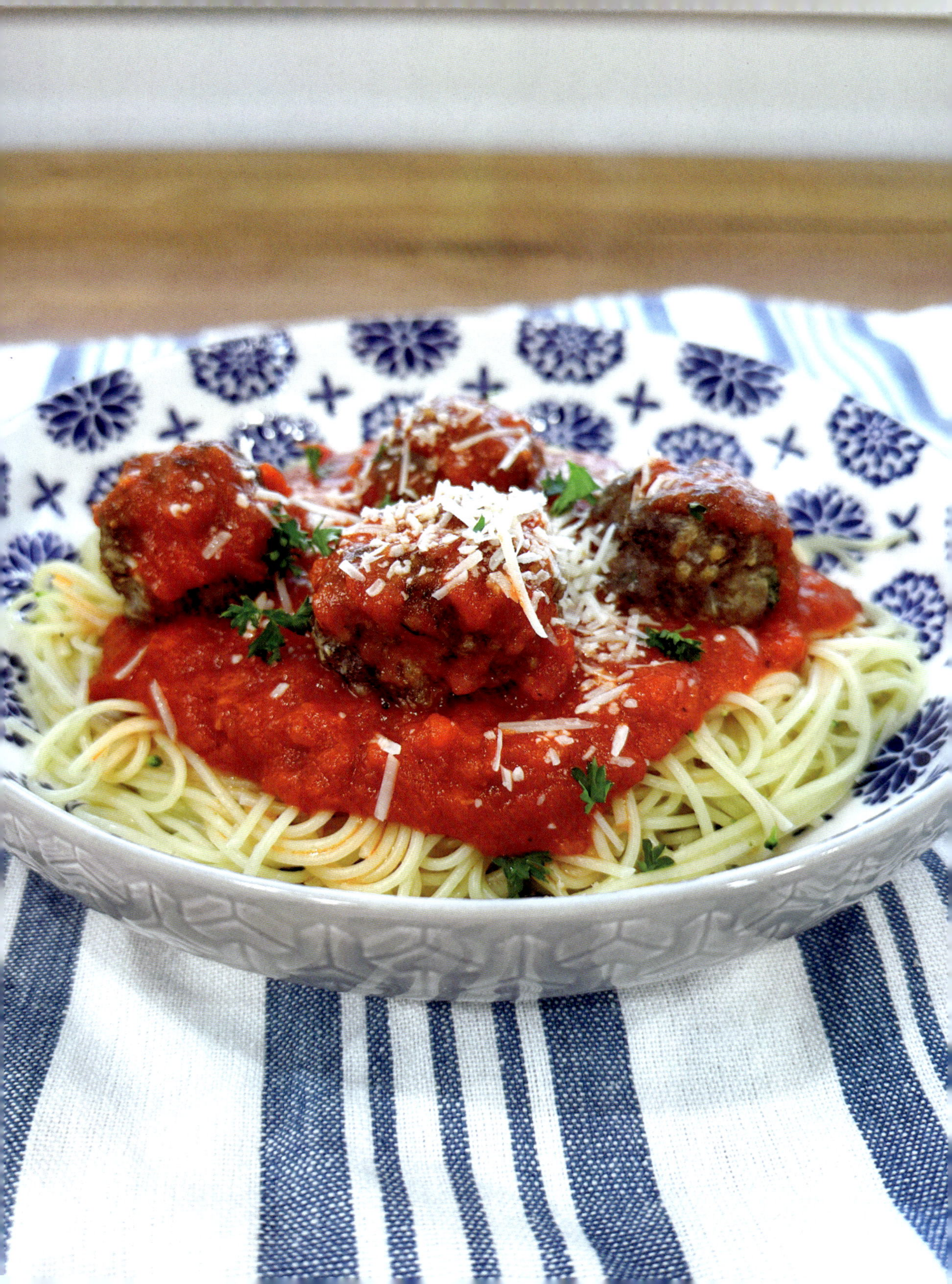

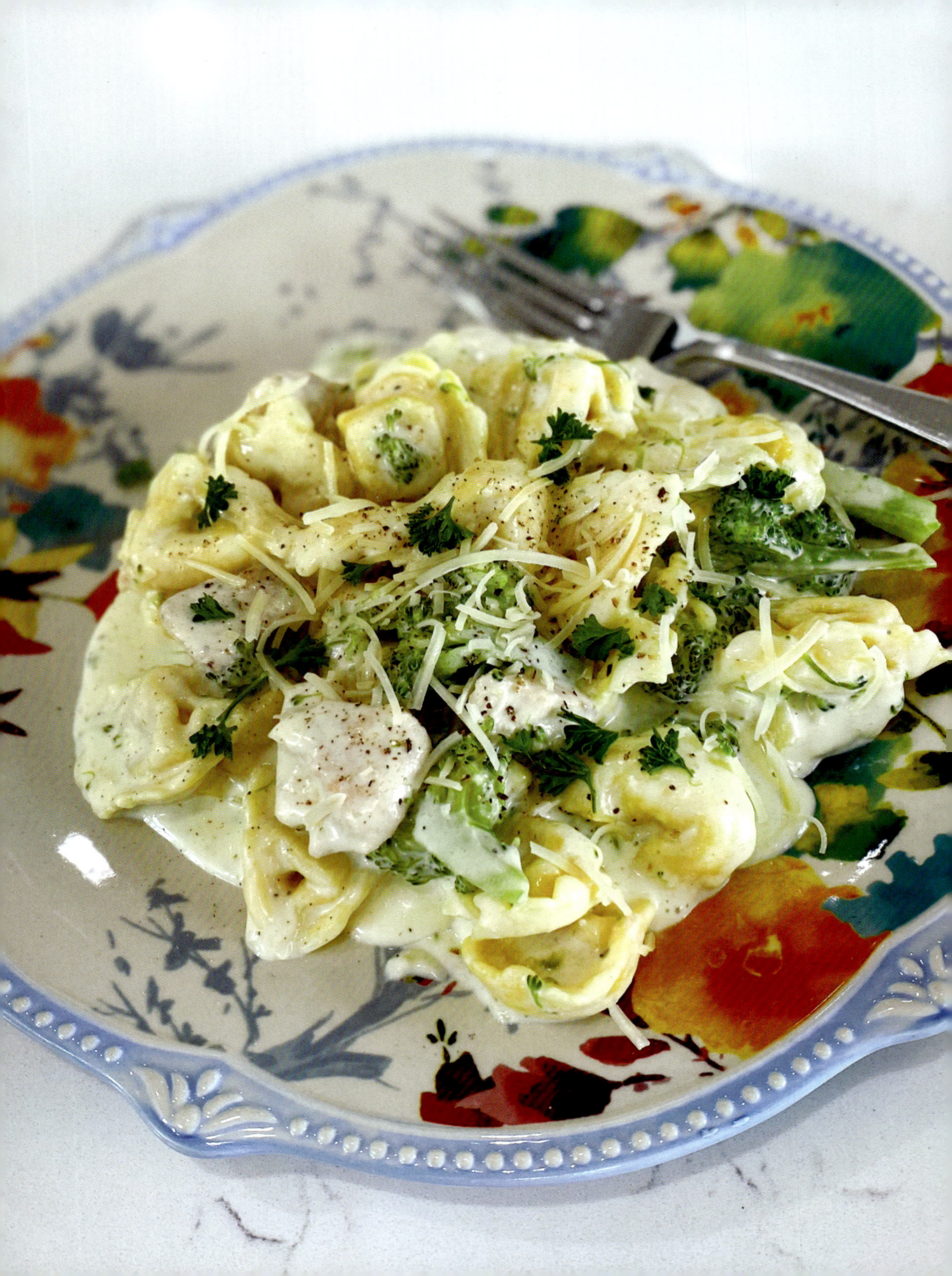

20-Minute Chicken Broccoli Tortellini

Chicken and Broccoli Tortellini is a classic dish that everyone loves, and it only takes 20 minutes and one pot to make.

Prep time: 5 mins   **Cook time:** 20 mins   **Servings:** 4

INGREDIENTS

- 1 lb chicken breast, cubed
- 1/2 tsp salt
- 1/2 tsp pepper
- 1 tsp Italian seasoning
- 2 tbsp olive oil
- 1 tbsp minced garlic
- 1 1/2 cups chicken broth
- 1 cup milk
- 20 oz refrigerated or frozen cheese tortellini
- 1 head of broccoli, chopped
- 1/2 cup Parmesan cheese
- 8 oz cream cheese, cubed

DIRECTIONS

1. Season the chicken on both sides with salt, pepper, and Italian seasoning.
2. To a large Dutch oven or pot, add the oil over medium heat. Once the oil is hot, add the chicken and cook for 7-8 minutes, or until it is cooked through. Remove the chicken from the pan and set aside.
3. To the same pot you cooked the chicken in, add the minced garlic and cook for about 20 seconds or until fragrant. Add in the broth and milk and bring to a gentle boil. Add the tortellini and broccoli, and let simmer, stirring frequently, for about 5-6 minutes.
4. Turn the heat to low and add in the Parmesan cheese and cream cheese. Add the cooked chicken back to the pot. Stir frequently, until the cream cheese melts. Serve and enjoy!

Garlic Parmesan Chicken with Zucchini

Garlic Parmesan Chicken is your lifesaver on a busy weeknight. Cheesy chicken and yummy caramelized zucchini is all made in one skillet!

Prep time: 5 mins   **Cook time:** 15 mins   **Servings:** 4-5

INGREDIENTS

- 1 lb chicken breasts, cubed
- 2 tsp salt
- 1 tsp pepper
- 2 tsp Italian seasoning
- 1 tsp garlic powder
- 1 tsp onion powder
- 3 tbsp olive oil, divided
- 1 tbsp butter
- 1 medium zucchini, diced
- 1 yellow squash, diced
- 1/3 cup grated Parmesan cheese

DIRECTIONS

1. Heat 2 tablespoons olive oil in a pan over medium heat. Add the chicken and season with salt, pepper, Italian seasoning, garlic powder, and onion powder. Cook until the chicken is cooked through, then remove from the pan and set aside.
2. To the same pan, add 1 tablespoon more olive oil and 1 tablespoon of butter. Once hot, add in the zucchini and squash, and season with a dash of salt, pepper, and Italian seasoning to your liking. Cook until tender.
3. Add the chicken and Parmesan cheese to the pan. Stir to melt the cheese and serve. Enjoy!

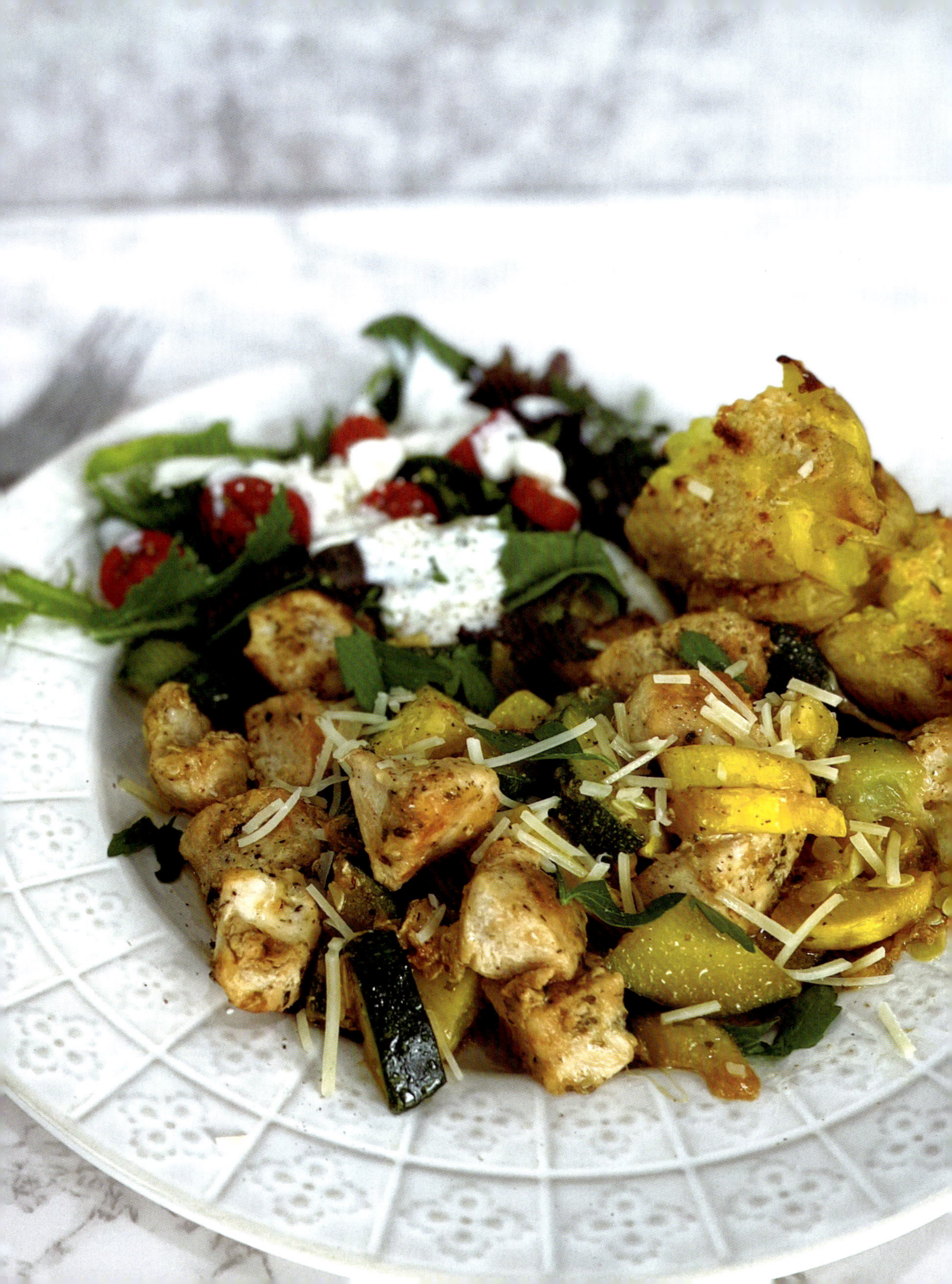

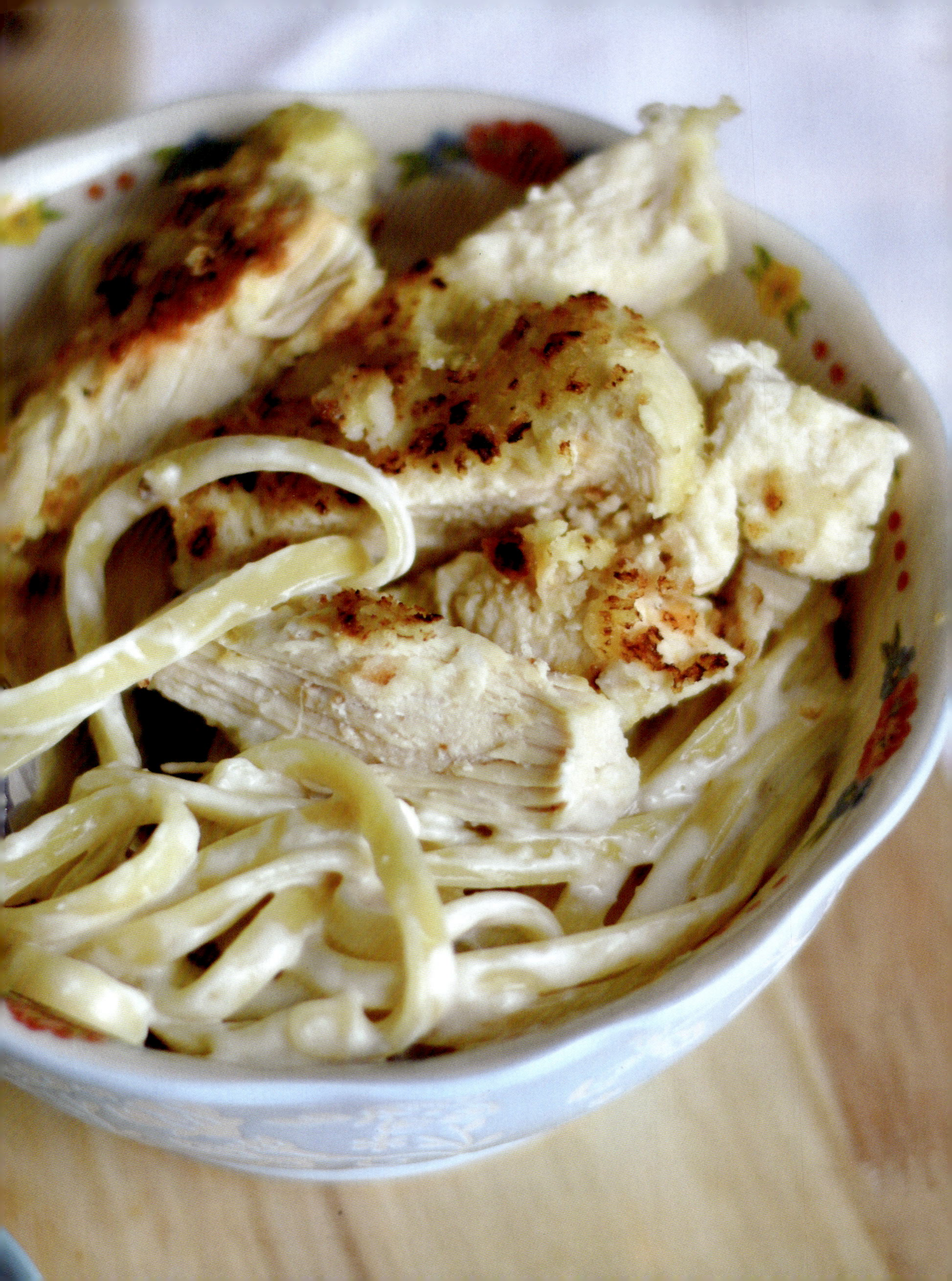

Lemon Chicken Pasta

Crispy panko-breaded chicken is served atop creamy and perfectly lemony pasta for an elegant meal.

Prep time: 10 mins **Cook time:** 20 mins **Servings:** 4-5

INGREDIENTS

Chicken & Pasta
- 12 oz fettuccine pasta
- 1 egg
- 1 tbsp milk
- 1 cup panko bread crumbs
- 1/2 tsp salt
- 1/8 tsp black pepper
- 1 lb chicken breast, sliced in half horizontally
- 2 tbsp olive oil
- 2 tbsp fresh lemon juice

Sauce
- 2 tbsp unsalted butter
- 2 tsp minced garlic
- 1/4 tsp onion powder
- 2 cups heavy whipping cream
- 1/2 tsp salt
- 2 tbsp fresh lemon juice
- 1/3 cup Parmesan cheese
- 1 tbsp parsley

DIRECTIONS

1. Cook fettuccine noodles to *al dente* according to the package instructions. Before draining, reserve 1/2 cup of the pasta water and set aside.

Chicken

1. In a small bowl, whisk one egg and 1 tbsp milk. In another bowl, combine the panko crumbs and salt and pepper. Dip each piece of chicken into the egg wash, then into the bread crumbs.
2. In a large skillet over medium heat, add the olive oil and sauté chicken 3-4 minutes per side or until cooked completely through. Transfer the chicken to a cutting board and pour 2 tbsp lemon juice over the chicken. Cut into strips.

Lemon Cream Sauce

1. In the same skillet you used for the chicken, melt the butter over medium heat. Add the garlic and onion powder and cook for 1 minute until fragrant.
2. Add the heavy cream and salt. Bring the sauce to a simmer, stirring often. Lower heat and whisk often while incrementally adding in 2 tablespoons of lemon juice. Turn off the heat. Add the Parmesan cheese and mix until melted.
3. Add the pasta and mix to combine well. Add some of the reserved pasta water if the sauce is too thick.
4. Serve the pasta with strips of chicken on top. Garnish with parsley. Enjoy!

French Bread Pizza

Prep time: 30 mins | **Cook time:** 40 mins | **Servings:** 4

INGREDIENTS

- 1 large loaf of French bread

Garlic Butter

- 5 tbsp butter, melted
- 1/2 tsp onion powder
- 1/2 tsp garlic powder
- 1/2 tsp Italian seasoning

Pizza Sauce

- 8 oz tomato sauce
- 1 tsp Italian seasoning

Pizza

- 8 oz mozzarella cheese
- toppings such as: pepperoni, peppers, onions, olives, sausage, or anything else you'd like

DIRECTIONS

1. Preheat oven to 425°F. Line a large sheet pan with parchment paper.
2. Slice open the French bread horizontally and place onto the sheet pan.
3. To a small bowl, add the melted butter and seasonings for the garlic butter and whisk well. Brush the garlic butter mixture on the inside of each side of French bread. Bake for 5 minutes.
4. Pour the can of tomato sauce into a small bowl, then stir in 1 tsp of Italian seasoning. This is your pizza sauce.
5. Once French bread is out of the oven, pour the pizza sauce over the top, then top with the cheese and your favorite toppings. Bake for 5-7 minutes or until the cheese is melts. Cut into thick strips and enjoy.

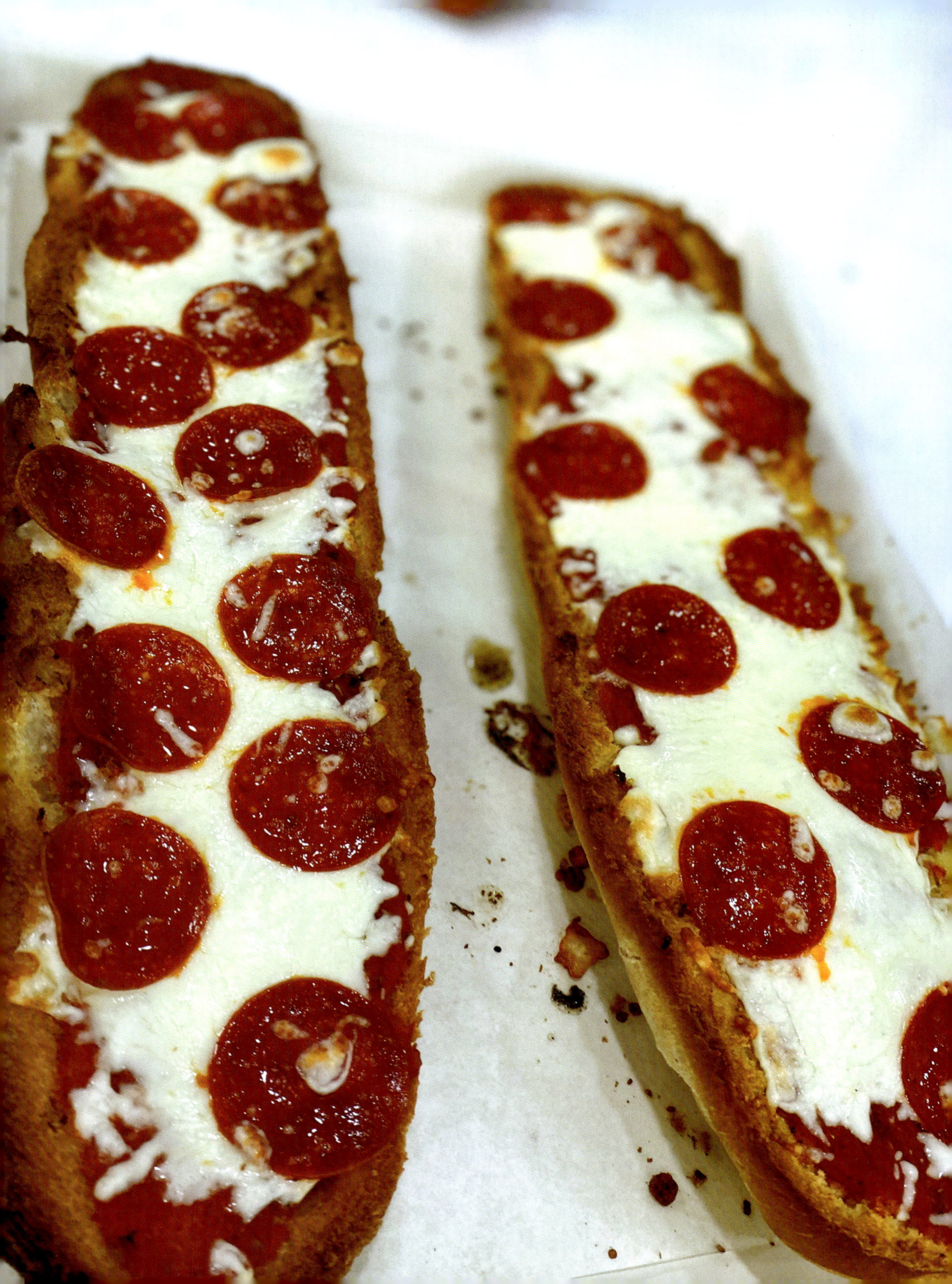

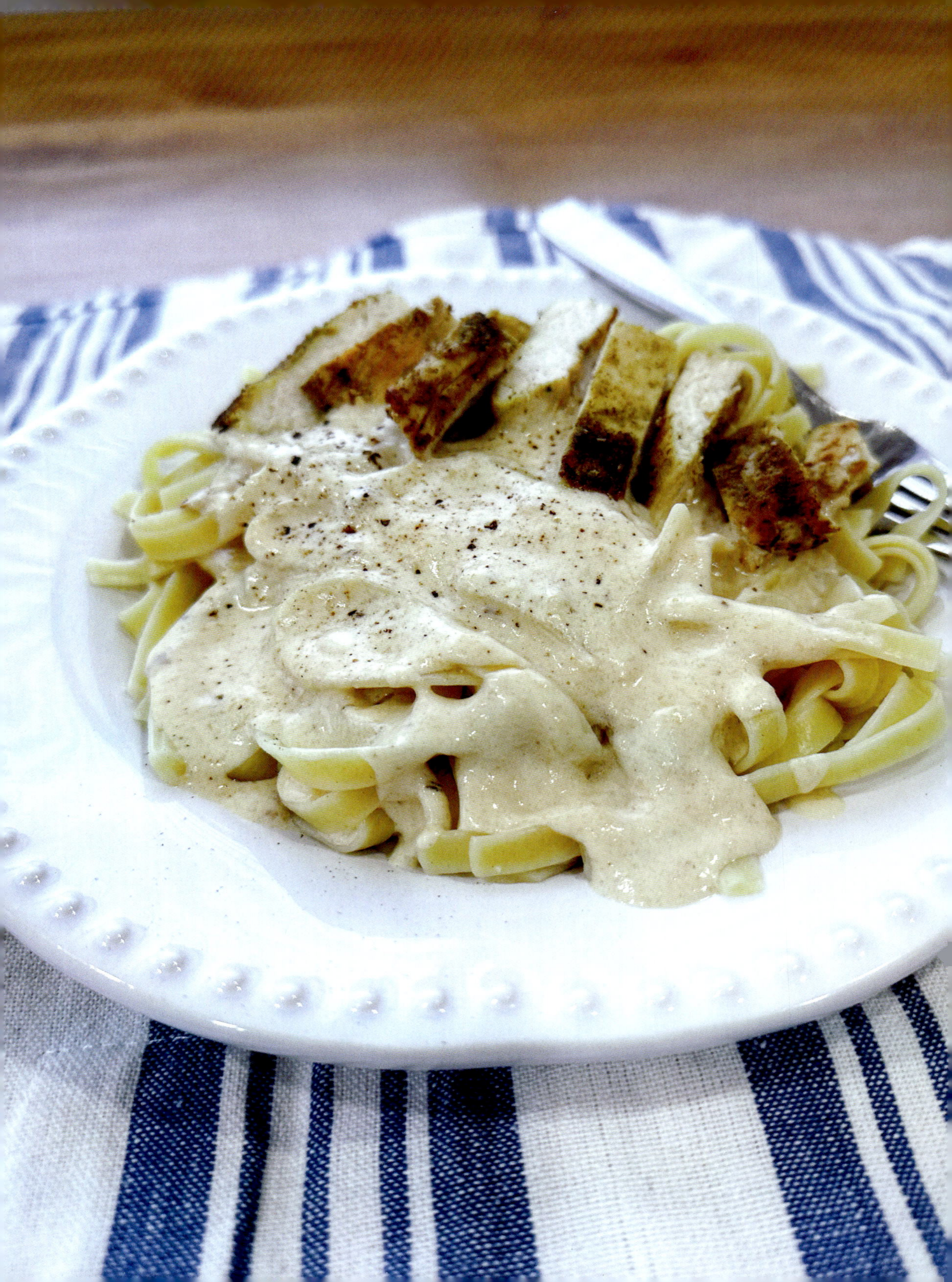

Classic Chicken Fettuccine Alfredo

With a deliciously creamy sauce and perfectly seasoned chicken, Classic Chicken Fettuccine Alfredo is everyone's favorite pasta dish.

Prep time: 10 mins **Cook time:** 20 mins **Servings:** 4-5

INGREDIENTS

- 1 lb fettuccine pasta
- 1 lb chicken breast
- 2 tsp Italian seasoning
- 1/2 tsp onion powder
- 1/2 tsp garlic powder
- 2 tsp salt
- 2 tbsp olive oil
- 1 tbsp minced garlic
- 2 cups + 3 tbsp chicken broth, divided
- 1 cup heavy cream
- 2 cups Parmesan cheese
- 1 tbsp cornstarch
- 1 tbsp water

DIRECTIONS

1. Bring a large pot of water to a boil on the stove. Cook the fettuccine according to the package instructions. Once the pasta reaches your desired tenderness, strain and set aside.
2. Season the chicken on both sides with Italian seasoning, onion powder, garlic powder, and 1 tsp of salt.
3. To a large sauté pan over medium heat, add the oil. Once hot, add the chicken and cook for 4-5 minutes on each side, or until the chicken is completely cooked through. Remove the chicken and set it aside, covered with aluminum foil to keep the chicken warm.
4. In the same pan you cooked the chicken in, add the minced garlic and 3 tablespoons of the chicken broth. Stir the garlic around and scrape the flavorful bits off the bottom of the pan. Add the remaining chicken broth and bring to a simmer.
5. Once simmering, stir in the heavy cream and heat for a few minutes. When the heavy cream starts to simmer, stir in the Parmesan cheese. Turn the heat to low and let the Parmesan melt, stirring occasionally.
6. Make the cornstarch slurry by stirring the cornstarch and water in a small bowl until smooth. Pour into the Alfredo sauce and let the sauce thicken.
7. Cut the cooked chicken into bite-sized pieces and add to the sauce. Serve over the fettuccine and enjoy.

NOTES

DESSERTS

These sweet treats are a tribute to my mom. So many of my memories growing up include coming home from school and being greeted with a snack and something sweet! I hope you enjoy these family favorites.

Peanut Butter Chocolate Pie No-Bake

A cream-filled cookie crust, dreamy peanut butter filling, chocolate shell, and peanut butter cups make this no-bake pie a rich and indulgent treat.

Prep time: 20 mins   **Cook time:** 2 hours   **Servings:** 6

INGREDIENTS

Cookie Crust
- 1/4 cup melted butter
- 10 oz cream-filled cookies

Peanut Butter Filling
- 1 cup creamy peanut butter
- 5 oz cream cheese, softened
- 8 oz whipped topping

Chocolate Shell
- 1 1/2 cups semi-sweet chocolate chips
- 1/2 cup heavy whipping cream
- crushed peanut butter cups

DIRECTIONS

Cookie Crust
1. Crush the cream-filled cookies using a food processor or in a large plastic bag and a rolling pin. Mix the crushed cream-filled cookies and the melted butter.
2. Press into bottom and sides of a 9-inch pie pan.

Peanut Butter Filling
1. Add the peanut butter and cream cheese in a medium bowl. Beat together until well combined. Beat in the whipped topping until well combined. Spread this mixture over the cookie crust. Refrigerate while you work on the chocolate topping.

Chocolate Topping
1. To a microwave safe bowl, add the chocolate chips and whipping cream. Place in the microwave and heat for 30 seconds at a time, stirring after every 30 seconds, until it is completely melted. Pour over the top of the pie. Refrigerate for at least two hours. Garnish with crushed peanut butter cups and enjoy!

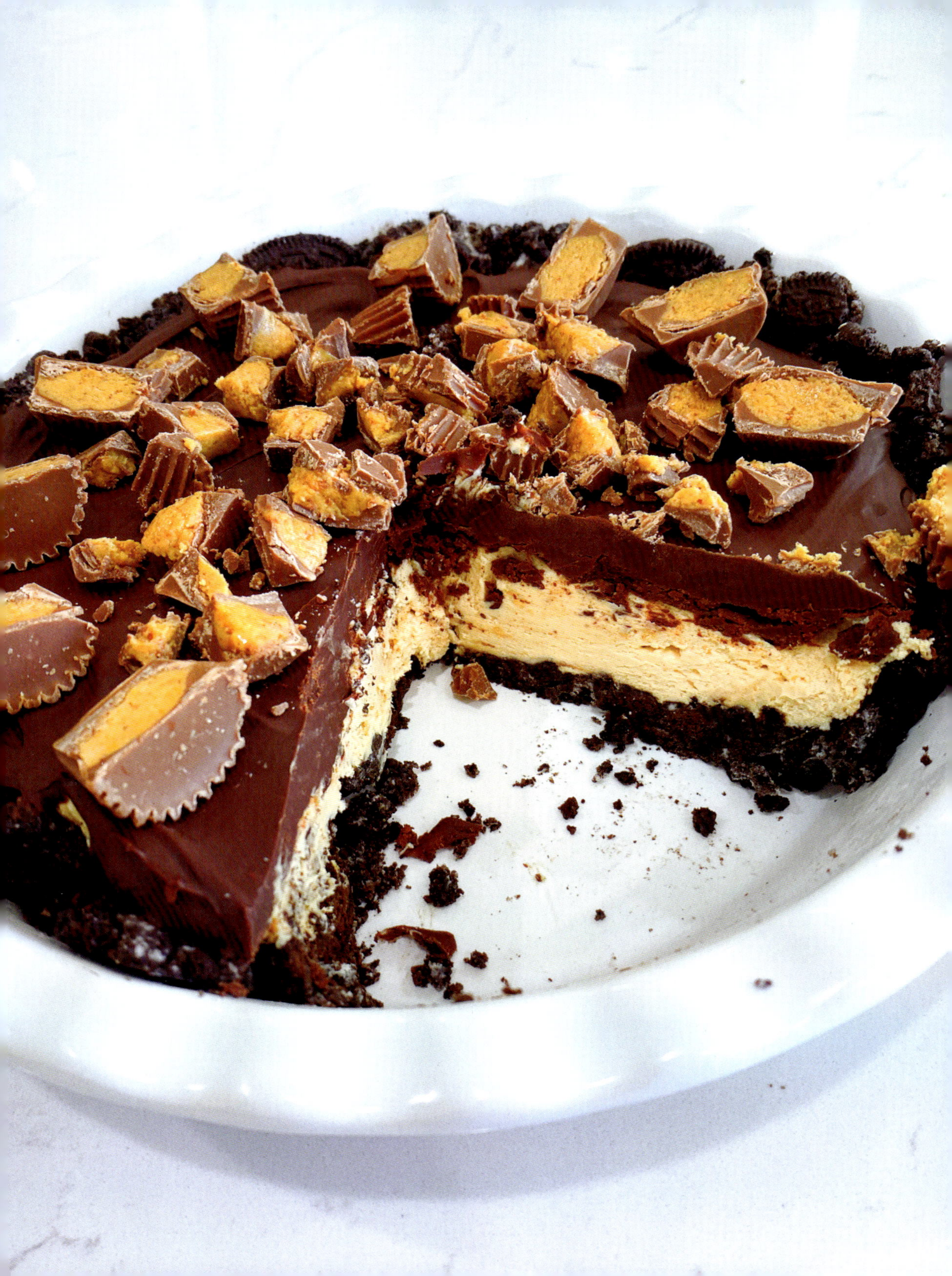

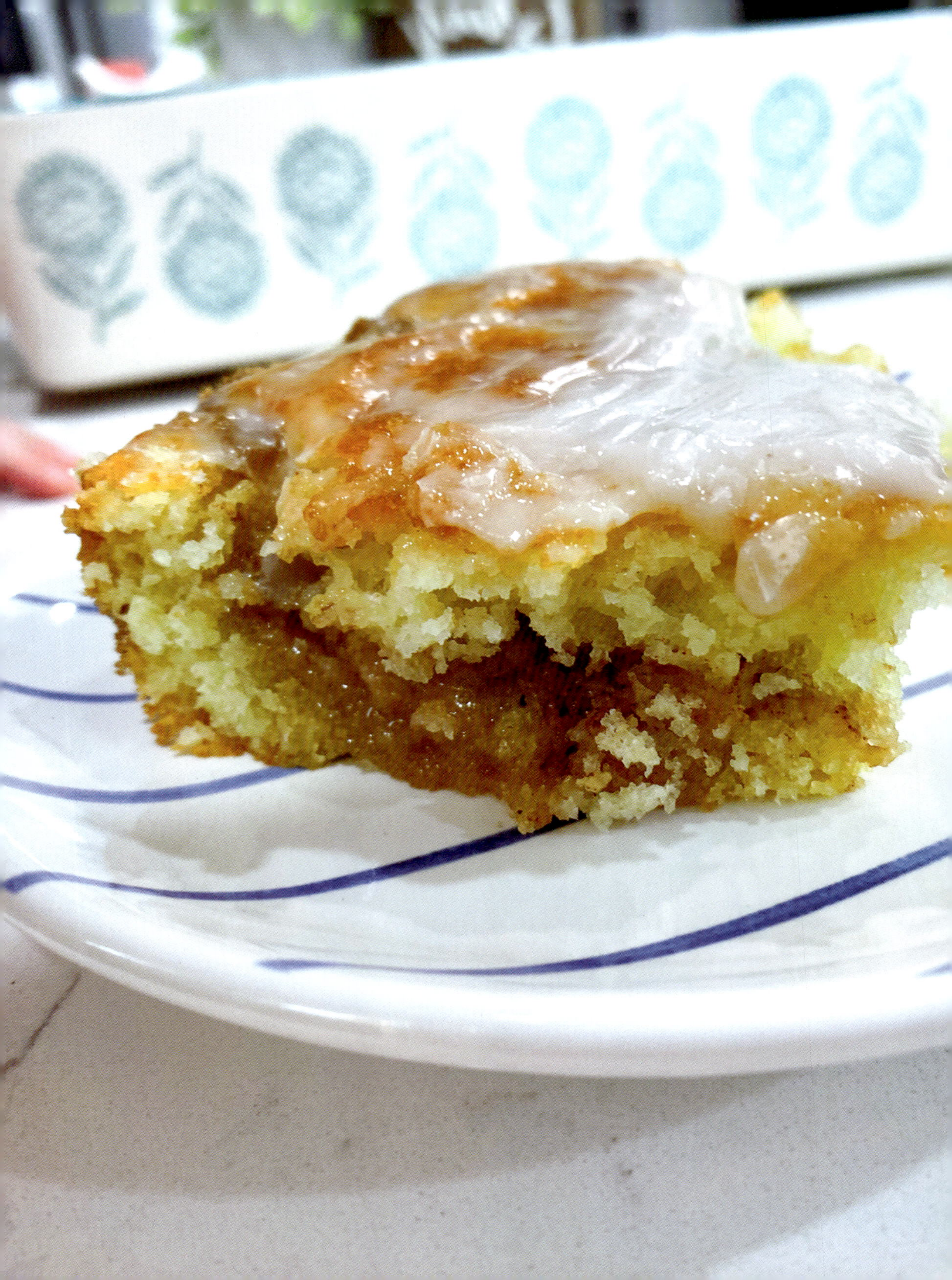

Honey Bun Cake

Moist cake layers are filled with a yummy brown sugar and cinnamon filling then topped with a simple glaze. This Honey Bun Cake is to-die-for good!

Prep time: 20 mins   **Cook time:** 35 mins   **Servings:** 4-5

INGREDIENTS

Cinnamon Layer
- 1 cup brown sugar
- 1 tbsp cinnamon

Cake
- 1 box yellow cake mix
- 4 eggs
- 1/2 cup vegetable oil
- 8 oz sour cream

Glaze
- 2 cups powdered sugar
- 1/4 cup milk
- 1 tsp vanilla extract

DIRECTIONS

1. Preheat oven to 325ºF.
2. Make the cinnamon layer. In a small bowl, whisk together the brown sugar and cinnamon set to the side.
3. Make the cake batter. To a large bowl or electric stand mixer, add in the cake mix, eggs, oil, and sour cream, and mix until well combined.
4. Grease a 9×13 baking dish with non-stick spray and pour half of the batter into the pan and spread out. Sprinkle the brown sugar and cinnamon mixture evenly over the top of the cake batter. Pour the remaining cake batter over the top. Bake for 35 minutes or until cooked through.
5. While the cake is in the oven, make the glaze. To a medium-sized bowl add the powdered sugar, milk, and vanilla. Whisk until smooth.
6. Once cake is out of the oven pour the glaze over the top. Serve and enjoy!

Hot Cocoa Cookies

Hot Cocoa Cookies are unlike any other cookie you've had before: chocolate cookies are baked with melted marshmallows on top and covered with a hot chocolate glaze and sprinkles.

Prep time: 20 mins **Cook time:** 35 mins **Servings:** 4-5

INGREDIENTS

Cookie ingredients

- 1/2 cup butter, softened
- 12 oz semi-sweet chocolate chips
- 1 1/2 cups all-purpose flour
- pinch of salt
- 1/4 cup unsweetened cocoa powder
- 1 1/2 tsp baking powder
- 1 1/4 cup brown sugar
- 1 tsp vanilla extract
- 3 eggs
- 12 marshmallows

Hot Cocoa Glaze

- 2 cups powdered sugar
- 4 tbsp butter, melted
- 1/4 cup unsweetened cocoa powder
- 1/4 cup hot water + 3 tbsp if glaze is too thick
- 1/2 tsp vanilla extract
- sprinkles

DIRECTIONS

Hot Cocoa Cookies

1. To a microwave-safe bowl, add the butter and chocolate chips and microwave for 30 seconds at a time, stirring after each time you microwave, until the chocolate chips and the butter are well combined and melted. Set to the side.
2. To a separate bowl, add the flour, salt, cocoa powder, and baking powder and whisk together.
3. To a large bowl or stand mixer, add the brown sugar, vanilla, and eggs. Mix until well combined. Stir in the chocolate sauce that you set aside and combine. Stir in the dry ingredients. Cover with cling wrap or a lid and refrigerate for 1-2 hours. This will help keep the cookies from spreading out too much inside of the oven.
4. Preheat oven to 325°F.
5. Line a large cookie tray with parchment paper. Using a cookie scoop, scoop out some of the dough and roll it into a ball with your hands. Place onto your cookie tray. Make sure the cookies are about 2 inches apart so they don't overlap while baking. This makes about

24 cookies so I normally bake these cookies in batches.

5. Bake for 11-12 minutes. While baking, cut each marshmallow in half. Once out of the oven, place each marshmallow half on the center of each cookie and bake for another 2 minutes to get the marshmallow melty. Let cool on the cookie tray for two minutes, then move to a cooling rack. Let cookies cool down completely before you glaze them.

Glaze

1. To make the glaze, add all of the glaze ingredients into a bowl and whisk together. You don't want the glaze super thin and runny, but you don't want it too thick like a frosting. Add a little bit more water if it appears too thick.

2. Once the cookies are cooled, drizzle some of the glaze on each cookie - it's ok if some of the glaze falls off the cookies - and sprinkle the tops of the cookies with sprinkles. Let the glaze sit for 20 minutes before eating. Enjoy!

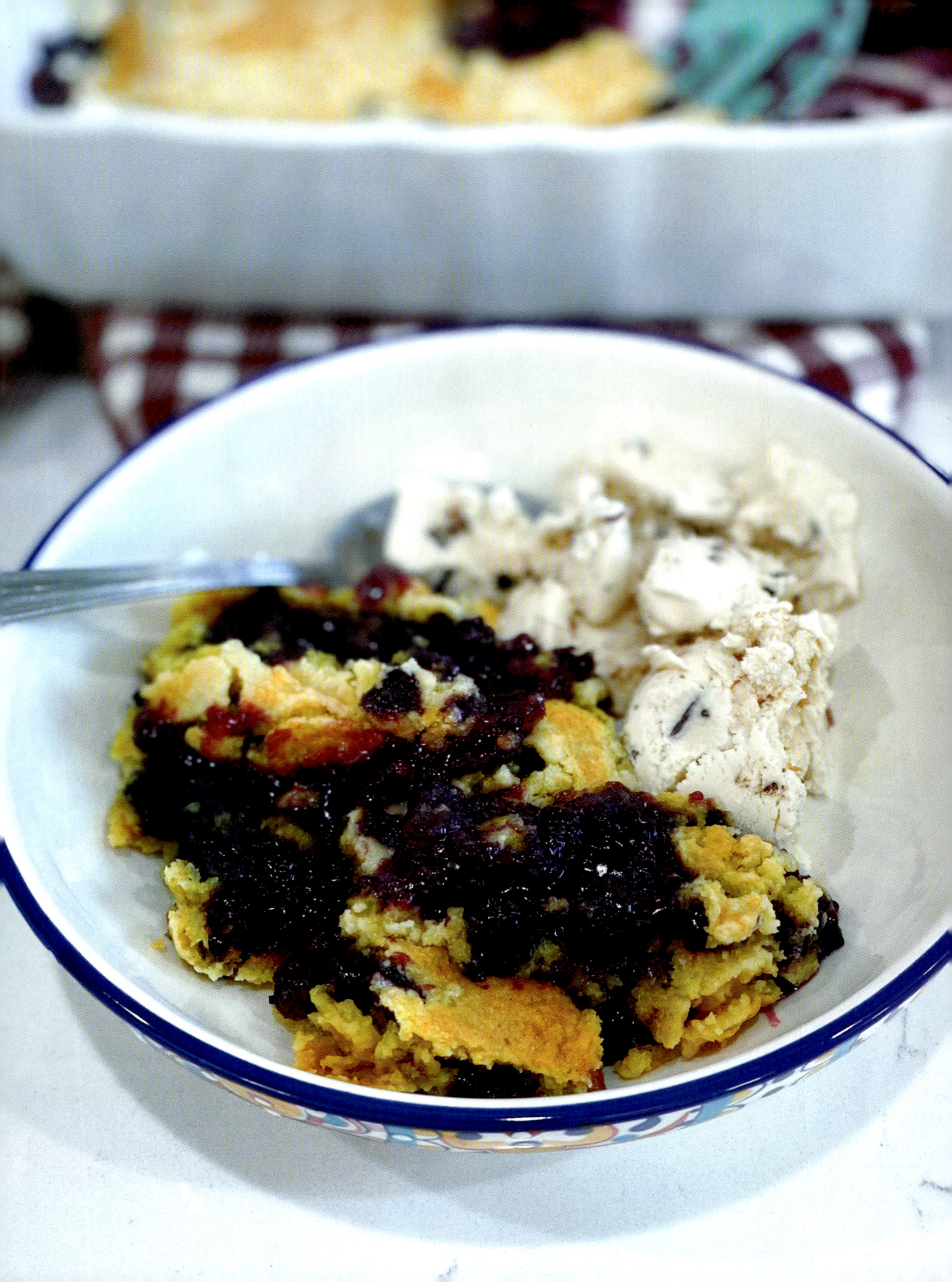

Blueberry Crumble Cake Mix Recipe

This Blueberry Crumble Cake has a secret: it's made using a store-bought cake mix. It's so simple to make and amazing to eat.

Prep time: 10 mins   **Cook time:** 40 mins   **Servings:** 5

INGREDIENTS

- 4 cups fresh or frozen blueberries
- 1 lemon juiced
- 3 tbsp brown sugar
- 1 box yellow cake mix
- 8 tbsp butter, sliced thinly

DIRECTIONS

1. Preheat oven to 350°F.
2. Add the blueberries to a large bowl, along with the lemon juice and brown sugar. Stir well to dissolve the brown sugar.
3. Grease a large baking dish with non-stick spray. Add in the blueberry mixture, then evenly sprinkle the cake mix over the blueberries. Top with slices of butter.
4. Bake for 35-45 minutes, or until the cake is golden and everything is bubbly. Serve warm with vanilla ice cream and enjoy!

Raspberry Lemon No-Bake Cheesecake

Fresh raspberries, lemon juice, and cream cheese give this Raspberry Lemon No-Bake Cheesecake a punchy zing and a deliciously creamy texture.

Prep time: 15 mins   **Cook time:** 2 hours   **Servings:** 6

INGREDIENTS

- 16 oz cream cheese, room temperature
- 1/2 cup powdered sugar
- 1 lemon, juiced
- 1 cup whipped topping
- 1 cup fresh raspberries, mashed
- 6 oz store-bought graham cracker pie crust
- toppings like fresh raspberries, lemon zest, whipped cream

DIRECTIONS

1. To a large mixing bowl add the cream cheese and powdered sugar and beat well. Add in the juice from the lemon and beat well. Stir in the whipped topping and the mashed raspberries.
2. Pour the cheesecake mixture into the pie crust. Cover and place in the refrigerator to chill for at least two hours.
3. Top with the toppings, slice, and enjoy!

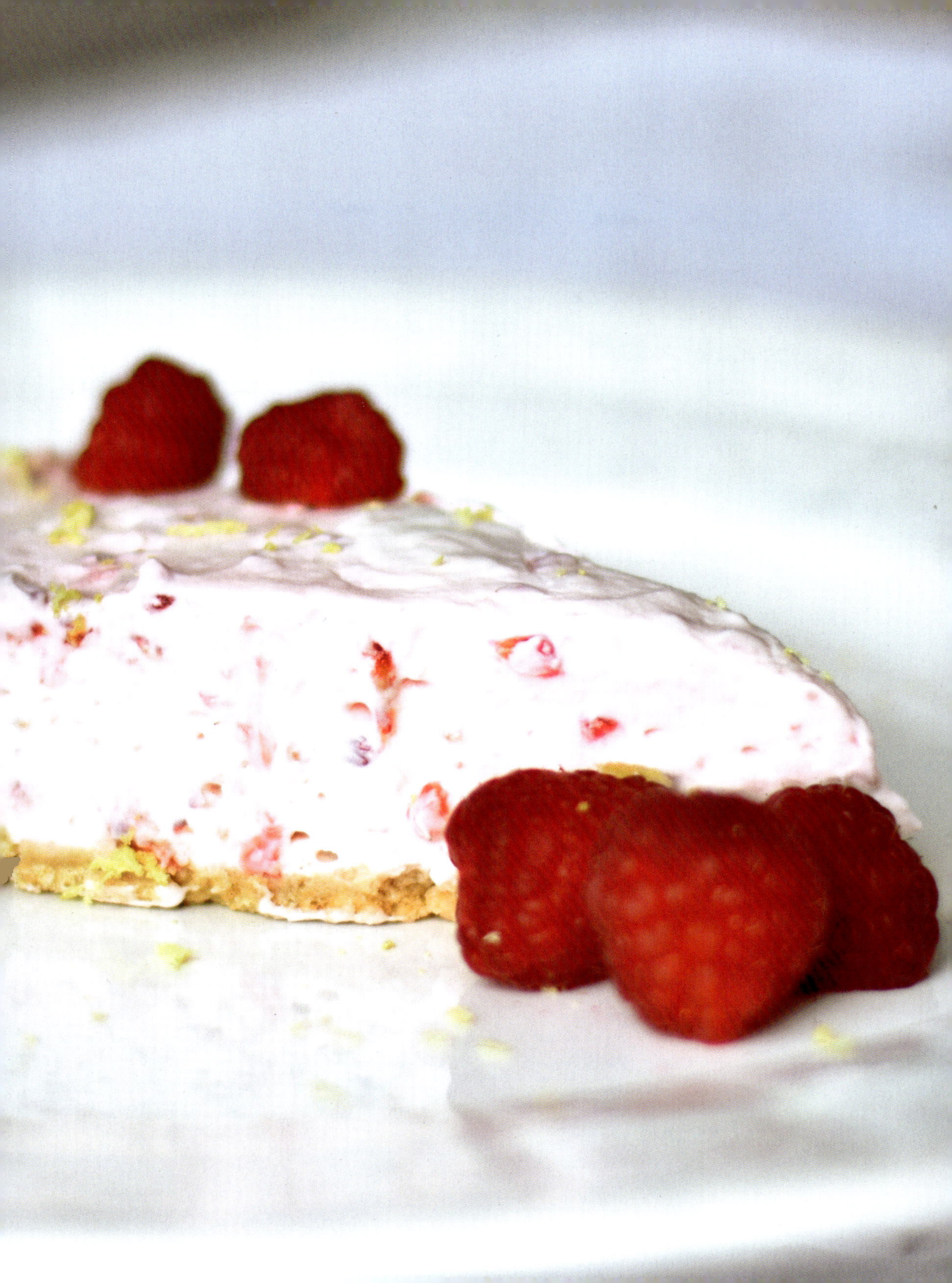

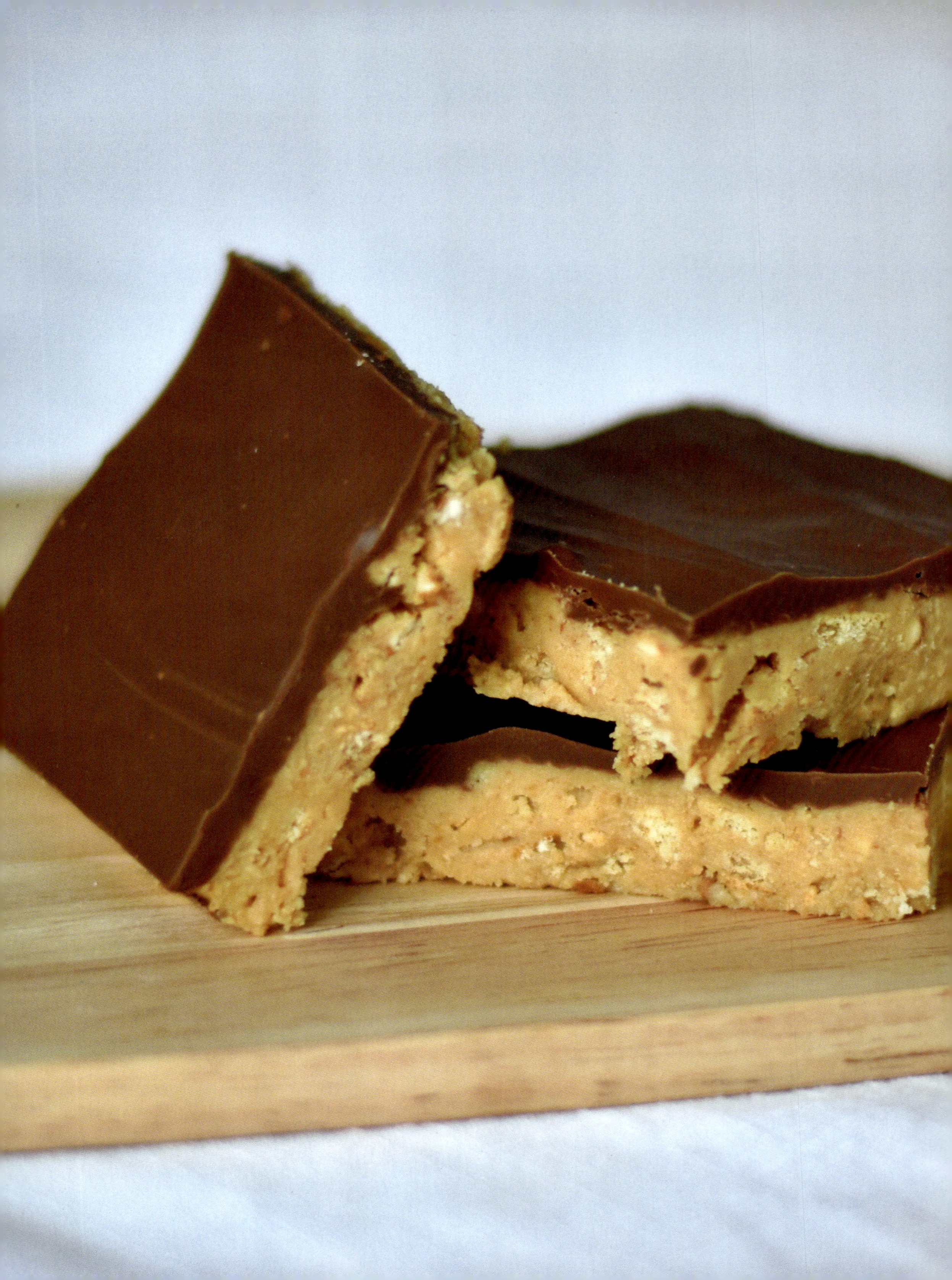

No-Bake Peanut Butter Bars

No-Bake Peanut Butter Bars are so easy to throw together and are perfect to make when you want something sweet but don't want to turn on the oven.

Prep time: 10 mins   **Chilling time:** 2 hours   **Servings:** 10

INGREDIENTS

- 1 cup salted pretzels
- 1 sleeve of graham crackers
- 1 cup unsalted butter
- 2 cups powdered sugar
- 1 1/2 cups creamy peanut butter

Topping:

- 10 oz semi-sweet chocolate chips
- 1/4 cup creamy peanut butter

DIRECTIONS

1. Add the pretzels and graham crackers to a food processor and pulse until they are small crumbs. Add the butter, powdered sugar, and peanut butter and process until the ingredients are fully combined.
2. Grease a 9×13 baking dish with non-stick spray, and spread the mixture out into the pan.
3. To a microwave-safe bowl, add the chocolate chips and 1/4 cup of peanut butter. Place in the microwave for 30 seconds at a time, stirring after every interval, until melted and smooth. Spread over the peanut butter layer.
4. Refrigerate for at least 2 hours. Slice into bars and enjoy!

Cake Mix Monster Cookies

Cake Mix Monster Cookies are chock full of everything you love: peanut butter, chocolate chips, oats, and chocolate candies!

Prep time: 10 mins   **Cook time:** 12 mins   **Servings:** 4-5

INGREDIENTS

- 1 box yellow cake mix
- 1/2 cup brown sugar
- 1 1/2 sticks butter, softened
- 1/2 cup peanut butter
- 3 tbsp water
- 1 egg
- 1/2 cup mini chocolate candies
- 1/2 cup mini chocolate chips
- 2 cups quick oats

DIRECTIONS

1. Preheat oven to 350ºF.
2. To a large bowl or electric stand mixer, add the cake mix, brown sugar, butter, peanut butter, water, and egg, and mix until well combined. Stir in the mini chocolate candies, chocolate chips, and oats.
3. Line a cookie sheet with parchment paper or spray with non-stick spray. Using a cookie scoop, scoop the dough and place it onto the cookie sheet, leaving 2-3 inches in between each cookie. Bake for 12-13 minutes. Let cool on the cookie pan for 2 minutes then transfer to a cooling rack. Enjoy!

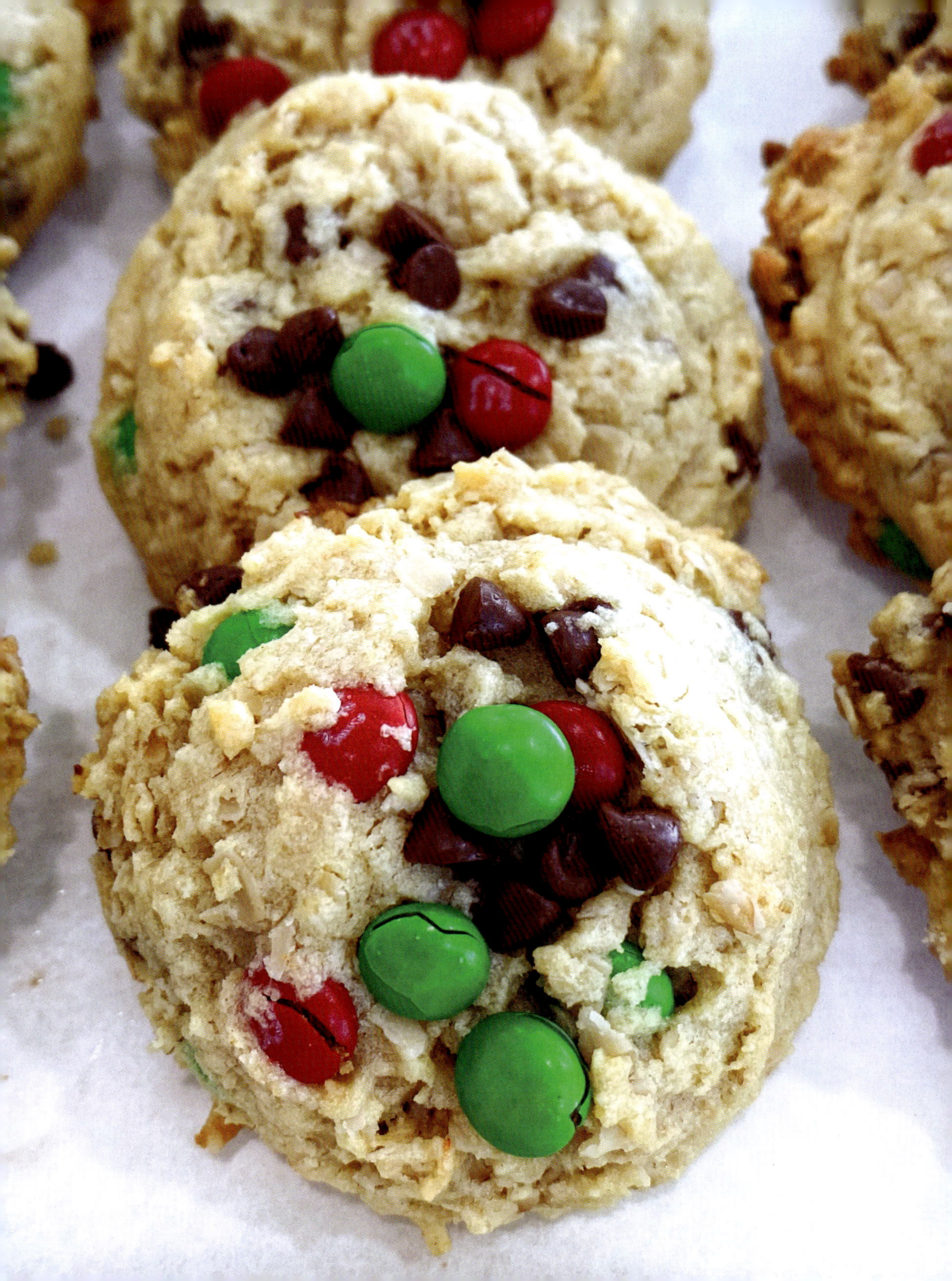

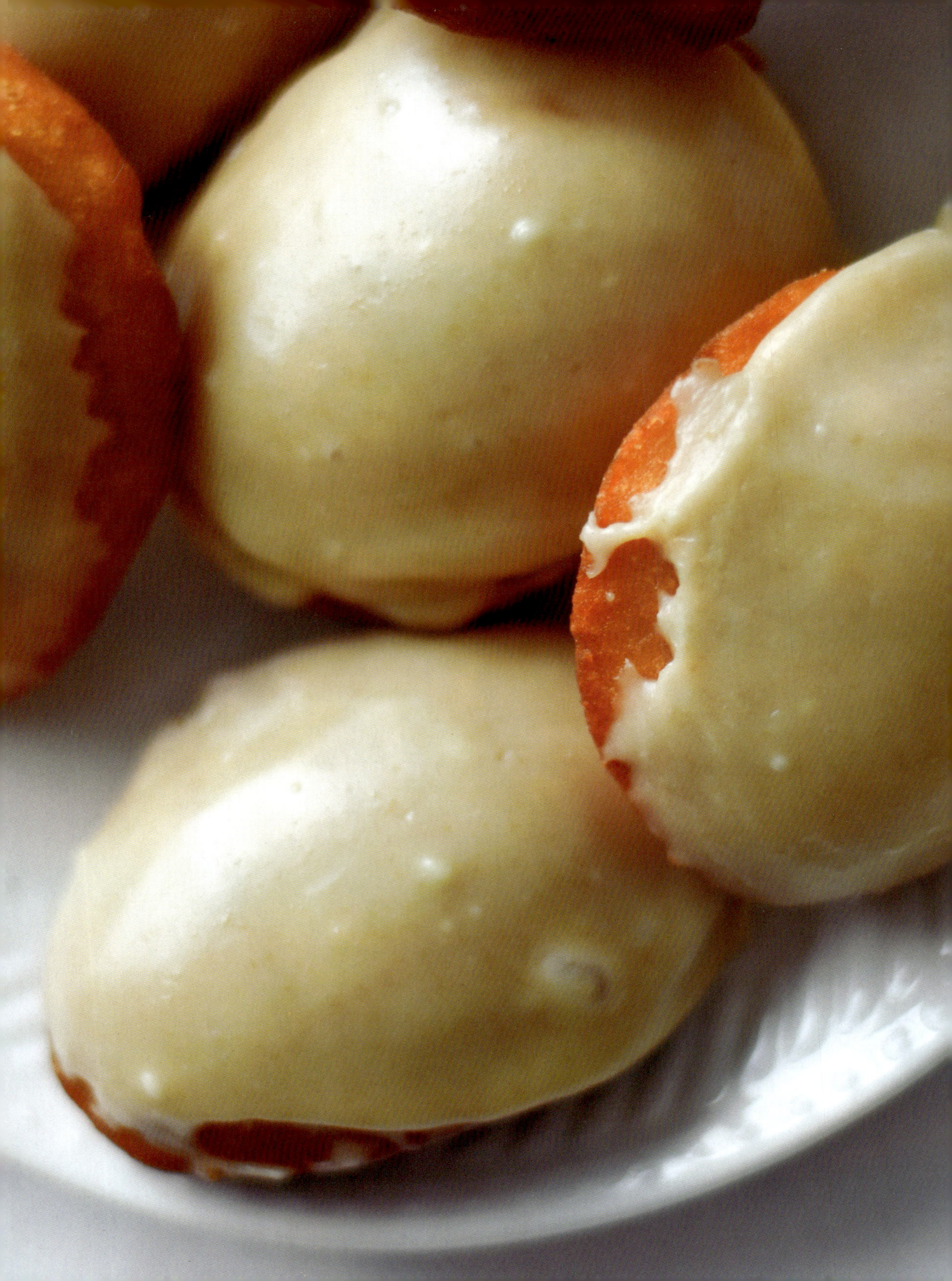

Maple Bars

These Maple Bars are so simple to make and taste amazing. Have hot and fresh donuts right at home in just about 15 minutes.

Prep time: 10 mins **Cook time:** 10 mins **Servings:** 8

INGREDIENTS

- 18-count can of biscuits
- 2 cups frying oil (I use canola)

Maple Glaze

- 1/4 cup butter
- 1/2 cup brown sugar
- 4 tbsp milk, plus more if needed
- 2 tsp vanilla or maple extract
- 2 cups powdered sugar

DIRECTIONS

1. Add the oil to a large pot on medium-low heat.
2. Gently stretch the biscuit dough into oval shapes.
3. Once the oil is hot, add the dough in batches and fry for 1-2 minutes on each side.
4. To make the glaze, add the butter, brown sugar, and milk to a saucepan over medium heat and whisk frequently for 3-5 minutes, or until the sugar is dissolved.
5. Remove the pot from the heat and add the vanilla. Slowly whisk the powdered sugar in 1/2 cup at a time. Add a little more milk if the glaze is too thick.
6. Dip the donuts into the maple glaze and enjoy!

Christmas Crack Toffee Bars

The graham cracker base, crunchy pecans, and rich chocolate make these Christmas Crack Toffee Bars the most amazing and addicting holiday treat.

Prep time: 20 mins **Cook time:** 15 mins **Servings:** 16

INGREDIENTS

- 1 sleeve honey graham crackers
- 5-1.55 oz chocolate bars
- 1 cup butter
- 1 cup light brown sugar
- 1 cup chopped pecans

DIRECTIONS

1. Preheat oven to 350°F.
2. Line a 9×13 baking dish with parchment paper or spray with non-stick spray.
3. Place the graham crackers side by side in the bottom of the baking dish.
4. To a saucepan over medium heat, add the butter and heat until melted. Add the brown sugar and pecans and bring the mixture up to a boil. Boil for 5 minutes, stirring constantly.
5. Remove from heat and pour over the graham crackers. Spread the mixture evenly over the graham crackers. Bake for 8 minutes.
6. Once out of the oven, immediately unwrap the chocolate bars and place them in a single layer over the toffee layer. You may need to break a few of the bars into sections.
7. Cover the baking dish with aluminum foil and let sit for 7 minutes to melt the chocolate.
8. Once the chocolate is melted, remove the aluminum foil, and using a spatula spread the chocolate out evenly over the top. Let cool completely, break into smaller pieces, and enjoy!

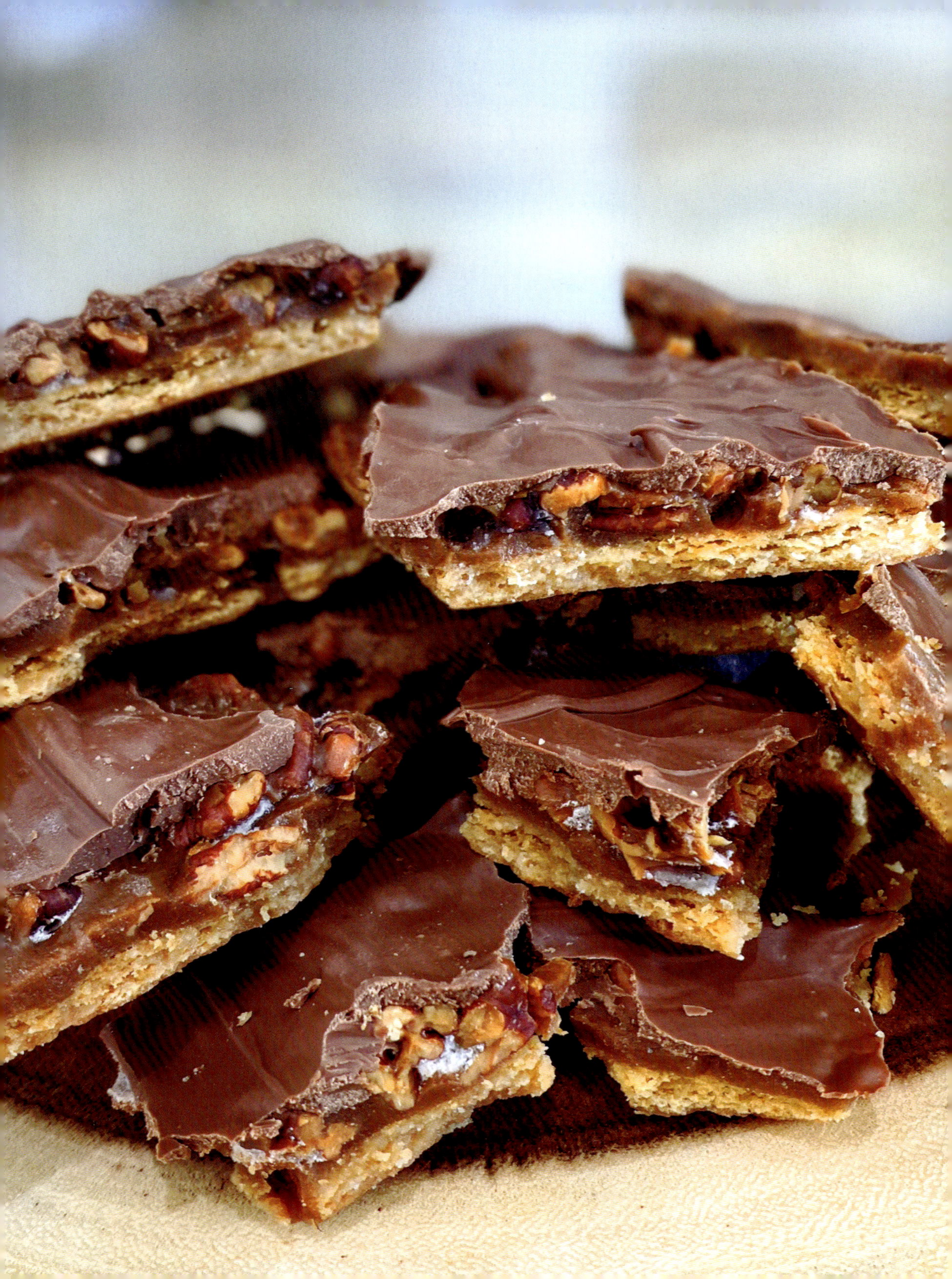

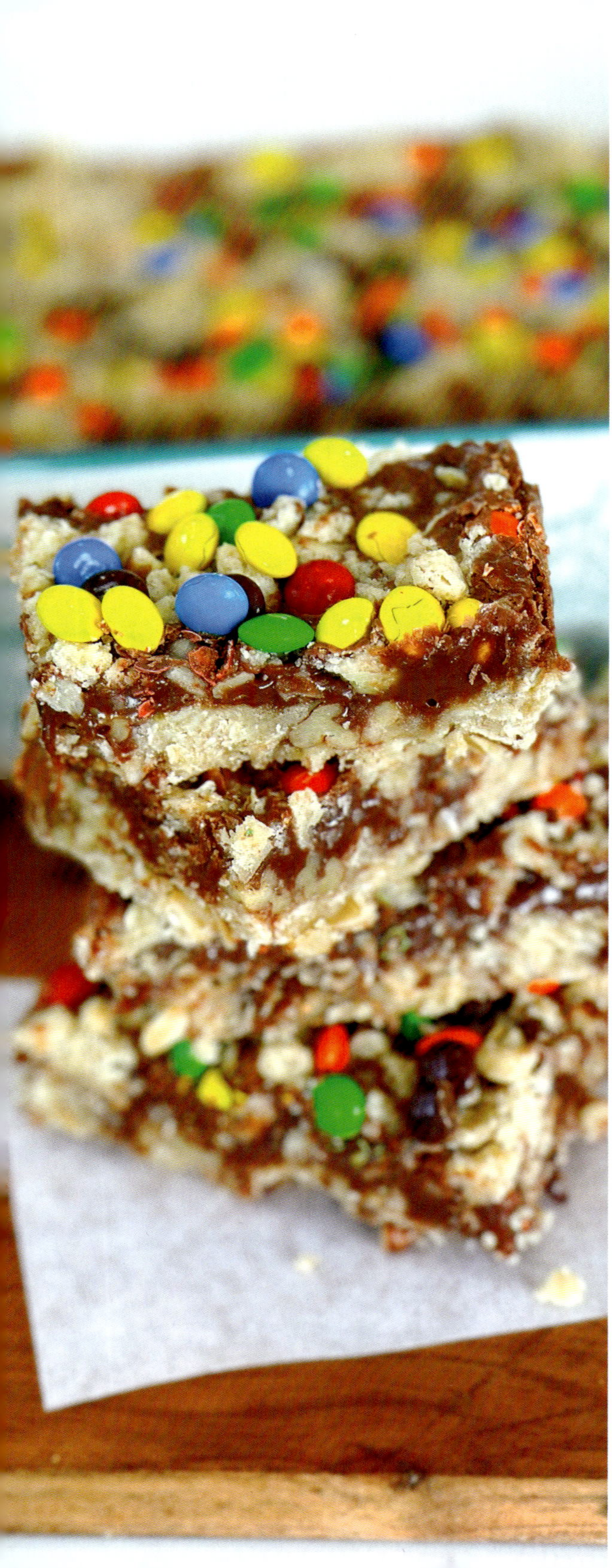

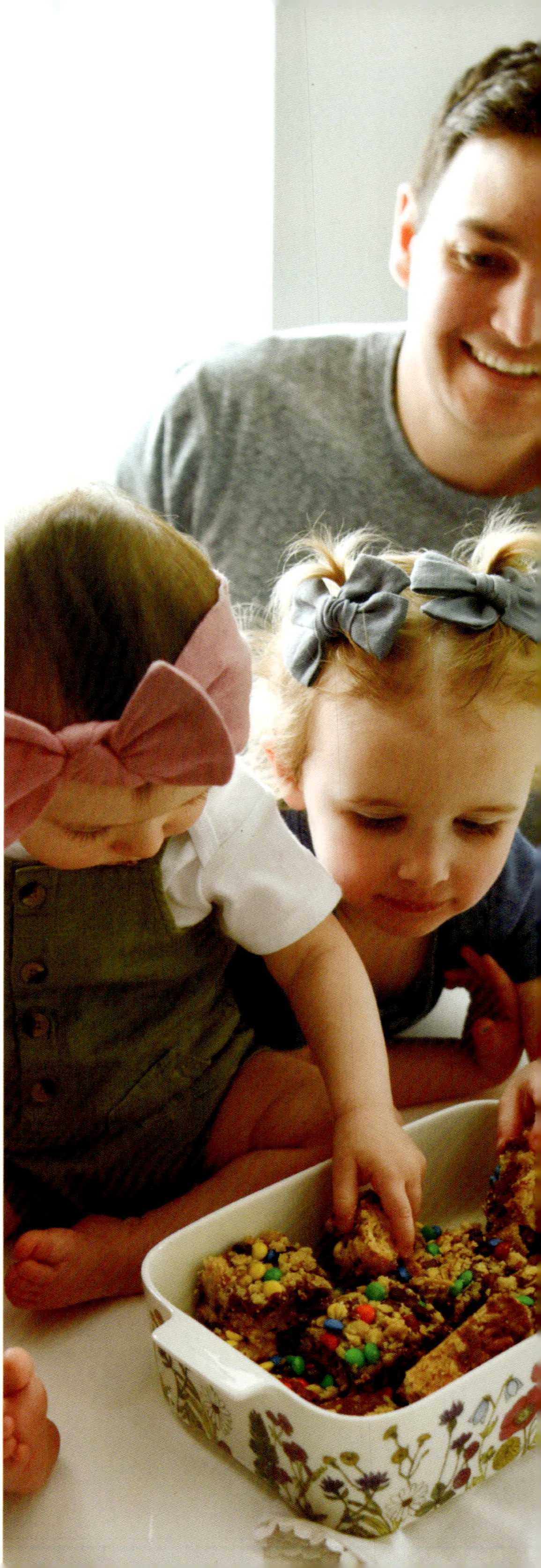

Fudge Filled Oat Bars

My mom's Fudge Filled Oat Bars were one of my favorite treats growing up. I love the combo of buttery oatmeal crust, soft, fudgy filling, and crunchy chocolate candies.

Prep time: 20 mins   **Cook time:** 15 mins   **Servings:** 16

INGREDIENTS

- 2 cups quick oats
- 1 1/2 cups all-purpose flour
- 1 cup brown sugar
- 3/4 tsp salt
- 1 cup butter, melted
- 1 cup pecans, chopped (optional)
- 14 oz can sweetened condensed milk
- 1 cup semi-sweet chocolate chips
- 2 tbsp shortening
- 1 cup mini chocolate candies

DIRECTIONS

1. Preheat oven to 350°F.
2. Grease a 9×13 baking dish with non-stick spray.
3. To a medium-sized bowl add the oats, flour, brown sugar, and salt. Mix well, then stir in the melted butter until crumbly. Stir in the nuts, if using. Remove 1 1/2 cups of this mixture and set aside.
4. Add the remaining mixture to the baking dish, spreading it out and pressing it into the pan to form a crust.
5. To a medium-sized saucepan over medium heat, add the sweetened condensed milk, chocolate chips, and shortening. Turn the heat to low and stir until the chocolate chips are melted. Spread over the crust in the baking dish. Sprinkle the remaining 1 1/2 cups of the oat mixture on top of the fudge. Top with the mini chocolate candies.
6. Bake for 20-25 minutes. Let cool completely, then slice into bars and enjoy!

Grandma's Carrot Cake

My mom and grandma have been making this cake for years and are famous for it. It's the only carrot cake I will ever make!

Prep time: 10 mins　　　**Cook time:** 35 mins　　　**Servings:** 8

INGREDIENTS

- 2 cups all-purpose flour
- 2 tsp baking powder
- 1 1/2 tsp baking soda
- 1 tsp salt
- 2 tsp cinnamon
- 2 cups sugar
- 1 1/2 cups vegetable oil
- 4 eggs
- 2 cups grated carrots
- 1 cup crushed pineapple (I use canned)
- 1/2-1 cup walnuts, chopped

DIRECTIONS

1. Preheat oven to 350°F.
2. Whisk together the flour, baking powder, baking soda, salt, and cinnamon in a small bowl. In a mixer, beat the sugar, oil, and eggs. Slowly add in the flour mixture to the wet ingredients. Once well combined and creamy, stir in the carrots, crushed pineapple, and walnuts.
3. Generously grease two 9-inch cake pans with non-stick spray. (You can also use a 9×13 baking dish and add 20 minutes to the baking time)
4. Bake for 35 minutes, or until a toothpick inserted in the center comes out clean. Once out of the oven, let cool completely.
5. Top with your favorite cream cheese frosting or use my recipe in this cookbook!

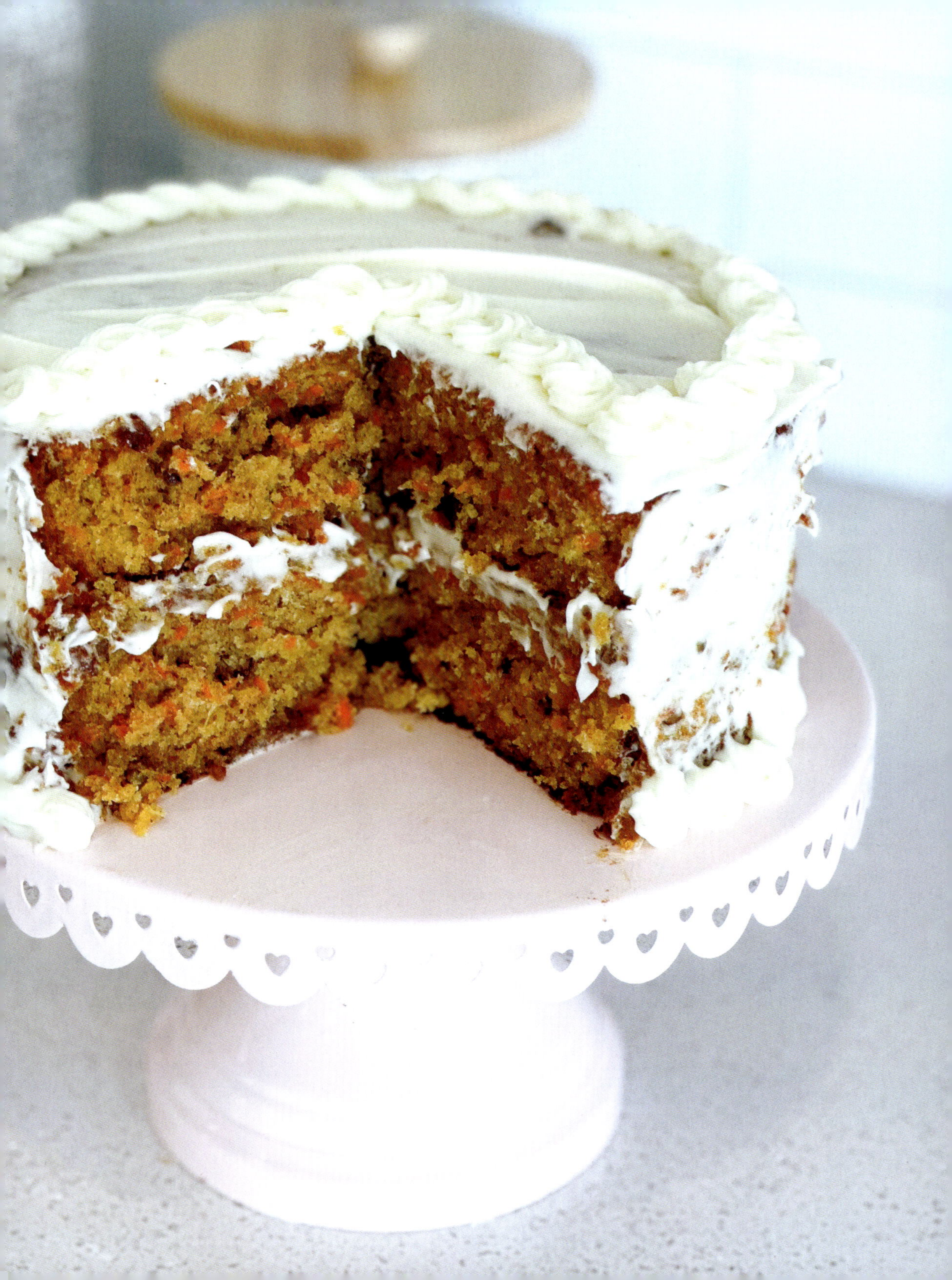

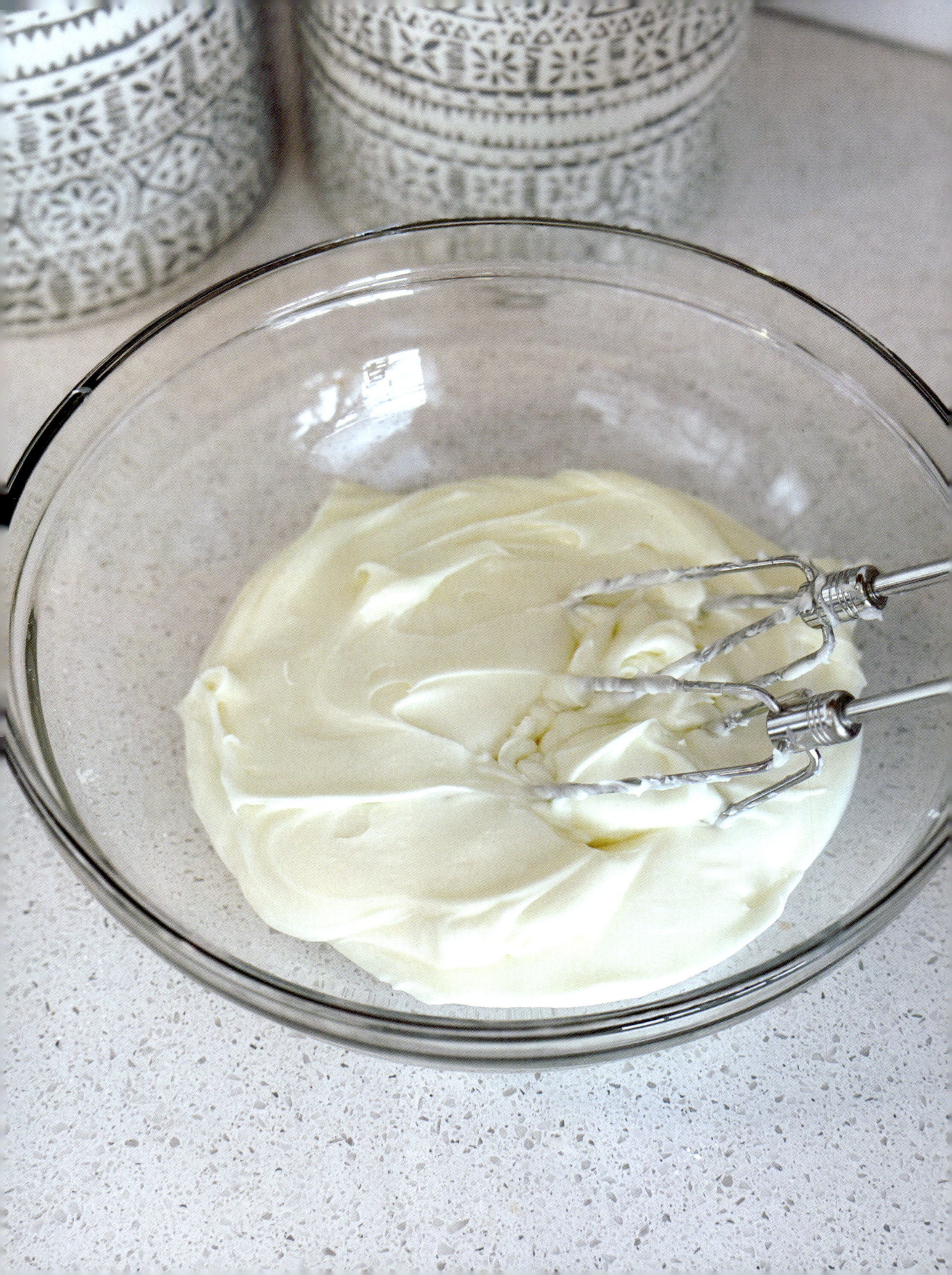

Cream Cheese Frosting

Cream Cheese Frosting goes well on everything: cakes, cookies, brownies, cinnamon rolls, or anything else you can think of!

Prep time: 10 mins   **Cook time:** 35 mins   **Servings:** 4-5

INGREDIENTS

- 8 oz cream cheese, softened
- 1/4 cup butter, softened
- 1 tsp vanilla extract
- pinch of salt
- 3 cups powdered sugar

DIRECTIONS

1. To a large bowl, add the cream cheese and butter and beat together until smooth. Add the vanilla, salt, and one cup of powdered sugar at a time, and beat until smooth.
2. Use this yummy frosting on a cake, cinnamon rolls, cookies, or anything!

Seven Layer Bars

Mom's Seven Layer Bars are the sticky, sweet, and nostalgic treat that you know and love!

Prep time: 10 mins   **Cook time:** 25 mins   **Servings:** 12

INGREDIENTS

- 16 graham crackers, crushed
- 1/2 cup margarine or butter, melted
- 8 oz butterscotch chips
- 9 oz semi-sweet chocolate chips
- 1 cup sweetened shredded coconut
- 1 cup walnuts, chopped
- 14 oz can sweetened condensed milk

DIRECTIONS

1. Preheat oven to 350°F.
2. Spray a 9×13 baking dish with non-stick spray.
3. To a medium-sized bowl, add the graham crackers and margarine and stir together until combined. Press the graham cracker mixture into the baking dish to form a crust. Over the crust sprinkle the butterscotch chips, chocolate chips, coconut, and walnuts, then drizzle the sweetened condensed milk over everything.
4. Bake for 20-25 minutes. Cut into bars once completely cooled and enjoy!

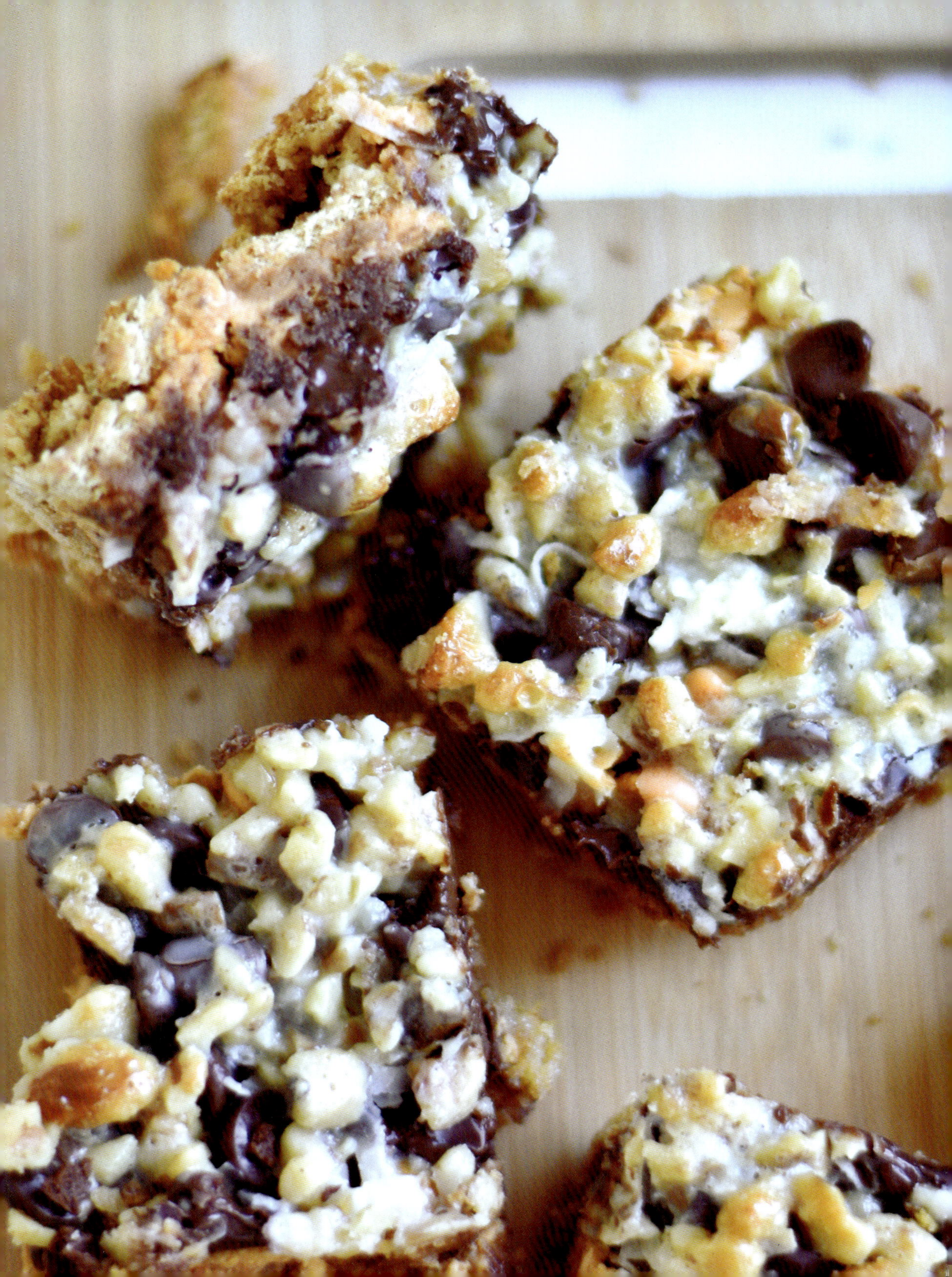

World's Best Cinnamon Rolls

These are the best cinnamon rolls that you'll ever make. They're perfectly pillowy and soft!

Prep time: 20 mins   **Cook time:** 35 mins   **Servings:** 4-5

INGREDIENTS

- 1/2 cup warm water
- 2 tbsp yeast
- 2 tbsp sugar
- 1 box instant vanilla pudding mix
- 1/2 cup butter, melted
- 2 eggs, beaten
- 1 tsp salt
- 6 - 8 cups flour

Topping

- 1/2 cup butter, softened
- 2 cups brown sugar, packed
- 4 tbsp cinnamon

Frosting

- 8 oz cream cheese, softened
- 1/2 cup butter, softened
- 1 tsp vanilla extract
- 3 cups powdered sugar
- 1 tbsp milk

DIRECTIONS

1. In a small bowl, combine water, yeast, and sugar. Stir until dissolved. Set aside. Yeast should bubble.
2. Make pudding mix according to package directions. Mix until slightly thickened. Add butter, eggs, and salt. Mix well.
3. Add yeast mixture and blend. Gradually add flour and knead until smooth.
4. Place in a large greased bowl. Cover and let rise in a warm, draft-free place until doubled in size, about 1 hour.
5. Punch down the dough and let rise again, about 45 minutes. Divide dough in half. Roll out to rectangle. Spread 1/4 cup melted butter over the rectangle.
6. In a small bowl, mix the brown sugar and cinnamon together. Sprinkle half over the top of the first dough rectangle.
7. Starting at the long edge of the dough, roll up very tightly. With a knife, put a notch every 2 inches making 12 notches (cut roll in half, then half again, then each of those halves into 3).

With string or thread place under the roll by the notch mark and cross over to cut the roll. Repeat with the second ball of dough.

8. Place rolls onto cookie sheets, 12 per sheet, 2 inches apart. Cover and let rise in a warm, draft-free place, until doubled in size.
9. Bake at 350°F for 15-20 minutes, or until golden brown. Do not over-bake.
10. Combine all frosting ingredients and mix until smooth. Spread on warm rolls. Serve warm and enjoy!

PREP AND FREEZE INSTRUCTIONS (OPTIONAL)

1. After shaping the rolls and placing them on the baking sheet, cover with lightly greased plastic wrap and a layer of tin foil. Store in the freezer.
2. The night before you want to serve them, take out the rolls and put them in the refrigerator. Let them thaw in the refrigerator for about 8-9 hours. Take them out of the fridge and let them rise until doubled. (If you have less time, you can take the rolls out of the freezer and let them come to room temperature on the counter, about 4 hours, then let them rise until doubled.)
3. Bake according to the recipe.

SUBSTITUTIONS

Cream of Mushroom Soup

- 2 tbsp butter
- 3 tbsp all purpose flour
- 1/2 cup vegetable or chicken broth
- 1/2 cup milk
- 1/2 tsp salt
- 1/4 tsp pepper
- 1/2 cup finely diced white mushrooms

How to Make

To a medium-sized saucepan add the butter. Allow the butter to melt down on medium heat for 2 minutes. Use a whisk to stir in the flour and incorporate. Remove from heat, and add the milk and broth a little at a time. Mix well before returning the pan to the low heat. Add the remaining ingredients and stir well until combined.

Cream of Chicken Soup

- 3-4 tbsp cream cheese softened or 1/2 cup sour cream
- 1/2 cup chicken broth

How to Make

Whisk ingredients together and add to replace canned soup.

Homemade Taco Seasoning

- 1 tbsp chili powder
- 2 tsp ground cumin
- 1 tsp garlic powder
- 1 tsp onion powder
- 1 tsp oregano
- 1 1/4 tsp salt
- 1 tsp paprika
- 1 tsp ground black pepper

How to Make

Mix all of the ingredients together and use the amount needed for each specific recipe from this batch.

Homemade Ranch Seasoning

- 1/4 cup Dried Parsley
- 1 tsp Dried Dill
- 2 tsp Garlic Powder
- 2 tsp Minced Onion
- 1 tbsp Dried Chives
- 1 tsp salt
- 1 tsp Black pepper

How to Make

Mix all of the ingredients together in a bowl and use as needed for the recipes.

SUBSTITUTIONS

Bread Crumbs

For 1 Cup of Breadcrumbs Use:

- 1 cup crushed saltines or any savory cracker

    -OR-

- 1 cup crushed croutons

Heavy Cream

For 1 Cup Heavy Cream Use:

- Combine 3/4 cup milk and 1/4 cup butter

    -OR-

- 1 cup evaporated milk

Mayonnaise

For 1 Cup Mayonnaise Use:

- 1 cup sour cream

    -OR-

- 1 cup plain Greek yogurt

Brown Sugar

For 1 Cup Packed Brown Sugar:

- Combine 1 cup white sugar and 1/4 cup molasses. Mix well in a separate bowl until well combined.

Cream Cheese

For 8 oz Cream Cheese Use:

- 8 oz sour cream

    -OR-

- 8 oz plain Greek yogurt

CONVERSIONS

SIMPLIFIED MEASUREMENT EQUIVALENTS

Dry Measurements	Ounces in Weight (oz)	Grams (g)	NOTES
1 tablespoon = 3 teaspoons	0.5 oz	14.3 g	
1/8 cup = 2 tablespoons	1.0 oz	28.3 g	
1/4 cup = 4 tablespoons	2.0 oz	56.7 g	
1/3 cup = 5 tbsp + 1 tsp	2.6 oz	75.6 g	
1/2 cup = 8 tablespoons	4.0 oz	113.4 g	
3/4 cup = 12 tablespoons	6.0 oz	170 g	
1 cup = 16 tablespoons	8.0 oz	227 g	

Liquid Measurements	Fluid Ounces (fl. oz.)	Milliliters (ml)	
1 teaspoon	0.16 fl. oz.	5 ml	
1 tablespoon = 3 teaspoons	0.5 fl. oz.	15 ml	
1 ounce = 2 tablespoons	1.0 fl. oz.	30 ml	
1/4 cup = 4 tablespoons	2.0 fl. oz.	60 ml	
1/3 cup = 5 tbsp + 1 tsp	2.6 fl. oz.	80 ml	
1/2 cup = 8 tablespoons	4.0 fl. oz.	120 ml	
2/3 cup	5.3 fl. oz.	160 ml	
3/4 cup	6.0 fl. oz.	180 ml	
1 cup = 16 tablespoons	8.0 fl. oz.	240 ml	

CONVERSIONS

SIMPLIFIED MEASUREMENT EQUIVALENTS

Fahrenheit (°F)	Celsius (°C)	Gas Mark
200°F	95°C	
250°F	120°C – 130°C	
275°F	140°C	1
300°F	150°C	2
325°F	160°C – 170°C	3
350°F	180°C	4
375°F	190°C	5
400°F	200°C	6
425°F	220°C	7
450°F	230°C	8
475°F	240°C	9
500°F	260°C	10

NOTES

INDEX

30 MINUTES OR LESS

20-Minute Cheeseburger Quesadillas, 178, 179

20-Minute Honey Garlic Chicken, 180, 181

20-Minute Spaghetti Bolognese, 176, 177

Alfredo Chicken Broccoli Skillet Lasagna, 120, 121

Baked Chicken Ranch Flautas, 184, 185

Baked Manicotti, 72, 73

BBQ Chicken Roll Ups, 46, 47

Beef Taquitos, 102, 103

Breakfast Biscuit Casserole, 20, 21

Breakfast Power Cookies, 16, 17

Cake Mix Monster Cookies, 214, 215

California Spaghetti Salad, 40, 41

Cheesy Chicken and Broccoli Pasta, 108, 109

Chicken Noodle Casserole, 66, 67

Christmas Crack Toffee Bars, 218, 219

Classic Chicken Fettuccine Alfredo, 198, 199

Crescent Roll Sausage Egg Casserole, 10, 11

Easy Chicken Noodle Soup, 134, 135

French Onion Chicken Casserole, 80, 81

Fudge Filled Oat Bars, 220, 221

Garlic Herb Mashed Potatoes, 42, 43

Garlic Parmesan Chicken w/ Zucchini, 192, 193

German Pancakes, 22, 23

Green Chile Chicken Enchiladas, 70, 71

Ham and Noodle One Pot Meal, 118, 119

Italian Chicken and Rice, 130, 131

Italian Chicken and Vegetables, 94, 95

Italian Vegetable Pasta One-Pot Dinner, 126, 127

Lemon Chicken Pasta, 194, 195

Low Carb Turkey Vegetable Skillet, 114, 115

Maple Bars, 216, 217

Meatballs, 188, 189

Mozzarella Stuffed Meatloaf, 92, 93

One-Pot Ground Turkey Pasta, 110, 111

One-Pot Mexican Quinoa, 112, 113

Parmesan Zucchini Skillet, 30, 31

Potato Salad, 54, 55

Pressure Cooker White Rice, 52, 53

Sausage and Tomato Gnocchi, 116, 117

Sausage Casserole w/Cauliflower Rice, 58, 59

Sausage Orzo Soup, 106, 107

Seven Layer Bars, 226, 227

Sheet Pan Burgers w/ Onions & Potatoes, 88, 89

Sheet Pan Chicken Tenderloins, 100, 101

Sheet Pan Loaded Quesadillas, 84, 85

Sheet Pan Steak Fajitas, 98, 99

Skillet Lasagna One-Pot, 122, 123

Sun-Dried Tomato Tortellini, 124, 125

Taco Rice Stuffed Peppers, 182, 183

White Chicken Chili, 136, 137

APPETIZERS/SIDES

Avocado Corn Salad, 34, 35

BBQ Chicken Roll Ups, 46, 47

California Spaghetti Salad, 40, 41

Coleslaw, 50, 51

Side Salad, 36, 37

Dinner Rolls, 48, 49

Garlic Herb Mashed Potatoes, 42, 43

Pressure Cooker White Rice, 52, 53

Parmesan Zucchini Skillet, 30, 31

Potato Salad, 54, 55

Ranch Bacon Pasta Salad, 38, 39

INDEX

Red White & Blue Cheesecake Fruit Salad, 44, 45
Twice Baked Potato Casserole, 32, 33

BREAKFAST
Breakfast Biscuit Casserole, 20, 21
Breakfast Power Cookies, 16, 17
Crescent Roll Sausage Egg Casserole, 10, 11
Egg & Ham Breakfast Enchiladas, 18, 19
German Pancakes, 22, 23
Sheet Pan Bacon, Eggs, and Potatoes, 14, 15
Slow Cooker Breakfast Burritos, 12, 13
Slow Cooker Breakfast Potatoes, 26, 27
Slow Cooker Hash Brown Casserole, 24, 25
Cinnamon Rolls, 228, 229

CASSEROLES
Baked Manicotti, 72, 73
Breakfast Biscuit Casserole, 20, 21
Cheesy Pierogi Casserole, 68, 69
Chicken Noodle Casserole, 66, 67
Chicken Stuffing Casserole w/Zucchini, 64, 65
Crescent Roll Sausage Egg Casserole, 10, 11
Fiesta Chicken Casserole, 62, 63
French Onion Chicken Casserole, 80, 81
Green Chile Chicken Enchiladas, 70, 71
John Wayne Casserole, 74, 75
Sausage Casserole w/Cauliflower Rice, 58, 59
Slow Cooker Hash Brown Casserole, 24, 25
Twice Baked Potato Casserole, 32, 33
Vegetarian Mexican Casserole, 78, 79
White Chicken Mushroom Spinach Lasagna, 76, 77

DESSERTS
Blueberry Crumble Cake, 208, 209
Cake Mix Monster Cookies, 214, 215
Christmas Crack Toffee Bars, 218, 219
Cream Cheese Frosting, 224, 225
Fudge Filled Oat Bars, 220, 221
Grandma's Carrot Cake, 222, 223
Honey Bun Cake, 204, 205
Hot Cocoa Cookies, 206, 207
Maple Bars, 216, 217
No-Bake Peanut Butter Bars, 212, 213
Peanut Butter Chocolate Pie No-Bake, 202, 203
Raspberry Lemon No-Bake Cheesecake, 210, 211
Seven Layer Bars, 226, 227
Cinnamon Rolls, 228, 229

ONE POT MEALS
Alfredo Chicken Broccoli Skillet Lasagna, 120, 121
Beef Stew, 128, 129
Cheesy Chicken and Broccoli Pasta, 108, 109
Easy Chicken Noodle Soup, 134, 135
Ham and Noodle One Pot Meal, 118, 119
Italian Chicken and Rice, 130, 131
Italian Vegetable Pasta One-Pot Dinner, 126, 127
Low Carb Turkey Vegetable Skillet, 114, 115
Minestrone Soup, 132, 133
One-Pot Ground Turkey Pasta, 110, 111
One-Pot Mexican Quinoa, 112, 113
Sausage and Tomato Gnocchi, 116, 117
Sausage Orzo Soup, 106, 107
Skillet Lasagna One-Pot, 122, 123
Sun-Dried Tomato Tortellini, 124, 125

INDEX

White Chicken Chili, 136, 137

SHEET PAN DINNERS

Beef Taquitos, 102, 103

Italian Chicken and Vegetables, 94, 95

Mozzarella Stuffed Meatloaf, 92, 93

Balsamic Chicken with Bacon, Potatoes, and Brussels Sprouts, 96, 97

Burgers with Onions and Potatoes, 88, 89

Burrito Bowls, 86, 87

Chicken Tenderloins, 100, 101

Greek Chicken Thighs & Potatoes, 90, 91

Loaded Quesadillas, 84, 85

Steak Fajitas, 98, 99

SLOW COOKER

Creamy Chicken Pasta, 166, 167

Beef Stew, 144, 145

BBQ Chicken, 154, 155

Baked Ziti, 148, 149

Barbecue Ranch Pork Chops, 170, 171

Barbecue Ribs, 140, 141

BBQ Chicken Drumsticks, 164, 165

Breakfast Burritos, 12, 13

Broccoli Cheese Soup, 152, 153

Chicken Enchilada Pasta, 150, 151

Chicken Tortilla Soup, 142, 143

Fiesta Chicken, 162, 163

Hash Brown Casserole, 24, 25

Honey Garlic Pork Tenderloin, 172, 173

Marry Me Chicken, 158, 159

Mexican Pasta, 160, 161

Pulled Beef Sandwiches, 156, 157

Shredded Chicken Tacos, 146, 147

Sweet Pork Burritos, 168, 169

SUBSTITUTIONS

Cream of Mushroom, 230

Cream of Chicken Soup, 230

Homemade Taco Seasoning, 230

Homemade Ranch Seasoning, 230

Bread Crumbs, 231

Heavy Creamy, 231

Mayonnaise, 231

Brown Sugar, 231

Cream Cheese, 231

SUPER QUICK DINNERS

20-Minute Cheeseburger Quesadillas, 178, 179

20-Minute Chicken Broccoli Tortellini, 190, 191

20-Minute Honey Garlic Chicken, 180, 181

20-Minute Spaghetti Bolognese, 176, 177

Antipasto Salad, 186, 187

Baked Chicken Ranch Flautas, 184, 185

Classic Chicken Fettuccine Alfredo, 198, 199

French Bread Pizza, 196, 197

Garlic Parmesan Chicken w/Zucchini, 192, 193

Lemon Chicken Pasta, 194, 195

Meatballs, 188, 189

Taco Rice Stuffed Peppers, 182, 183

NOTES

NOTES